PRAISE FOR THE GIRLS WRITE NOW ANTHOLOGY

"To write is to bring an inner voice into the outer world, to believe that our thoughts are worth entering the thinking of others, and to make real what has never existed in quite the same way before. What could be a better path to self-valuing than that? In giving young women in the five boroughs this biggest of all gifts, Girls Write Now is giving the rest of us the gift of those girls." — GLORIA STEINEM

"As a writer and reader, I was impressed and enraptured by these stories. As a teacher, I applauded! And on a simple human level, I was deeply moved. There's something about women helping women that generates a power unlike any other."
— JENNA BLUM, *THOSE WHO SAVE US* AND *THE STORMCHASERS*

"If only an organization like Girls Write Now existed in Chicago when I was in my late teens writing alone. It felt like I was putting a message in a bottle. Decades later the bottle was found by this wonderful endeavor and the message has proliferated. The more voices of young women of color that are heard the brighter the path for everyone."
— ANA CASTILLO, *GIVE IT TO ME*

"The young women of Girls Write Now are flowering into mature writers under the tutelage of women who have walked the path before them. Writing can be joyful or gut-wrenching, playful or painful — both the content and the process itself. How wonderful to see this next generation embracing the emotional risks of producing heartfelt work, and mastering a craft that changes the world in unexpected ways."
— FARAI CHIDEYA, *THE COLOR OF OUR FUTURE*

"The courageous young women of Girls Write Now know perfectly well the power of the written word to move hearts and influence minds. The writing you'll find in this anthology is powerful, resilient, and above all, true."
— DAWN DAVIS, VICE PRESIDENT AND PUBLISHER, 37 INK/ATRIA

"When girls write their truth in their particular way, with their particular vibrant edged rhythms and images, the door to the new world opens. Girls Write Now is a breathtaking liberation. The wild birds are flying free."
— EVE ENSLER, PLAYWRIGHT AND FOUNDER OF V-DAY

"The Girls Write Now anthology is an impressive collection from the next generation of women writers, representing the diversity of voices of today. Replete with honesty, inspiration, and bold creativity, these pieces pay homage to our most revered female authors of the past and present and portend a great future." — JANE FRIEDMAN, CO-FOUNDER AND CEO, OPEN ROAD INTEGRATED MEDIA

"Girls Write Now makes the extraordinary possible — helping girls find and give shape to their voices. Through their writing we are offered the stunning possibilities of what our world will become with girls like these continuing to write and create change." — ROXANE GAY, *AN UNTAMED STATE*

"Girls Write Now knows what happens when girls tell their stories. They soar! They write powerful, moving stories about their lives and the lives of others. They write uppity stories that question us and challenge the status quo. And every word on the page becomes a declaration of freedom." — MARCIA ANN GILLESPIE, TEACHER, WRITER, AN EDITOR EMERITA OF *MS.* AND *ESSENCE*

"Once I started reading this marvelous collection of memoirs, stories and poems, I found I could not stop. Each piece has such a strong, unique point of view and voice — there are so many perspectives, I learned something new with every page. These young writers are giving us the truth of who they are, and that is not only very powerful, but it is addicting." — ISABEL GILLIES, *HAPPENS EVERY DAY, STARRY NIGHT*

"Girls Right Now is an amazing program. Perhaps 'empowering' is an over-used word, but it couldn't be more appropriate. These young women are given the power of language, the power to shape their world into a narrative. And we are lucky enough to get to read it. The passion is right there on every page." — AJ JACOBS, *THE YEAR OF LIVING BIBLICALLY*

"Jewish tradition teaches that in the beginning, the world itself was created with the word. And there can be no question about the power of words to transform the world in myriad ways, both good and bad. By teaching these young women to powerfully articulate their own voices through the written word, Girls Write Now is participating in the great human endeavor of transforming and, in this case, repairing the broken world in which we live." — ROBERTA KAPLAN, PAUL, WEISS, RIFKIND, WHARTON & GARRISON LLP

"This year's anthology celebrates the idea of breaking through boundaries, and nothing could be more exciting than watching the writers of Girls Write Now do just that. With skillful guidance from their mentors, these girls have created astounding narratives. Their writing is honest, fearless, and triumphant." — CHRISTINA BAKER KLINE, *ORPHAN TRAIN*

"Girls Write Now gives the world an immeasurable gift: it offers young women fellowship on the path to finding their voice, and the courage to use it. This is a present that amounts to nothing less than the step we need to expand, heal, and illuminate this world."

— SARAH LEWIS, *THE RISE*

"Hold your ear to the Girls Write Now Anthology and hear the "barbaric yawp" of young women who have freed their inner warriors. Open its pages and see how the power of language has enabled these crusaders to say: I am here. We are here. They are writing not only their bravest selves into being, but a better world for us all."

— MARIE MANILLA, *THE PATRON SAINT OF UGLY*

"Much of the talent nurtured today by Girls Write Now's program will blossom into tomorrow's most celebrated authors, poets, playwrights, and journalists. But whether or not they become professionals, the opportunity to shape their thoughts into words and express their feelings on paper (or screen), and the experience of being well-mentored, is sure to contribute to the girls' enhanced self-esteem and a lifelong love of writing and reading." — LETTY COTTIN POGREBIN, AUTHOR, JOURNALIST AND A FOUNDING EDITOR OF *MS.*

"What a pleasure to read the works in this collection. Not only are they brave, beautiful, and filled with smarts, they've got insights and an emotional maturity about politics, the role of women in our culture, family, friends, and love that will resonate with readers of all ages. This isn't only the work of writers on the verge. These are the voices of writers who have arrived." — LIZZIE SKURNICK, EDITOR-IN-CHIEF, LIZZIE SKURNICK BOOKS

"The power of expression is in evidence in this anthology, which demonstrates the resonant effects that can take place between a seasoned writer and a beginning one; between an open mind and a blank page; and, in the case of this book, between a reader and a collection of strong, important writing." — MEG WOLITZER, *THE INTERESTINGS*

Girls Write Now
Breaking Through 2014 Anthology

EDITORIAL COMMITTEE

Molly MacDermot
Editor

Kirsten Reach
Anthology Committee Chair

Lizz Carroll

Meg Cassidy

Kristen Demaline

Amy Flyntz

Kathleen Scheiner

Joann Smith

Kara Thordarson

Laura Cheung
Communications Manager

Rebecca Haverson
*Writing & Mentoring
Program Manager*

Laura Stenson Wynne
Director of Programs

Maya Nussbaum
Founder & Executive Director

Lauren Harms
Designer

Luvon Roberson
Copy Editor

Dea Jenkins
Jackson Konyango
  Ongyango
Kristia Phillips
Emily Turner
Photographers

GMPC Printing
www.gmpcprinting.com

ABOUT GIRLS WRITE NOW AND OUR ANTHOLOGY

In today's changing landscape, Girls Write Now is paving the way for the next generation of women writers, one girl at a time. For sixteen years, we have been helping underserved teen girls discover their voices as they share their stories in a supportive community. Each girl is paired with a mentor who helps harness the power of her own creative and intellectual abilities. Girls Write Now's mission is to support and nurture these relationships.

Girls Write Now's program activities culminate each year with the publication of our award-winning anthology, which includes the best writing from the mentees and mentors in the program. For many girls, this is their first time seeing their work in print, and that experience has a profound effect on their image of themselves as writers. *Breaking Through: The Girls Write Now 2014 Anthology* includes original work by 62 mentor and mentee pairs. The poetry, fiction and essays in this book explore the personal relationships, expectations, and identities of the girls and their mentors. "It's really exciting to have my work published with other people, see it in a book form, and see everyone go buy it. It makes us feel important. It makes me feel like I'm getting somewhere as a writer," says Najaya Royal, a third-year mentee in the program, who contributed her story, "You Are..." (p. 205).

Through weekly pair sessions — often conducted in libraries, bookstores, and coffee shops across New York City — as well as workshops, portfolio building, and readings, our girls are gaining the skills and confidence necessary to share their stories. This year's anthology celebrates the theme of "Breaking Through," both in our lives and in our writing. Our Anthology Editorial Committee, comprised of active mentors in the program, had our own breakthrough as we guided the book, in design and content, to reach a broader audience in a market that is hungry to experience new work from the next generation of women writers. To highlight these powerful stories from our girls and pull the curious reader in, we followed the format of a traditional anthology by structuring the work alphabetically by writer's last name, followed by her mentor's writing. (All of us working with these amazing young women feel inspired to follow their energy and their talent!) We have also included a new addition in the back of the book, called "Ready, Set, Write!" which provides an accessible plan to help writers work on their skills with prompts and exercises; these activities can be used by individuals or groups. What makes this anthology unique is the celebration of the writers and their deep-rooted connection to each other, which is detailed in the profile that follows the writing. You will learn about each mentee-mentor pair and how their working relationship and growing friendship profoundly affects their work as well as their lives.

Girls Write Now started 16 years ago, and released its first anthology a few years later as a 30-page stapled zine, sincere in its devotion to celebrating girls, their mentors, and their collaborations. The anthology has grown into a substantial literary celebration that is winning awards, passionate fans and most importantly, the hearts of the girls and their mentors who are boldly breaking through their own personal boundaries to share their stories with us in this anthology. We can't tell you how excited we are to put their stories in your hands.

-ANTHOLOGY EDITORIAL COMMITTEE

AWARDS FOR GIRLS WRITE NOW

Girls Write Now's teens won a total of 52 gold and silver medals and honorable mentions, including four national awards, from the prestigious Scholastic Art & Writing competition.

The organization was distinguished twice by the White House as one of the top after-school arts and cultural organizations in the nation.

Our annual anthology has received the Outstanding Book of the Year Award and Independent Voice Award by the Independent Publisher Book Awards and has earned honors from the International Book Awards, The New York Book Festival, the National Indie Excellence Awards and the Next Generation Indie Book Awards. The anthology has also received Honorable Mention from the San Francisco Book Festival and the Paris Book Festival. Countless publications and recognitions are listed with all of the pair profiles in the anthology.

LITERARY PARTNERS

Algonquin Books

Alliance for Young Artists & Writers

Atria Publishing Group

Bonnier Corporation

Book Riot

Bust Magazine

Bustle.com

Children's Book Council

Dramatics Play Service, Inc

Girls Be Heard

Hachette Book Group

HarperCollins Publishers

Hive Learning Network New York City

Houghton Mifflin Harcourt

Jane Austen Society of North America

Mary Jo Band & Bread Loaf Writers' Conference

Library Journal

Little Brown & Company

Macaulay Honors College at CUNY

McNally Jackson

McSweeney's

Mentoring Partnership of New York

Middlebury College Press

National Book Foundation

Open Road Integrated Media

Parsons The New School For Design

Penguin Group USA

People StyleWatch

Poet-Linc at Lincoln Center

Poetry Society

Poets Out Loud at Fordham University

Power Poetry

Queens Library

Random House Children's Books

Riverhead Publishing

Romance Writers of America

Rona Jaffe Foundation

RT Book Reviews

Scholastic

She Knows

She Writes

Simon & Schuster

Story Bundle

Story to College

Swoon Reads

The Feminist Press

The MOTH

The New York Times

The Rumpus

Travel + Leisure Magazine

Ugly Duckling Presse

VIDA: Women in Literary Arts

Wave Books

Writers House

Yes Yes Books

Young to Publishing Group

ANTHOLOGY SUPPORTERS

We are grateful to the countless institutions and individuals who have supported our work through their generous contributions. Visit our webstie at www.girlswritenow.org to view the full list or download our most recent Annual Report.

Girls Write Now would like to thank Amazon.com, which provided the charitable contribution that made possible this year's anthology.

The anthology is supported, in part, by public funds from the National Endowment for the Arts; the New York State Council on the Arts, a State Agency; and the New York City Department of Cultural Affairs, in partnership with the City Council.

Breaking Through: The Girls Write Now 2014 Anthology

Girls Write Now, Inc.
247 West 37 Street, Suite 1800
New York, NY 10018
info@girlswritenow.org
www.girlswritenow.org

Printed in the United States

ISBN 978-0-692-02151-4

GIRLS WRITE NOW
BREAKING THROUGH
2014 Anthology from the Next Generation of Writers

Foreword

First Lady of New York City, Chirlane McCray

and he said: you pretty full of yourself ain't chu
so she replied: show me someone not full of herself
and i'll show you a hungry person
— Nikki Giovanni, an excerpt from
"Poem For A Lady Whose Voice I Like"

I was going to high school in Longmeadow, Massachu-
setts, when I read my first Nikki Giovanni poem. I was
always the only black kid in my class, and there were
times when I was the only black kid in the entire school,
which I had some pretty strong feelings about. For the
most part, I kept my opinions to myself. But when my
sophomore English class read Giovanni's poem, I felt
like I had a new friend. And she was sitting right in my classroom, talking to me.

I started talking back — expressing myself by writing every day. Poems mostly.
Some of them were good. Some of them were really bad. But I just kept writing until
I had a fat, spiral-bound notebook bulging with words. One day, I got up the courage
to submit some of them to our high school literary magazine, *Outlet*. Maybe, I hoped,
I could get one published.

The day *Outlet* came out, I discovered that 10 of the 30 poems published were
mine. What a moment. It changed everything for me. I felt like a real writer — a star!

Breakthroughs come in all shapes and sizes. Sometimes, as you're turning a page
in your notebook, you know you're also turning a page in your life. Other times, what
may seem like a whim or passing deliberation can later turn out to be life-changing.

This year's Girls Write Now anthology, *Breaking Through,* includes both types of
breakthroughs. There are poems and stories here that record growth that is as defini-
tive and permanent as a ring in a tree trunk. And there are the breakthroughs that
will emerge years later, when the author looks back and realizes that her experience
with Girls Write Now forever altered the trajectory of her life.

I invite you to meet our young writers, to hear their words that will rattle and
sway, and be fuel for progress. One girl at a time, Girls Write Now is challenging the
status quo and creating the next generation of women writers, "full of themselves"
and keenly attuned to the enduring power of words.

— **CHIRLANE MCCRAY,**
FIRST LADY OF NEW YORK CITY

Introduction

2014 Anthology

This anthology is proof that the mentee-mentor relationships of Girls Write Now have a power that extends well beyond those individual pairings. We readers also benefit greatly from this important work.

This year's theme, "Breaking Through," is woven throughout these 122 pieces in unexpected ways. This is writing about overcoming hurdles — internal and external — that also bears witness to the process of writing — to finding the courage to voice, and to name, one's experience. Whether it be in a story of privately overcoming a personal struggle, or in conquering a fear in public, these pieces are shot through with the desire to transcend limitations. From the closely-observed images of "The Feminist In Me" by Tuhfa Begum (p. 16), to the love/hate tribute of "You and Me," by Elshaima Omran (p. 170), the energy at the heart of Girls Write Now's mission — to help girls find their voices — is fully on display here.

I was lucky enough to hear some of these pieces live, read by their authors, at the Girls Write Now CHAPTERS Reading Series in New York City earlier this year. To see these girls reading their work in front of an audience — many of them for the first time — was a privilege. I was particularly moved by the girls who had chosen to read on stage with their mentors.

In one case, a girl and her mentor, Tema Regist and JoAnn DeLuna, read a piece they had written together which played with the very notion of the mentor-mentee relationship. Entitled "Adult/Teenager," the poem, written for two voices, showed both writers working through similar issues regarding adulthood, albeit in different ways. I was moved by it because it was not about a mentor imparting wisdom to her mentee. It was a true collaboration in which both partners fully and generously participated. The result — lucky us! — was great writing.

I think this is what makes Girls Write Now such an unusual, and smart, institution. Yes, their mission is about writing, but first and foremost, Girls Write Now is an organization dedicated to creating good relationships. I think this is a very wise emphasis. Ultimately, writing is much more than a craft to be taught or learned. Writing is a sharing of spirit. That Girls Write Now is grounded in the work of making good relationships in order to make good writing shows a great understanding of the truth of writing, as well as the truth of growing up in the world today. More than ever, we are aware of being one people on one globe. What each one of us does has a ripple effect. Writing and relating can't be separated.

To the writers in this year's anthology and the women who mentored them, thank you. And to the readers of this book, enjoy these breakthroughs and please consider making further breakthroughs possible: make a donation in support of Girls Write Now.

— AMY FUSSELMAN,
THE PHARMACIST'S MATE, 8 AND SAVAGE PARK

Table of Contents
Girls Write Now: Breaking Through 2014 Anthology

Confessions of a Self-Proclaimed Bitch

Nishat Anjum

To me, breaking through is the same thing as coming to a realization. This piece depicts my journey to realizing that no one should define me except for me.

A sick feeling twisted in the pit of my stomach. The words of one of my club members ran in circles inside my head as I walked to school. "Nishat's a total bitch sometimes." Passion Pit sang through my headphones while I tried to calm myself down. I used the melody of their instruments to meditate. I needed to get into "the zone" before starting the club meeting for that day.

Although I had been captain of my club for two years, I still felt a rush of apprehension before every meeting. Being in charge of something is scary. Being in charge of not one but two groups of people is frightening. It's not very easy presenting yourself to your peers and expecting them to give you their respect and compliancy. It is especially difficult when you're all teenagers; we have the attention span of a fly. We are also highly judgmental. I had begun to develop thicker skin during my years of being a captain, but criticism still stung deeply. I craved the approval of my other club members. In my high school, after-school clubs are a big thing. Forget the cheerleaders and football team, if you were captain of Indian Dance or Filipino Club you were in the "in crowd." By the end of my junior year I became captain of Asian Dance and Korean Fan Dance. But let me clarify, I am not "popular." If I had to label myself in the so called high school hierarchy, I'd be right below the popular people, friendly to everyone but not seen at parties.

I grew up in a semi-typical Bengali family. My parents expected me to do well in school and "bring honor to the family." My father wanted to brag that his daughter got into an Ivy League. And my mom wanted to brag that her daughter could already make the best tasting biriyani and pleat a sari skirt. I am much closer to my mom than to my father. But I am not my mother's daughter, no matter how much I pretended to be. She groomed me to be always polite and likable. To be complacent and agreeable, even if that meant lying to myself. All of her lessons had accumulated to the result that I had the reputation of the "good girl." When my friends' parents are being difficult about something, they point at me and say, "But look, Nishat's doing it, too!"

> "But I am not my mother's daughter, no matter how much I pretended to be."

When they need permission to go somewhere they point out that I'll be going, too, as reassurance to their parents.

But I hated lying to myself. Constantly trying to emulate someone else is exhausting and depressing. Instead of being true to ourselves, most of us strive to become someone else's ideals — whether it's our parent's, friend's, boss's, or crush's. We shrink away from what we really want to do and say for the sake of blending in.

I have always been stubborn and opinionated. As a child, stating my opinions sometimes got me into trouble. As a young woman, this labeled me as being a bitch. As a result, I shied away from stating my opinions. I didn't want to be that girl, the one who always shakes the boat. The girl that no one liked. But I didn't want to be the girl that everyone pushed around. I wanted to find a middle ground, a state of existing that I could be happy with. Becoming captain of a club led me to that state.

Being a captain was probably the best and worst experience of my life. It was the best because I became more confident and gained new experiences. It was the worst because being a leader is similar to putting yourself out there. I basically set myself up for criticism and at my worst I was very, very self-conscious. Every decision I made was analyzed. I cross-examined others' comments and began to fall into this pit of self-loathing. My lowest point was when my mom criticized me for being too harsh towards my club members and I completely fell apart.

Then I decided to put myself back together. After some deep soul searching and playing therapist on myself, I realized that true happiness can only be obtained when you are happy with yourself. It's an old adage, but something that you need to experience for yourself. Words only have the meaning we decide to attach to them. One of the best epiphanies of my life occurred the moment when I realized that yes, I was indeed a bitch, but so what? To me, that word simply means that I know what I want and that I'm not afraid to go after it. To me that word is simply a more passionate way of saying strong, authoritative, and smart.

Recalibrating

Julie Salamon

Nishat has used Girls Write Now to dig deep into her sense of identity, to probe, to question and to appreciate who she is. I am constantly inspired by her willingness to confront hard questions with passion and without fear.

I applied to be a mentor at Girls Write Now because my younger child was leaving for college and I was facing The Empty Nest — a major moment to break through. Once again I had to reassess and recalibrate my relationships to my husband, my children, myself — and yes, even to the dog and the cat!

The reflections of my mentee Nishat on breaking through at age 17 remind me of how many such crossroads I've contemplated during my much longer lifetime: some exhilarating, some painful, many a poignant blend of pleasure and sorrow. It makes sense that a writing program — Girls Write Now — would be the place for me to puzzle through this new phase of life. Ever since I can remember, writing has been the way I figure things out. First came diaries and letters, then stories followed by a career in journalism that led to another career as an author, all adding up to hundreds of thousands — actually millions — of words. Writing is my profession but it is also my essential process, the chisel that chips at the giant inchoate mass of thoughts and feelings which jam my brainwaves until something gives.

Through non-fiction writing and journalism, my personal inquiry has been nurtured and challenged by what I've learned from other people's stories. Writing fiction has forced me to confront lapses in narrative that sometimes reflect carelessness or laziness, but just as often signal fear of facing why the gaps might exist.

> "Writing helps me believe, at least for a while, that I understand what it's all about."

Writing helps me believe, at least for a while, that I understand what it's all about. That feeling was never brighter than the day I picked up my first book — a novel — from the copy shop. That was 26 years ago, long before email existed, a lifetime before I sent an entire book to my editor as a word attachment. Back then, you delivered a typed manuscript, usually in the grey cardboard box provided by the copyshop. I remember carrying my book — still in the form of typed pages in a grey box — across Washington Square Park. The sun bounced off the Arch and I felt as if I'd entered the Promised Land. I was an author.

Since then I've written many more books and crossed many more milestones, most precious among them becoming a mother. For 23 years, from the time my daughter was born until my son left for college, life was a balancing act — managing family and career. Now, The Empty Nest has thrown my balance off-kilter; it's the narrative gap still waiting to be filled. I'm calling it a breakthrough in progress.

Nishat Anjum

YEARS AS MENTEE: 2

GRADE: Senior

HIGH SCHOOL:
Susan E. Wagner
High School

BORN:
Chittagong, Bangladesh

LIVES: Staten Island, NY

COLLEGE:
Brooklyn College

PUBLICATIONS AND RECOGNITIONS:
Scholastic Art & Writing Awards, Honorary Mention for Portfolio

I come from a very traditional Bengali family. Before Girls Write Now, my world was limited to what I saw with my family and what I saw at school. Julie has completely changed that. Not only have I gained more knowledge about writing, but Julie has broadened my world by making me independent and unafraid to try new things. We've had many breakthrough moments, but the major one occurred recently. College decisions are hard and college rejections are even worse; Julie had been teaching me that it doesn't matter where you go but what you do once you get there.

Julie Salamon

YEARS AS MENTOR: 2

OCCUPATION:
Author

PUBLICATIONS AND RECOGNITIONS:
Wendy and the Lost Boys, Cat in the City, The New York Times, The New Yorker, Vanity Fair, Vogue, The Wall Street Journal

This year we've spent a lot of time on Nishat's college applications so we are always thinking about what it means to break through, in many ways. Like Nishat I had immigrant parents and ricocheted between opposing desires. I wanted to conform to their wishes, to reward them for their perseverance and courage by being the best girl possible; I also wanted to fly free, break their rules and become the authentic me, whoever that was. Nishat reminds me that the process continues.

The Lost Boys

Maxine Armstrong

*Bay is the protagonist in a coming-of-age story
about belonging and regret. He tries to break
through the misconception that he is nothing but
another troublemaker. I've returned and left this
story many times but can never seem to fully let it go.*

The snow blankets insignificant cars that line the bare streets of Red Hook.

Underneath me, the world screams beneath a pair of old boots that are poorly insulated and are only held together by laces.

The streets stand irregularly silent, the snow red with the luminescent light of the liquor store sign. The shadows of old women on the stoops of decaying brownstones singing in Spanish hymns and blessings for their sons are gone. All that is left of them is the lingering smell of Sunday dinners that seep through unhinged front doors and building exhausts. I stand alone at a green streetlight in the center of a virgin street, staring at the black sky coated with an armor of approaching clouds.

Allie is on the corner of Dwight Street. He is stiffer than usual, violently shoving a cigarette into a frozen corpse. His uncombed wheat hair escapes out of his black wool hat; he shoves his red hands into the pockets of his leather jacket and stares with a purpose at the still night ahead of him. My breaths are uneven against the bitter gusts of December wind as I approach him. We don't greet each another.

> "My breaths are uneven against the bitter gusts of December wind as I approach him."

Allie instead mirrors my smirk and grabs my jaw. His sly smile fades, dark brows arching. "Where'd you get the bruise, Bay?" I bite down on my lip, incapable of feeling my teeth against my skin.

Allie opens his mouth and I move my jaw out of his grip.

"I thought you quit," I say, looking down between his feet covered by black boots where a discarded cigarette lay.

Allie grumbles underneath his breath, gesturing for me, unmoving, to follow him as he walks. Something in him, the silence as he watches every corner and shadow reminds me of Mac. His hazel eyes watch the Red Hook houses with a certain caution; he runs his fingers over his unshaven face.

"What happened between you and Mac?" he asks. "I mean lately, you been crashing at my house more than home."

"Who says that's home?"

I avoid his glance by watching my boots wage war against the pavement, leave my mark on the world in unstable footsteps. We walk almost aimlessly into the maze of project apartments and homeless men who have known colder realities than the weather.

Bette Davis, M.D.

Kathleen Scheiner

Feeling nervy before our midyear interview, Maxine and I worked on our starlet series. My assignment — what would Bette Davis do? Fifteen minutes later, I read my scene to Maxine and got a solid laugh out of her. Bette had broken through.

Bette liked Tennessee — a neurotic Aries who was a perfect complement for her overbearing Aries personality. She played the part of Maxine, an aging hotel owner, in the production of *Night of the Iguana*, and one thing Bette excelled at was projection. So much so that her voice carried over all the other actors when they were on stage, making them resent her. They made jokes about putting rat poison in the blue glass bottle in her dressing room that she claimed contained medicinal herbs — but everybody else knew it was vodka.

"So, darling, I'm thinking of adding this step," said Bette, eating up the stage with her arms in the shape of an "L." All of a sudden, Bette was front and center when she was supposed to be in the background mixing drinks.

Tennessee sat in the front row of the theater at this impromptu rehearsal that Bette had called — and he was in extreme pain, oily sweat dripping off his brow. "Yes, yes," he mumbled. "Beautiful."

"Tenny, you have to stand up so you can see it."

"I-I can't."

"Well, why not? I've made an effort to make your words brilliant."

"My ank — " and his head fell backward, dark hair flopping, his eyes rolling up.

"You're so cruel. You can see that I'm in pain."

Bette screamed and leapt off the stage, as if she'd practiced many times.

Tennessee's legs were splayed out in front of him, no shoes on his feet. Bette could see checkered socks that had no more stretch in them because the feet and ankles were enormous, swelled up to the size of Easter hams.

She slapped Tennessee's cheeks, taking great relish in doing this, and gradually he came around, throwing the actress off him.

"Stop it — I've had enough."

"What's wrong with your feet — they're absolutely enormous." She nudged one of them with her pointy-toed shoe and Tennessee howled.

"You're so cruel. You can see that I'm in pain."

"Then do something about it, or is this an incurable disease?"

Tennessee shaded his eyes from the stage lights and he could see the mad gleam in Bette's eyes. The vodka shine he was all too familiar with. "I don't like doctors. They scare the bejesus out of me."

"I always travel with my own personal physician. Let me go get him." And Bette was off, a tiny tornado in red lipstick.

Tennessee flapped his hand weakly. "No more. No more rehearsal today. I'll see you back at the theater at seven."

The lights went off, the actors left the stage, and Tennessee felt better. He felt like a bit of an ass for getting himself in such a predicament. Chicago wasn't one of his cities. He liked New York and New Orleans and Key West, but he shunned the Midwest — it was too damn cold.

Maxine Armstrong

YEARS AS MENTEE: 2

GRADE: Junior

HIGH SCHOOL:
Brooklyn School for
Collaborative Studies

BORN: Brooklyn, NY

LIVES: Brooklyn, NY

COLLEGE:
Pace University

SCHOLARSHIPS:
Pace University
Presidential Scholarship

PUBLICATIONS AND RECOGNITIONS:
Scholastic Art & Writing Awards Honorable Mention in Short
Story (2013), Second Pick at Scenarios USA Competition,
Scholastic Art & Writing Awards Silver Key in Short Story (2014)

*Coming into junior year, there was a lot on my plate: SAT prep,
Regents, PBATS, and exams. Our weekly meetings are an oasis
away from the hectic reality I know as high school. Filled with
prompts and American Horror Story conversations, our meetings
are always the highlight of my week.*

Kathleen Scheiner

YEARS AS MENTOR: 3

OCCUPATION:
Freelance Writer
and Editor

PUBLICATIONS AND RECOGNITIONS:
Horrorfeminista.com

*Maxine has been busy her junior year cramming for SATs,
writing papers, and deciding what colleges to apply to next
year, while I'm busy with my own writing and editing work.
We both have a lot of writing work that's un-fun. When we get
together, we assign each other prompts and the game is to come
up with a scene, a little story within fifteen to twenty minutes.
This is my fun time. It reminds me why I love writing and went
into publishing.*

Firm Believer in the Cooties

Misbah Awan

*I wrote this right after I tried convincing my mom
to let me go to a school dance, but found myself
not really wanting to go deep down. This was a
breaking through moment because I went with my
gut and, with the help of a friend, convinced myself
it was okay not to go.*

I stared at the carpeted floor, sitting at the top of my bed with my knees touching my chin. Sat there for 45 minutes, probably more, thinking, *Should I go? Should I not go?* The cool air pushed itself through the one inch window space, creating erect hairs on my arms. Through the window, I heard the laughter of my peers — boys talking about how wonderfully round her butt was, and girls squealing about how the blue eyes that glanced at them for a nanosecond were drop-dead gorgeous.

From where I sat at the tip of the bed, I leaned back and saw the dim light flickering in the library of the main building of my school. The gymnasium was across the street, tucked in between two six-story buildings, one of which was mine. In spite of the bedroom window being almost closed, I didn't have to strain to hear the beat of Miley Cyrus' loopy song next door, from the gym. I hated that song and I hated the hyper sexualized message it sent across and I wasn't in the mood to hear Miley talk about how there's "Red cups and sweaty bodies everywhere" and "Bet somebody here might get some now."

I leaned forward again, this time wrapping my arms around my knees. The softness of the striped blue dress was a cruel reminder of how I'd previously ironed the cloth and joyously stepped into the bathroom. I was dressed up, ready for it all and had already told my mom the details, from A to Z — there would be music blasting, boys (though I emphasized how there'd be few of them), and friends who were waiting for me. Near me, my kid brother's hands flipped the pages of a slim paperback. *Should I go? Should I not go?* It wasn't that my mom decided to suddenly change her mind and say "no." That actually comforted my heart since I knew, deep down, it wasn't where I wanted to be.

I stood up, tired of sitting, and walked towards the dresser to touch the person that stood before me. I hated how it had the boldness to dare mimic my every move. My cheeks were flushed — a red, rosy, burning color. My lips were pale. My hair, not

> **"I was dressed up, ready for it all..."**

dried yet, was bunched together in a bun, baby curls falling in the front of my face. Closer to the window now, the previous and distant laughter of the students was now louder than ever and Miley still belted on, this time about how she's "Dancing with Molly" and "And we can't stop."

Bzzzzz! My mother's callused, yet somehow soft hands outside the bedroom folded clothes while the mouth cursed the buzzer. I was hesitant, but I said it's probably my friend. She was dressed up, too — leather black jacket, red band shirt, and jeans. I almost wanted to smile, but I didn't and she guided herself towards the bedroom, greeting my mother a "hello," and sat on the bed. I didn't want anyone to see me cry so I tried to scrunch myself up into a ball near the headboard, out of sight from the working hands outside. The pages of the slim paperback continued to flip on the bunk bed beside mine. She asked what was wrong and I couldn't speak, so instead I reached for the white on black polka-dot covered phone and typed what I was so torn apart with. *Should I go? Should I not go?* The tears reached my lips. Tasted of salt, perhaps a more stale taste — metal. She didn't try to hug me immediately or exhaust me with her words. Instead she knitted her brows together, trying to form phrases out of letters that didn't quite come out.

After once again convincing my mom I'd be home in an hour, I closed the apartment door behind me and we reached the 5th floor, one floor below mine, barely reaching the landing when I came to a halt.

I knew my place wasn't there. In truth, the weed that reeked off the school gym's wall, the booming of music that would make your head throb, the one-on-one grinding — all under the hawk eyes of teachers — wasn't where I wanted to be. I didn't want to be squished in between Miley's sweaty twerk team and I couldn't say "yes" to Molly when she asked for this dance. I didn't need a confirmation.

Footsteps turned towards us. My neighbor's eyes looked at my eyes, bloodshot red, and he sighed a heavy breath, turning towards the final flight of stairs. I shook my head and she reached her hand out to comfort me with a hug this time. The ringing of her phone didn't even make her rush her hug or loosen her stance.

I moved away and told her to "go" — her walk to the 4th floor staircase hesitant and mine, back to the 6th floor, one of triumph.

Wanderer

Lilly O'Donnell

I was reminded of my own struggle to break through at a young age — that inkling of new awareness just out of sight. This piece is a scene from that time in my life, and that feeling of searching, reaching to grow, and the breakthrough of realizing I already was.

I didn't sleep much as a teenager. Usually just laid in bed, waiting, but some nights I was propelled as if by external force out the door and onto the street. Sometimes I would pick a stoop and scribble frantic poetry in my notebook until sunrise. Other nights I walked in zigzags across lower Manhattan, singing softly to myself, "I am not sleepy and there is no place I'm going to." I walked across the Williamsburg Bridge at dawn to watch the sun rise over the water. I told myself stories about the places I passed, true and made up.

> "I walked across the Williamsburg Bridge at dawn to watch the sun rise over the water."

When I saw people heading for work I knew it was time to go home and sneak back into bed before my mother woke up.

I was searching for something on the streets, but I didn't know what. I often imagined my moment of epiphany, but the image was too blurry to see what it was that I'd realized. I'd sigh and keep walking, scrutinizing pieces of trash on the ground, as if any one of them might be the final clue in the puzzle of finding happiness.

One rainy night I was in bed, hoping for sleep. The room was so dark that even though I'd been lying there with my eyes open for at least an hour, I couldn't see anything. During the day my window looked out onto a brick wall, that night it looked out onto more darkness. There was just the sound of rain. I spent half an hour or so thinking about how active and alive that rain sounded, how purposeful, determined and exciting. I was jealous of the rain, of the ground the rain was falling on.

I got up and felt my way around the room, finding the clothes I'd worn that day by texture: the thick, heavy jeans, the scratchy wool sweater, and the already-wet-from-earlier boots. I pulled them all on clumsily, and walked slowly toward the door with my hands on the walls, kicking a houseplant on the way. I opened the door as little as possible so as to not let in enough light to wake my mother. Once I was finally able to see, I was overwhelmed by the bright fluorescent lights in the hallway, and I stood at the top of the stairs with my eyes closed for almost a minute.

Once I'd adjusted to the blinding light I ran down the stairs, flying downward like the rain. I hesitated for just a moment at the downstairs door; I hadn't even thought to bring an umbrella. I walked quickly with my head down for the first block, but once I'd been thoroughly soaked by the downpour my steps became slow and purposeful, and I looked up at the streetlights, letting the rain run over my face and wash away my nerves. I wandered in the rain for hours that night, smiling, because I wasn't searching anymore, just enjoying a walk.

Misbah Awan

YEARS AS MENTEE: 1

GRADE: Sophomore

HIGH SCHOOL:
The Young Women's Leadership School of Astoria

BORN: Pakistan

LIVES: Queens, NY

My first year as a Girls Write Now mentee was a fascinating ride, full of bumps and laughter. While I was eager to jump into breaking the rules and creating something that didn't even have flesh yet, my mentor encouraged me to focus on abiding by the rules first, so I could break them better. She gave me constructive criticism, was always honest, and never sugar-coated the faults in my writing. I reluctantly took her edits, but now I'm learning to trust her more and more and I now understand that the reader is a significant factor in the equation.

Lilly O'Donnell

YEARS AS MENTOR: 1

OCCUPATION:
Freelance writer

PUBLICATIONS AND RECOGNITIONS:
New York Magazine, Bust, Narratively NY

Every conversation with Misbah has been a breakthrough, in our communication with each other and in the process of writing, which really comes down to breaking an idea out of your mind like you would a friend out of jail, leading it into the light of the page where it can live its own life. To write is to learn the various tunnels and escape routes, and mentoring has been like sharing my hand-drawn map to freedom.

Keji

Dahnay Bazunu

This poem depicts the breakthrough of a young girl
who is forced to realize that her self-centered nature
could end in tragedy; it's her reality check. I was
inspired to write it after reading Omar Tyree's
"Flyy Girl."

Gold on her throat, diamond on her fingers,
Perfume so strong that when she leaves the room it lingers,
Name brands so fresh but no respect for higher authority,
I mean who needed manners when fashion was Keji's biggest priority?
The girl the boys loved, yet the one girls envy,
But opinions never fazed Keji as long as her pockets weren't empty.
Fifteen years young with a grown woman's mentality,
"Ms. Had It All" was determined to portray she was living lavishly.
"Slow down, Keji!" – Requests from her mother she'd ignore,
Besides her parents always valued their overtime more.
So one night, Keji got dressed in one of her best outfits,
It was Harlem's biggest party, an opportunity she couldn't forfeit.
She snuck out of her room, and met up with a couple of girls,
Keji had no idea that tonight would change her fairy tale world.
She got to the club, swaying her hips to the rap beat,
Flattered by the occasional whispers in her ear and compliments on the
latest Nikes on her feet.
It was the time of her life, but soon she was ready to go,
She looked for friends but realized she was all alone.
Suddenly a strange face complimented her on how well she matched,
Before she could reply, she felt fingers on her throat and her chain was snatched.
She wrapped her hands around her throat, only to realize it was bare,
She looked around for comfort, but met only the accomplice's cold stare.
Tears stung her eyes as she became afraid,
She began to curse herself for the stupid decision she made.
She pushed through the crowd of preying drunken men,
At that moment she swore she'd never do something this dumb again.

This

Raquel Penzo

Being paired with someone who mainly writes
poetry was a challenge for me because I struggle to
understand the genre. My piece is an attempt to step
out of my comfort zone — trying to remember the
trappings of teen life, based on what Dahnay wrote
in her poem.

This.

This is the last time.

Yesterday Sheri got an early acceptance letter
to Harvard.
We were supposed to be roommates
We were going to change that school, that
city, the world.
We were going to prove statistics wrong —
We were not destined to fail because of
our zip codes.
We would make it out and then come
back to say, "Look what we did. See how
great we turned out?"

Yesterday was my fifth trip to the local
precinct.
These pigs are tired of seeing my face and
calling my mom to come get me.
My mom is tired of threatening to leave me
out in the street to fend for myself.
The judge is not going to want to tell me
again to stay out of trouble "or else."
They're all going to stop caring whether or
not I fade away in the system.
Soon I'll be too old to get away with it all. I've
been too old for this for a while now.

So this is the last time.

The last after-midnight sale I make.

The last pill I bag. The last party I attend.
The last high I chase.

This is the last boy I will kiss and the last shirt
I will take off as this person I've become,
This non-me.

This is the last 40 I drink, the last page I answer,
the last red lipstick I reapply.

This is the last girl I fight, the last dress I
boost, and the last chain I snatch.

This is the last time I say it's the last time,
so that tomorrow can be the first time I
greet the sun with no burdens

Dahnay Bazunu

YEARS AS MENTEE: 1

GRADE: Senior

HIGH SCHOOL:
  Midwood High School

BORN: Queens, NY

LIVES: Franklin Park, NJ

COLLEGE: Pace University

My mentor has opened my eyes to new kinds of writing besides poetry. I see a lot of me in her, and I'm pretty sure we have many more breakthrough moments to come.

Raquel Penzo

YEARS AS MENTOR: 1

OCCUPATION:
  Copywriter, Brooklyn
  Public Library

Working with Dahnay has been like a trip back in time for me. We had similar stories and struggles, and I'm glad I was able to let her know (and realize for myself) that things work out for the best, always, as long as you put in the work.

The Feminist in Me

Tuhfa Begum

This piece is close to my heart. It is a testimony to the
relationship I share with my mother, as well as the
three years I have spent with my mentor, breaking
through, day by day. Twenty-three revisions and
one panic attack later, here is my story.

It started with an insult, when we collided at the front door of school at 8 o'clock on a Monday morning and I dropped an armful of feminist posters. They scattered across the threshold and back down the steps. He stood watching as I struggled to pick them up and tuck them under my arm.

"What's the matter with you anyways?" he asked. He had that slouchy look on his face that some boys covet.

"Excuse me?"

"Why don't you take cooking class like the other girls do? At least you'd learn something useful."

Before I could answer, the bell rang and we went our separate ways to class.

I was a feminist long before I knew what the word meant. I was born in Bangladesh, unaware that I was the first female in my family to be delivered in a hospital, the first to receive a birth certificate. Later, my grandfather defied gender norms by teaching me to read and write in English. In the mosque, he seated me up front with him and the other men, rather than placing me in a dark corner with the other women and children.

My mother never received these benefits. When she was born, my grandparents were young, poor, and living in a backwards village. They arranged her marriage to my father at a young age. Our female ancestors married young, then spent most of their time relentlessly cooking, cleaning, and caring for children. Even today in Bangladesh, the expectation for a girl is to have no expectations.

"While other little girls followed Disney princesses, I imagined a princess who could save herself and her kingdom."

I immigrated to the United States with my parents when I was three years old. While other little girls followed Disney princesses, I imagined a princess who could save herself and her kingdom. I identified with Susan Pevensie, who was cast out of mythical Narnia because she refused to conform.

In middle school we had to create a board game using historical events. I added a new category to my board called "The Suffrage Movement and Feminism." A family friend studied my board and asked, "What about men's rights? We carry the burden of your feminine nonsense."

In ways I didn't fully appreciate, my mother was my role model. While the mothers of many of my classmates were doctors or lawyers, my mother juggled working a minimum wage job serving fast food and taking care of her family. If others disparaged me, my mother encouraged me to work hard and persevere against obstacles.

In high school, I took extra courses, volunteered at the Housing Works Bookstore, raised money for United Nations' programs, and received the many benefits of belonging to Girls Write Now. Last summer, I interned at the Bella Abzug Leadership Institute, founded by the daughter of "Battling Bella" herself. Here, feminism came alive as we declared that women's rights *are* human rights.

At that point, my beliefs turned into activism. I began making posters about the global subjugation and abuse of women and taping them up at school. I staged little events in the hallways and handed out flyers. Mostly, my efforts were ignored.

My mother always stood by me, from the warm glasses of milk she would hand to me during late-night study sessions, to the Girls Write Now annual public readings, where she clapped the loudest when I read my work. Even so, her long work hours and my demanding academic schedule meant that we spent little time together.

One afternoon, after having two wisdom teeth removed, I sulked around the house until, finally, I followed my mother into uncharted territory — the kitchen. I never helped out in the kitchen. My mother understood that I feared stepping inside even once would lead to never stepping out.

As I stood in the doorway, watching her — she was wearing her faded blue jeans and *salwar kameez* while she prepared dinner — I saw that she looked happy. She was gossiping on the phone with a friend and chopping onions at the same time. (I don't know *how* she does this.) I had never wondered if my mother was happy or not. I took for granted that she was always there, providing everything we needed.

My mother said "goodbye" to her friend, hung up the phone, and continued working. Her black hair caught the light, and streaks of gray glimmered as she pushed her hair off her face. She hummed along to the Beatles on the radio, and I remembered what my writing mentor once told me: "Even in spaces of confinement, women can find liberation."

I lingered in the doorway until she noticed me. "It's just dal,"she said, stirring lentils that were soaking in a pot of water. "Come, clean the next bag. Pick out the tiny stones."

First step. Second step. On the third step, I found myself inside the kitchen, standing close to my mother. I opened the other bag of lentils. We sang "Lucy in the Sky with Diamonds" as we worked.

The next time someone tells me to abandon my posters and take cooking class, I'll say, "I already know how to cook. My mother taught me!"

Hot

Josleen Wilson

We meet at the library equidistant between
her school and my home office. My short walk
typically turns into a nightmarish hike through my
neighborhood. I vent for two minutes after I arrive.
"Write it down," Tuhfa says. So, I return the same
way, writing it down.

I'm walking in my widest-tread sneakers — the only shoes safe to wear on the uneven pavement — going uptown on the west side of First Avenue. (If you're thinking of wearing your Jimmy Choo look-a likes, better to reserve a door-to-door car service.)

My eyes are fixed on the cracked sidewalk, rather than the window displays of the shops that line both sides of the avenue. I'm not complaining, because there's nothing to see there anyway: all those fun-filled windows now have "For Rent" signs or they're boarded over, thanks to the relentless, ongoing wreckage known as the construction of the Second Avenue Subway, the phantom tunnel that goes nowhere. They've been working on it on and off (mostly off) for the last 100 years; its original cost estimated at $86 million, now expected to top $17 *billion*.

Five years ago, our congresswoman decided it was a good time to try to finish it, again; just think of all the manly labor needed to blast, gouge, and destroy everything in its path below and above ground. The only stores in this neck of Manhattan are new Duane Reades and Chase banks. But, no, I'm not complaining.

Out on First Avenue the traffic flows one way, going in the same direction I am walking. First Avenue has always been the preferred street for trucks, buses, and taxis, but now its five lanes are narrowed by 1) a bike lane, in which bikers ignore the stop lights and one-way signs, 2) a parking lane, 3) a double-parking lane, 4) a bus lane, and 5) another parking lane.

To interpret the white hieroglyphics etched onto the black tarmac requires analytical thinking unsuitable to New Yorkers on a miserable, sweaty August afternoon.

> "An elderly woman clinging to her walker stands paralyzed in the crosswalk..."

When I reach 86th Street, four different traffic lights are blinking: 1) a straight arrow 2) a left turn arrow, 3) a bicycle symbol, 4) a walking-man symbol. The red, yellow, and green lights dance like heavy-metal rockers — and suddenly stop at all red.

An elderly woman clinging to her walker stands paralyzed in the crosswalk, the bumper of an SUV trying to turn left from the middle lane nearly touching her. Horns start blasting from all sides. I zigzag into the middle of the street and touch the woman's arm. "Which way, ma'am?" She points across the street in the direction she is facing. The driver of the SUV lowers his window and curses us. I point my index finger and thumb straight between his eyes. If he moves his car an inch either way I will shoot.

I hold her arm and together we break through to the relative safety of the opposite curb, the street suddenly quiet. But, no, I'm not complaining.

Tuhfa Begum

YEARS AS MENTEE: 3

GRADE: Senior

HIGH SCHOOL:
Vanguard High School

BORN: Sylhet, Bangladesh

LIVES: Bronx, NY

COLLEGE:
New York University

SCHOLARSHIPS:
Full scholarship to
New York University

PUBLICATIONS AND RECOGNITIONS:
Scholastic Art & Writing Awards National Silver Medal in Memoir, Silver Key in Humor, Silver Key in Senior Portfolio, Gold Key in Memoir, Silver Key in Memoir

We're sitting on tiny chairs in the children's room at the 79th Street Public Library. Instantly, we lose ourselves in conversation, ignoring the librarian who reminds us that the library will close. "I found the Dorothy Parker collection," Josleen says, handing me a thick book.

"I'd like you to know her before she fades from history." She shows me "Big Blonde" and "You Were Perfectly Fine." We talk rapidly about the Algonquin Round Table, humorists, feminism and global warming.

Josleen Wilson

YEARS AS MENTOR: 6

OCCUPATION:
Writer and Author

I'm compelled to plant as many writers into Tuhfa's head as possible before she graduates. She is my memory bank, with more little gray cells than Hercule Poirot. "Who's Mary McCarthy?" I challenge. "Who's Nicholas Kristof?" she parries. Oh, we do go on. Time is my enemy, but not hers. She breaks through, breaks through. I know where she's going, going....

Emmy's Interview

Brenda Bota

*This story is about a girl called Emmy who became
a model. This is the interview she had after landing
a major modeling contract.*

After the party revealing Emmy as the face of Burberry's spring ad campaign, many paparazzi and reporters wanted to interview Emmy. She was so excited, and wanted to do as many interviews as she could, but the crazy mob of people mixed with media presenters was overwhelming. As Emmy finally made her way through the mob to the restroom to cool down a little bit — not to mention, make sure her makeup was still holding up — she met eyes with a reporter who had just walked out of the restroom.

"Hey! Great — I'm so happy that I met you here. I love your style, no wonder you are a model. But anyway, congrats on your big shot! The picture is beautiful, that is a really great opportunity, you know, this is just the beginning!" the woman said eagerly.

"Thank you so much, I really appreciate it!" Emmy said back politely.

"Oh my, excuse my manners, my name is Melissa Hutson. I'm a contributor at *Vogue* magazine," she reached out and shook Emmy's hand. "I was wondering if I can interview you for our 'Model of the Year' section".

"Oh, yes! I would love that."

"Okay, great! Well, let's get to it, follow me," Melissa said, taking the lead.

> "...taking a deep breath and trying to bring herself back to the time before all this madness."

They walked away from the restrooms and into a side room and took a seat. Emmy was so relieved. She had finally gotten away from the mob of people and media presenters and was sitting with the one publication that truly matters — *Vogue*. She was in a room that was bright red with bright lights that made her feel welcomed. It was so cozy — giant throw pillows were tossed onto the chairs, and the table had a pile of perfectly stacked fashion photography books. Melissa finally got her papers together and held her pen in her hand and smiled.

"Okay, so how did all this begin? The modeling and everything?"

"Well..." Emmy said, taking a deep breath and trying to bring herself back to the time before all this madness.

"It was back in 2004 and at that time I was living with my father, who is a businessman in New York. He worked for a large company and was always busy and never seemed to have time for me. However, whenever I needed something from him, I'd go visit him at this office and he usually, well always, just gave it to me.

"One day after I got home from school I received a letter from my first-choice college, Harvard, saying that they had accepted me. I was so excited I quickly rushed to my dad's office to tell him and so he could give me the money I needed to make the deposit. When I got there, one of my dad's workers named Ben Sarpong, whom I had met from time to time during my visits, stopped me from bursting into his office and told me that my dad was in a super important meeting so I had to wait.

"While sitting in the reception area, I began talking with Ben. He told me how proud he was of me for getting into Harvard and wanting to pursue a psychology career but — and it was the weirdest thing ever — he then said he just couldn't picture me there. I laughed and asked him what he could picture me doing. He said something fashion-related because of the way I dressed and carried myself. I told him that while I loved fashion, I just wasn't sure of how many career options I had in fashion. A degree in psychology was the safer call. Then he went off on a tangent about how important it was to always go after your heart's desires even if you feel it'll be hard getting your hands around what you want. He then told me about a female friend who was a well-known designer in the city and that he could get me an internship with her; she could help me find my way into the fashion industry.

"Gladly, I started to intern with his friend Celibra McIntosh. The dresses she made were simply the most gorgeous things I had ever seen. After interning with her for a while, she started using me to do the fittings. She said I had the right body she needed to make sure her dresses were fitting the way she wanted. Over time she started having professional photographers come in and take pictures of me in her latest designs. She'd hang them up in her office and in the hallways of her building to promote her designs. After a while I started realizing that other than designing, I loved modeling and fitting. So that's when I got myself involved with Chromville, which is an agency that helps upcoming models. Through the agency, I started doing more backstage work for models, like fitting, designing, and modeling in small mini-shows.

"One day about a year after I graduated from high school, one of the marketing directors from my agency gave me good news. They were going to start putting me in more runway shows, as I was older, and they were beginning to get requests from a lot of people. Basically from there, I began doing New York Fashion Week and shoots for designers. Then, by chance, I got a call from Burberry, which brings me to where I am now. It's really crazy that a few people believing in me and my own self-confidence led me to where I am now.

"So, that's how it started," Emmy concluded.

For the rest of the night, Emmy and Melissa carried on with the interview, engaging in interesting conversations that brought both a lot of joy. It was the start of a friendship.

Runner-Up

Maddy Zollo

*Brenda's piece is about a girl named Emmy and
her big modeling debut, so I thought it'd be fun to
write from the perspective of another model who is
insanely jealous of all the press Emmy is getting.*

That bitch. Her stuck-up, goody-two shoes face was staring at me from all angles. It
was like my own personal hell: in front of me, she was writhing on the side of a building in an orange-studded trench coat. To the right, there she was again rocking a
metallic pair of aviators and to the left was a series of
her and her teeny little waist splashing around in a river
looking like it was the best day of her life. Too bad a croc-
odile didn't appear in the water and take a nice big bite
out of her bony little leg. Burberry's spring face missing
the half of her calf? Not a chance. Then they would've
called me (well it *should've* been me anyway until dear sweet Emmy came galloping
in the day I was out "sick" to go work on my chi in the Hamptons).

> "Too bad a crocodile
> didn't appear in the
> water and take a nice
> big bite out of her
> bony little leg."

I took the last gulp from my champagne glass and grabbed something that
appeared to be a violet-tinted mojito from the baby-faced server who was parading
around with the cocktail trays. I took a sip from the silver straw and despite it tasting
like what I'd imagine a bouquet of flowers would taste like if they were blended into a
smoothie, I kept drinking.

You see, I wasn't even going to come, but my manager said everyone who's anyone
will be here so I might as well get my face in the mix to remind them just how much
prettier (and what better cheekbones) I have than the new plain-faced "it" girl who
probably doesn't even know how to spell Balenciaga. Plus, I'm not going to lie, I look
damn good tonight — my lime bandage dress was hugging my frame in all the right
places (thank you, green juice) and my maid finally returned my beloved white Val-
entino pumps she had "borrowed" for a wedding (shocker since I thought those had
immediately gone to eBay for my maid's renaissance costume fund).

"Excuse me, excuse me?" I feel someone tap me on the shoulder. Finally — someone has noticed me, it's about time. I swing around and see Stanley O, only the most
respected street style blogger.

"Why yes," I flip my hair over a shoulder and turn towards him.

He raises his eyebrows at me.

"Oh hello, Bria — it's you." He laughs. "I didn't realize that the puffy figure stuffed
in that little puke green number was you. Just thought it was some wannabe model

who I could guide in the right direction before she ends up on a What Not to Wear list, but since it's just you — carry on."

Brenda Bota

YEARS AS MENTEE: 2

GRADE: Senior

HIGH SCHOOL:
Bronx Career and College Preparatory High School

BORN: Yonkers, NY

LIVES: Bronx, NY

Maddy's a great person. During these last two years, she has helped me break through as a writer and woman. This year, we broke through by sticking to our goal of trying a new type of writing. We worked towards this and I submitted two pieces of fiction instead of poetry, which is what I usually write. She has made me a better woman because she is a woman of her word; she is truthful and says whatever is on her mind. She is also very kind. I have learned that I can express my feelings in a kind way and be truthful at all times.

Maddy Zollo

YEARS AS MENTOR: 2

OCCUPATION:
Assistant Beauty Editor at *People StyleWatch*

PUBLICATIONS AND RECOGNITIONS:
People StyleWatch, People.com

Every Friday, I sneak away from my desk and go downstairs to the Le Pain Quotidien to meet with Brenda. We usually sit at a table by the window — her with an apple juice and me with a green tea. Sometimes we write and do exercises; sometimes we'll sit and chat about prom and college. Since this is our second year together, we have really bonded and have developed a special friendship. Even though Brenda will be at college doing amazing things, I'll miss our afternoon meetings.

Pila

Arnell Calderon

*This is one of a series of vignettes about a girl named
Alberta and her relationship with her family. Writing
this story made me step out of my comfort zone.*

His car smelled of pine and old newspapers. As I walked towards the brown rusty
door, looking forward to the obnoxious heat in his car, a wind gently pushed the pink
barrettes of my hair. He always walked a little in front of me, with his hands in his
black nylon jacket. His light footsteps took his right hand out of his pocket, pulling out
a metal key with a black plastic casing. The cuticle on his right thumb was of snow, a
flake that hit an onyx stone. The knuckles of his hands were experienced; they knew
what it was like to walk around a steering wheel, and they knew what it was like to
empathize with one who missed the bus. They were the epitome of empathy and flaw.
Cracked, white with splotches of brown, but they understood struggle. The day those
knuckles made love to petroleum jelly will be the day my father has left for me clean-
liness and luxury.

He opened the door to his driver seat. I pulled the metal handle of the other door,
but it was still locked. I looked at him through the window and he held his hand up
for about three seconds. I saw the engraved brown lines in his hands. As soon as I
heard a click sound I opened the door and entered. His car was warm as always. He
reached his hand toward the radio. There was dust in the cassette space. I loved how
he never cleaned that space. His index and thumb finger
lightly squeezed and turned the "tuning" circle, I heard
static, "GOOOOOOOOOL, news stations, and merengue.
He decided to leave it on the merengue station. All you
heard was La India's childlike voice, "Es un gran necio,
un estupido!" He looked at his side view mirror and fixed
his cap, put his seatbelt on, and looked at me and chuck-
led. I gripped on the black crank below the handle; I wound it to the right and wind
made its way through my twists, sending chills to my scalp and bumps on the right
side of my neck.

> "...wind made its way
> through my twists,
> sending chills in
> my scalp and bumps
> on the right
> side of my neck."

Looking through the windows of cars was always my favorite part. Whirling
sounds and conga sounds danced through my ear with rhythm. The green leaves of
trees responded to the sound with violent sways, enough to intimidate a jazz singer.
I turned and stared at him, his eyes focused on the road, and his ear slowly moving
up and down. I saw the things on the side of his jaw that always stung me every time
he reached for a kiss. Those things were grey, black, short, and upright. They pushed

against the smoothness of my cheek, causing comforting interruption. As I watched him, he asked, "How was school?" "Good," I replied. "Make sure you get 3's and 4's," he said. "Don't worry, I will," I responded with a smile.

Our conversations always moved in simplicity. Words flew out of our mouths and created ideas and thoughts that lacked complexity, but were bathed in feeling and thought. We shared words that definitely did not paint the room with an array of colors, but an array of honesty. There was not really much to say, and we appreciated that, and translated through blemished streams of words. He stopped the car and parked near the "4" train station. We walked to the dentist, well, he walked, and I rode on his back. I wrapped my two hands around his neck that stung and tickled. The sun reflected on his black rectangular sunglasses. And before I knew it, the tonsils of my sandals touched the warm black concrete and he opened the door. A strong wind went through the upper halves of our bodies, cooling the water running down my underarm, and blowing the navy blue linen shirt of my father's.

Bien domesticada

Morayo Faleyimu

My story arrived over the course of several hours, bidden by weeks of listening to Colombian rock music and rereading Garcia Marquez's great work, 100 Years of Solitude.

Es difícil de domesticar el inglés. Mientras el español me recuerda del gato, el inglés me recuerda del lobo. El primero es un animal curioso que corre de patas seguros: la n, la erre, la p, la aspiración de la jota. Cada sonido une uno con otro. Las monjas hablan del mismo tipo de unidad, la que las ata a Dios. No es posible atarse al inglés de tal manera. ¿Te provoca preguntar el por qué? Pues, es que el inglés es la lengua del lobo. No se puede confiar en él. Los consonantes le muerden la lengua. Las vocales se naufragan contra los dientes. Hablar inglés es hablar con canicas en la boca. Es por los sonidos crujientes de inglés que hablo de susurro, mi voz fuerte se pone, de repente, débil. En espanol, tengo muchos relatos de decir. Pero decirlos en inglés – me pierdo por la selva de verbos y sustantivos.

> "Las vocales se naufragan contra los dientes."

El varón se convierte en la hembra – *he es she y she him* – y no puedo producir más que uno de cualquier cosa. I have two shoe. My father have many wash. *Relojes.*

Wash-es? ¿Cómo es posible que una lengua me empobrece tanto?

Tengo un cuento bien cortito. Había una vez una niñita que tenía dos mascotas – un gato gris y un lobo marrón. Su padres le reglaron el gato por su primer cumple. El gato era fiel. Pasaba los días sentado por los hombros de ella. Al cumplir los 10, sin embargo, el padre le quitó de su pueblo y la instaló en una ciudad grande de edificios que tenían ojos translucientes y temerosos. La ciudad tocó la puerta y cuando ella no la contestó, lanzó por la ventana el lobo. El lobo no era fiel. Siempre tenía hambre. Pasaba los días en seguir a ella. Contra él la niña cerraba las puertas, pero el lobo no necesitaba llave para entrar. El lobo merendaba la n, la fe, la p de ella, hasta que llegó el día lluvioso que el lobo la saltó por los hombros y se lo comió el gato entero.

And from that point on, she lived with the wolf forever and ever. But she could still hear that cat meowing, lost somewhere in the wolf's stomach.

Arnell Calderon

YEARS AS MENTEE: 1

GRADE: Junior

HIGH SCHOOL:
NYC iSchool

BORN: NY, NY

LIVES: NY, NY

My relationship with Morayo has opened me to many possibilities in writing. I've gained an understanding in consistency. Her ability to experiment with words and ideas has forced me to expand my limits in writing, to the point where there aren't any limits at all. Before Morayo, I often fidgeted and was overwhelmed with anxiety when it came to expressing my ideas and writing. Luckily, I was blessed with someone who helped me develop as a writer.

Morayo Faleyimu

YEARS AS MENTOR: 2

OCCUPATION:
Campus Director,
Citizen Schools

Me inspira el ambiente viviente que produce Arnell cuando escribe de su gente garífuna.

In other words, working with Arnell has helped me break through my English and find characters who speak in an entirely different language — Spanish.

Breaking Through: Negativity

Kaytlin Carlo

The breakthrough that Ashley and I have discovered this year is positive thinking. I told her I think negatively a lot of the time, and she challenged me to swap those thoughts for positive ones for an entire day.

6:30 a.m.: Instead of cursing out the alarm, I realize that it's a blessing to wake up and see another day.

8 a.m.: Yes, I'm leaving my house late once again, but at least the trains and buses won't be so crowded!

9:15 a.m.: Smile at Ms. Gilmore and stay on task for the entire class. And ignore all the kids scoffing that you're always late; at least you're trying to get to class on time.

11:30 a.m.: Refrain from yelling at 13-year-old freshmen holding up the line in the staircase. Instead, calmly remind them that they have to be in class in two minutes as well.

12:07 p.m.: Don't be ashamed that you're still hungry after your salad. Go eat a granola bar and drink some water.

2 p.m.: Don't argue with Mr. Greenblatt that pre-calculus is unnecessary. Appreciate the opportunity to get an education for free and remember that limit does not exist!

3:30 p.m.: The kids are rowdy and fresh out of school on the J train. Instead of giving a dirty look and scoffing some words underneath your breath, turn your music up louder and look the other way.

4:36 p.m.: Don't curse out the sidewalk; you were just being clumsy and so happened to trip.

5 p.m.: Just throw out the garbage, don't argue with your mom. It's not worth it.

7:55 p.m.: Procrastinating once again. Just start your homework even if you're a senior with two months left. You have not graduated yet!

9:30 p.m.: Mom made mashed potatoes again. Instead of reminding her how disgusting they are, make a sandwich and call it a night.

10 p.m.: No cold water? It's okay; you can shower in the morning. Anyway, you hate falling asleep with your hair wet.

11:30 p.m.: I know you aren't tired, but you need to go to bed. Attempt to be early to first period tomorrow and break in some more positive habits.

Breaking Through: Negativity

Ashley Howard

When we were discussing the topic of breaking through, Kaytlin told me she's constantly trying to break through the negative thoughts she battles with. I could absolutely relate. So, we challenged each other to dedicate one day to turning all of our negative thoughts into positive affirmations.

8 a.m.: Instead of waking up annoyed that I have to get out of bed, I remind myself how lucky I am to have a means of making money.

9 a.m.: I'm having a bad hair day, but I focus on being blessed with a healthy, thick set of locks.

9:30 a.m.: Smile at the man who holds the subway doors open too long, maybe his wife is in the hospital and he's racing to be by her side.

12 p.m.: Eat a bag of chips with No. Guilt. At. All. Maybe I'll even order a cookie today!

2:30 p.m.: Don't get frustrated about being stuck in the office when it's beautiful outside. Appreciate that this company believes in my potential and is essentially giving me a free education.

4 p.m.: Feeling the gratitude of being in a committed relationship, rather than looking at my phone every five minutes and obsessing over when my boyfriend will call.

5:30 p.m.: Today I remain in my own yoga practice and accept the level I have reached, not the level of those around me.

6:30 p.m.: A taxi almost runs me over in the crosswalk and reminds me how much I love the fast-paced hustle of Manhattan.

7 p.m.: The burn in my legs from my sixth floor walk-up apartment almost sets me off, but I am so lucky that it's so safe and quiet where I live.

8 p.m.: My fridge is pretty empty so it looks like I'll be having oatmeal again for dinner; it beats the bologna sandwiches I once ate for a month straight while volunteering for under served communities in Africa.

10 p.m.: No motivation to write my freelance article. I'll just get up early and start the day with a creative writing prompt!

Midnight: Staring at the ceiling with an uncontrollable flood of thoughts. I close my eyes and tune-in to everything around me: a comfortable bed, heat and hot water. There's so much to be thankful for, not even one sneaky thought of negativity could pull me away from this feeling of gratitude.

Kaytlin Carlo

YEARS AS MENTEE: 3

GRADE: Senior

HIGH SCHOOL:
  Pace High School

BORN: Brooklyn, NY

LIVES: Brooklyn, NY

During my time with Ashley, I have done some things I would have not done if it weren't for her. The breakthrough that Ashley and I have discovered this year is positive thinking. Whenever I'm with her she makes me feel excited about writing and more curious about where my life may take me.

Ashley Howard

YEARS AS MENTOR: 3

OCCUPATION:
  Freelance Writer

This past year with Kaytlin has really been an amazing learning experience. During our pair sessions, she has helped me find a healthy balance of unpolished creativity and refined discipline. We've broken through writing skills, deadlines and even trust issues. Most of our time spent together became very positive moments of creativity and I hope we continue our friendship when she heads off to college in the fall.

Self-Betrayal

Sabrina Cevallos

*Not every relationship a person has is a good one
and many times people get hurt when they are
blinded by love. This piece relates to breaking
through by providing a different perspective.*

I walk into the party but as I approach the door my stomach fills with "butterflies." As I reach for the door handle, someone from the inside grabs a hold of it first and pulls me along with it. "Hey Chloe!" Cammy says to me. "Sorry, I was about to step out to go get more soda but I'll be right back."

"Hey, Camm, where's Andy?" I ask.

"Oh, I forgot tonight's your little date. Well, last time I saw him he was in the kitchen with his 'friends,'" she says rolling her eyes while laughing.

"What friends and why are you laughing?"

"Because...he's...you'll see," she says strangely. As I walk over to Andy, I see the back of his head but as I come around I can't help but notice a girl who looks like Megan Fox. I tap him on the shoulder and he turns slowly, laughing at the conversation he's having with her.

"Hey!" I say with a grin. "Who is this?"

"Oh, Chloe. I didn't know you were going to be here," he says.

"Yes, you did. Camm's my best friend. I told her to invite you."

"Oh, well — talk to you in a bit," he says and turns his back towards me. Twenty minutes later, Cammy walks in, and I ask about the girl. She tells me her name is Megan. What are the chances, right? She says that Megan and Andy are apparently close friends from middle school.

As I twiddle my thumbs over the situation, I decide to twiddle them away in a text to Andy. I tell him to come meet me by the bookcase in the back of the studio apartment. From a distance, I can tell that he got the message just by the look on his face. "What?" he says with disgust.

"Can we talk? What's up with you? You said you liked me. I thought we were going to hang out but you are hanging out with another girl. What if I was hanging out with another guy?" I yell.

"Why would I even care?" Andy says.

"Wow!"

"Chill, why are you getting mad?" He asks.

"Because I know you would be upset."

"I really wouldn't!"

"Are you kidding me? So, you're telling me I can hang out with other guys?" I ask.

"Yea, cause I wouldn't care."

"Well thank you for that clarification. I'm glad I know that now, and I will."

"That doesn't mean you should."

"You just said that you didn't care so…"

"Fine!" he says in a rage. "Go ahead!"

"I wasn't even going to."

"Whatever!" he says as he walks away angrily.

As I wonder what just happened, I can't help but spot Megan from across the room. I decide to talk to her. "Hi," I say as I get closer. "I'm Chloe."

"I'm Megan. Nice to meet you."

"Likewise," I say. She tells me about Andy in middle school and how close they were. She mentions how they went out back then and were too little to understand the meaning of love but now that she's a little older, it's clear to her that love is what she felt for him all along.

"That's why I want to ask him to get back together," she continues "We've been talking these past couple of months. He told me that he's been feeling the same way as well."

"Oh, really," I say.

Andy sees me talking to Megan as he walks back into the party. Megan and I are on the couch. Suddenly, Andy grabs my arm forcefully and lifts me up. As he does this, I feel every blood vessel in my arm tighten up. "Why are you talking to her?" he asks.

> "I feel every blood vessel in my arm tighten up."

"We were just talking about her life. Let go, you're hurting me!" He lets go, frightened because everyone in the room is looking at him with judging eyes. By his facial expression, it isn't hard to see that he is angry. He guides me to the corner of the room. "What the hell is wrong with you?" he asks.

"What?"

"You know what! Don't talk to Megan!"

"I was just asking about her life and you."

"About me — don't ask people about me!" he says as he pushes both my shoulders up against the wall; I have to stand on the tip of my toes. I feel my arm rub against the dark brick wall.

"Dude , you're hurting me, Andy!" I say. His friend quickly runs over; he laughs at my situation.

"Yo man, want to go play spin the bottle?" Kylie asks completely ignoring my pain.

"Nah man, I have to deal with this one!"

"This one has a name!" I yell.

He grips my arms tighter and I look past his face towards the other end of the room. There, my closest friends are huddled with drinks in their hands, whispering.

While I start to wonder who are my real friends, Megan runs towards me.

"What are you doing to her?" she yells to Andy.

"Come talk to me over there. Now!" she says, pulling him towards the kitchen. I rest my heels back on the floor and catch my breath. Cammy catches up to me,

"Hey, where's that jerk?" she asks.

"What jerk?" I ask.

"The one who put his hands on you. Are you okay? I heard something happened!"

"I'm fine," I say. I catch Andy's eyes looking at me. He winks and I blush. I look back at Cammy. "Now I know he finally cares," I say. Later on, as Andy walks me out of the party, I stop and say goodbye to Cammy. She whispers in my ear, "Don't go with him. Please don't." I smile back at her and grab his hand and let him lead me to the door. I look at Andy and say, "You're perfect for me, I'm sorry I was getting upset." I look back once more and hear Cammy tell my friends, Tasha and Remy, "She doesn't understand how violent that relationship will be... she won't until it's too late. That's the problem with her."

Walking Through Time

Rachel Cline

I have spent most of my life compelled to review and re-examine my past. Capturing a specific time and place in writing helps me release myself from that obsession.

My walk up Montague Street takes me past a thousand things that I can sometimes see through younger eyes: the polished brass water main, the dented and over-painted fire call box, the lost glove impaled on the cast iron fence. Across Hicks Street, the Thai restaurant occupies the storefront where I used to gaze at Barbie outfits and molded plastic kits for manufacturing replicas of the Mummy, the Bride of Frankenstein, et cetera. Back then, monsters were big business — and not human. When I look down at the pebbly surface of the sidewalk, I know how it felt when my roller skates encountered the smooth softness of slate sidewalk after this aggregate, which is called "Cosmo-krete" or maybe "Cementine." (The brass badges that brand the pavement are still here, worn almost illegible, but I know what they say.) I must have been a happy kid at some point, because these waves of nostalgia knock me sideways, sometimes.

I try to recollect the way Montague Street felt to me, in 1972: A paradisiacal fragrance beckons from Ebinger's Bakery — inside, the women in dresses with white collars wrap boxes in red-ticked string fed from a device on the ceiling and cut with a special ring worn on their index fingers. Nick unloads fruits and vegetables from a dark green truck, in front of Bohack's, across the street the shoe repair guy in his long, blue apron smokes a filterless cigarette, awaiting customers. He frightens me but I don't know why. Across Henry Street, I peer cautiously up at Prana, the newly arrived hippie store, which is up a flight of stairs. It isn't open in the morning, of course, but contains all the clothes in the world that I want but don't come in my size, as well as incense and posters. Past the hardware store, the variety mart, the store where we buy my cotton underpants from cardboard boxes stored way above eye-level and retrieved by the grumpy Italian woman who can tell my current size without measuring tape.

"All these experiences are linked by the missing presence of my mother..."

Next door, Meunier's, is where I buy presents — silver jewelry and onyx eggs, and, at Christmas, little brass candle holders whose flames induce two silhouetted angels to spin and strike a tinny bell. All these experiences are linked by the missing presence of my mother, whose scent I am following as she shops and browses and flirts. Once I saw her coming and didn't recognize her, in her fully lipsticked and coiffured state, on her way to meet a man, although she never told me that in so many words.

Sabrina Cevallos

YEARS AS MENTEE: 1

GRADE: Senior

HIGH SCHOOL:
Manhattan Village
Academy

BORN: NY, NY

LIVES: Queens, NY

Rachel has always pushed me to be more creative in my writing. No matter how complete I feel a piece is, she will help me realize how much more potential a story has. I have realized that when I have a limited time to write, I become more productive. She has also helped me realize that writing dialogue has to be purposeful. She has truly allowed me to be more thoughtful in my writing.

Rachel Cline

YEARS AS MENTOR: 1

OCCUPATION:
Writer and Editor

Watching Sabrina's bravery in tackling difficult material about her family history has made me question my own reticence about my family stories. Watching the way her pen flies across the page whenever I give her a timed assignment reminds me of the girl I once was, and the way that writing enabled me to say what I wanted or needed to say — even though I rarely shared that work with anyone. Sabrina is braver than I ever was, but I am catching up!

To You, My Daughter

Ashley Christie

This piece was inspired by the idea of accepting and moving on. A void is filled when a baby girl, Myhonesty, arrives.

Dear Myhonesty,

As a mom I vow to be there every day, to support you, to love you, to hold you, to show you. I wish other parents would understand the significance of support. I remember the first time I felt you kick. Oh, how reassuring it was. I was in the middle of a presentation and someone walked in and said that my mother was on the phone. My palms began to sweat, *she never calls me at work*, I thought. The night before, I told my mother about my promotion and the party the staff was throwing me. I knew she would love it. I was so excited and so sure that she would agree to come but I should have known better. When does she ever show up? She crushed me the way construction workers devour their lunch. Unconsciously. I excused myself from the meeting and ran into my office leaving a trail of my tears to follow. Once again, I felt like I was alone and my success mattered to no one. I worked this hard and I have no one to share my victory with. After a few minutes of drowning in my sorrow, I felt something pushing my naval outwards — it was you. You reminded me that there was someone else here. I held my belly and cried out passionately. For the first time in my entire life, I felt like I was not alone. That someone was you, Myhonesty.

Six months later, I am sitting here watching you sleep. I have never seen anything more beautiful. The way you wiggle your nose every few minutes brings joy to my heart. Your curly black hair is relaxing on your small head, your eyes are protected by these thick fringes of eyelashes, and your mouth is open.

> "...kiss you on your forehead. "Do not worry, Mommy will always be here..."

You inhale and you exhale, creating this pacifying monotone. The music only a mom can cherish. You hear how your name flows, your breathing inspiring me. You stretch the "y" in my, then you embrace the honesty after. I stare at you lying in my arms so peacefully, trying to figure out what was so important that your dad could not be here right now. Maybe his mistress assistant had something more alluring to show him. I rub your head gently, hold you a little tighter and kiss you on your forehead. "Do not worry, Mommy will always be here," I whisper. You are more precious than she is.

As a mother I vow to bathe you and make sure you are clean; to clothe you to make sure you are warm, to feed you and make sure you do not starve, to send you to school and make sure you have an education. All of which society demands me to do. But as a mom I vow to make sure your life doesn't "stink." There are too many flowers in our garden that need picking. As a mom, I vow to cuddle you so you will never be cold. My bed is big enough to comfort us both. As a mom I vow to make sure no meal goes eaten alone. There is nothing more depressing than sitting at a big table with your shadow. As a mom, I vow to listen to your stories. Perhaps we can create one together. You see, there is a difference. A mother just makes sure the job is done; a mom is there to guide her child through. Now that I hold your hand, the journey has just begun.

EXCERPT FROM

The Yellow Notebook

Chana Porter

Working with Ashley has changed the writing of my new novel from traditional to a YA Sci-Fi novel based around journal entries of a smart, young woman coming of age in strange times.

Tonight, Angela and I snuck into Heather's house with mocha brownie ice cream. Diary, we keep trying to be vegan but it's ridiculously hard — everything good has cheese in it. Heather says not to worry because ice cream is proof that God loves us. Angela got an organic kind that she said wasn't full of antibiotics and GMOs. Heather's mom is still being totally controlling; I don't know how Heather puts up with it. I mean, who doesn't let their daughter hang out with her platonic, female friends on Valentine's Day? I would probably run away if my parents were like that. We whispered on her bed about college, eating from the carton and passing one plastic spoon. Angela is still hoping for pre-law at Howard University. I found out Heather got in early decision to MIT, but she is probably going to be first in our class so I shouldn't be so surprised. I suffered existentially for a minute that my two best friends are so much smarter than I am. I don't mean to sound whiny, I know I'm good at reading and art. But it's so difficult for me to pay attention to things that don't interest me. So, I guess it's more a matter of discipline than brains. Anyway, after throwing a self-pity party for like a minute, I filled them in on the latest Frankie-Brad-Chelsea drama. I met Brad in the parking lot today like always, after Drama Club. He had just come from cross country and was really sweaty (remind me to tell you what hugging him smelled like . . . desire is an object I can hold in my hands. I cannot believe how bad I want to get naked with him. Is this normal? No one else seems to be as hormonal as I am.) So we get to his car and there's a note that says "open me" on the trunk. We were pretty nervous because Mallory Elmstead gave a speech last week in English about animal suffering and factory farming and the stupid lacrosse jocks totally covered her car with raw meat. I had to listen to them congratulate each other all during Biology because I sit in front of them. Finally, I turned around and told them to shut up, and Mr. Matthews came to the back of the room and said, "Chelsea, stop flirting and pay attention!"

> **"I hate that man with nuanced, surprising depth."**

I hate that man with nuanced, surprising depth.

Brad slowly opened the trunk to reveal a writhing mass of red shapes. For a moment my stomach felt cold and sick.

Then they started floating upwards, first just a few, then dozens of red balloons cascading up into the sky. We held hands as we watched them float away, so vivid against the blue-black of dusk. There was a note at the bottom of the trunk. It read, "I tried to fit in 99 but your trunk is too small. Next time, buy American. Love, Frankie."

Ashley Christie

YEARS AS MENTEE: 2

GRADE: Junior

HIGH SCHOOL:
Urban Assembly School
for Law and Justice

BORN: Brooklyn, NY

LIVES: Brooklyn, NY

Chana Porter has made a huge impact on my life as a young writer and a young woman. She inspires me to try new things and supports all my decisions. She gives me books to help expand my vocabulary and develop a "me" writing style. Her smiling face and compassionate spirit welcomes me every time. I look forward to spending my last Girls Write Now year with her and will make it my priority to make sure we maintain a relationship after that.

Chana Porter

YEARS AS MENTOR: 2

OCCUPATION:
Writer, Yoga Teacher

Now in our second year together, Ashley had the marvelous idea to start a book club. So far we've been reading coming-of-age novels that I read when I was her age, such as Zora Neale Hurston's Their Eyes Were Watching God *and Anne Frank's* Diary of A Young Girl. *It's amazing to relive these literary experiences of my adolescence with Ashley, who has so much grace, poise, and wonder (more than I did as a 17-year-old, I suspect.) She helps me experience these familiar characters anew.*

Cancer Girl

Corrine Civil

*Over time, I have learned that it takes the greatest
deal of strength for one to accept and break through.
Janet does so in the story, and I hope readers will
recognize this.*

Janet took her final pose on the stage with a huge grin on her face and happiness in her eyes. Wearing her pink wig, "Tabby," speckled with glitter and pride, she walked off with the sound of applause ringing in her ears.

She had come such a long way from a few months ago, when the doctors declared her cancer-free after a long, hard battle with leukemia.

People in the audience still whispered about it, as she knew very well. "Isn't that the cancer girl?" She remembered when she was just Janet, the brown haired girl with big eyes and a broad smile. Now, she was cancer girl, who wore wigs even after her hair had grown back into a short cut.

> "...cancer became this struggle that had taught her what true strength really was."

"Why would she want to be reminded of what she went through with those wigs?" The whispered questions never ended, and sometimes, she preferred pity over their constant complaints.

Cancer was always going to be her enemy, something that frightened and plagued her for months. But now, after being able to participate in the school musical and live an almost normal life (the wigs were strange, even she had to admit it), cancer became this struggle that had taught her what true strength really was. Janet wasn't grateful for it, but if she could be cognizant of what it had shown her, why couldn't other people be as well?

"Hey Janet, we're gonna go for pizza to celebrate," Ian said to her as she brushed Tabby in the tiny mirror backstage. "You should come, if you're not too tired or something." Or something. There goes the pity, Janet thought. She could never win. She beat leukemia, for crying out loud, and people still treated her like a brand new crystal snow globe.

Before she thought of a sarcastic remark to complement her refusal, she replied with a simple and sweet, "No thanks," knowing it was exactly what was expected of her — to go home while everyone else partied and lived life, as if life were only able to be lived to its fullest if you had never been a petite, young girl who recently recovered from a devastating illness.

She wasn't really tired. She just said she was because it was easier than trying to convince them that she could be treated like anyone else.

Janet sighed as she looked in the mirror once more, grabbed her coat, and walked out to the parking lot. There, her mother and father were waiting with huge, genuine smiles on their faces.

"You did so great, honey," her dad said, followed by a quick hug.

"Are you feeling okay?" her mother asked, her smile suddenly becoming nervous and concerned.

Janet glanced up at the sky, silently praying to God, hoping he would ease up on the pity tonight. "Yes, mom," she said brusquely.

She knew that going home and straight to bed was the temporary solution. She knew that feeling powerless and misunderstood wouldn't seem too awful after a cup of tea and eight hours of dreaming.

In her dreams, the people around her admired her. She was never cancer girl, although she wore her wigs. She could run through the streets and do cartwheels when she got excited. Sleeping reminded her of what it felt like to be free. Then, she would wake up, and the feeling of helplessness would set in. At that point, even chamomile tea couldn't take away the pain.

But Janet was tired of pretending to be tired. If she went home and spent the night in, nights like this one would happen again. People would continue to ask her to get pizza or to roller skate or party out of obligatory courtesy, knowing she would always say no.

If she went with Ian and the rest of the theater crew, all night people would ask her how she felt, and look at her with solemn eyes before they moved on to a more interesting conversation with the next person they saw. On the other hand, if she went home, she would always just be existing rather than living.

She grabbed her coat from the back seat of her parent's car, told them she was going out and would see them later on, and walked back to the school.

In This Creaky Body

Robin Marantz Henig

I was thinking about a woman trapped in an aged body while still feeling young. She ignores the physical decline so her inner spirit can break through. The character is fictional, but any resemblance to my real-life mother is not coincidental.

The snowy day made her feel more hemmed in than ever. It was hard enough to wake up in this creaky body day after day, staring in the mirror stunned anew every time she got a glimpse of the old-woman face that greeted her. But somehow if she could get outside, she could forget the way that craggy, wrinkled face really looked, could forget the gray hair and the bent back and the legs that didn't quite get her moving as fast or as sure as she wanted to. She could get outside and think of herself as she always did, eternally 21 and with her whole life ahead of her.

But with the snowy day, she was truly and deeply 89.

"I know I need to get out of my own head," she told her daughter, who telephoned her every morning at 9:15 sharp. "I know this isn't good for me, staying alone in my apartment for so many hours." Her daughter agreed, as she always did, and urged her to go downstairs for the exercise class that was held in the basement of her building.

So she went. She looked around at the other old people sitting on chairs in front of the DVD player, getting ready to lift their arms and shake their torsos in time to the instructor on the video, and she felt worse, not better. "How did I get here?" she wondered. "How did I get so old?"

Oddly, the other people in the exercise class, most of them women, had big smiles on their faces. They didn't seem to mind being old, or living in this senior housing setup, or being reduced to exercising out of a chair instead of the way they used to, by running in the park or skiing down mountains or lifting real weights in a real gym. This was their life now, they seemed to be saying, and this was good enough.

"Reach up for the sky. Stretch those arms, stretch that back, feel yourself getting taller and taller."

"Stretch, one, two, three," the video instructor chanted in her slightly-annoying singsong. "Reach up for the sky. Stretch those arms, stretch that back, feel yourself getting taller and taller." She was still sitting in the chair, just like everyone else was, but the stretching was working. This was her life now, and this was good enough.

Corrine Civil

YEARS AS MENTEE: 2

GRADE: Junior

HIGH SCHOOL:
Young Women's Leadership School of East Harlem

BORN: NY, NY

LIVES: NY, NY

PUBLICATIONS AND RECOGNITIONS:
Brown University Global Program; Kenyon Review Young Writers workshop

"I'm going to meet with my mentor, Robin." My friends have probably heard me say this more than 100 times, but cannot imagine how much she has helped me develop as a writer and a person. Sharing my work with others was never really an easy task, but since last year, meeting with Robin for an hour to talk, write, edit, and breathe in the smell of coffee has forced me (in the best way) to be open with my writing. By giving me compliments and constructive criticism, she has helped me build confidence and appreciation for myself and others.

Robin Marantz Henig

YEARS AS MENTOR: 6

OCCUPATION:
Freelance Journalist

PUBLICATIONS AND RECOGNITIONS:
American Society of Journalists & Authors Best Article award, Honorable Mention, *Twentysomething*

When Corrine and I sit together on a beat-up couch at Max Caffe, we clatter away on MacBooks, writing on our own. Sometimes we work on one laptop, passing it back and forth, writing alternate paragraphs — a literary version of the "Exquisite Corpse" game. I realized how intertwined we'd become when I looked through the writing from our year together. Occasionally, I'd stumble on a story unsure whether I'd written it on my own. Suddenly, I realized Corrine and I had broken through to a new level of collaboration, where her voice and my voice had become almost interchangeable.

Black Cherry Soda

Samori Covington

For me, writing this story was my way of breaking through because the process of writing about my surroundings was something that I had never done before.

School is finally over. I walk over to my locker. Locker number 206. *12-2-32* right left right. It's 2:45 p.m. and I have to meet Brooke at 3 p.m. I speed walk out the massive foam-green front door trying to remember to use my muscles to open it. I say bye to the security guards, but as usual they just look at me. I walk past Yogurt-land thinking about how good frozen strawberry yogurt would taste even in the winter. Every street is white and covered with snow. I cross a red light and now I'm on Third Street. I look up at the trees and I notice how lonely they look without their leaves. I'm meeting Brooke at our usual place, a café called s'Nice. I'm just a block away and I can see the brick-stone restaurant on the corner.

> "I look up at the trees and I notice how lonely they look without their leaves."

I can taste the fizzing black cherry soda that waits for me there, *mhmm*, and picture catching up on the latest gossip and writing about whatever comes to our minds. "I'm almost there," I say to myself, wishing that the snow would stop.

Apricot Tea

Brooke Borel

For Samori and I, our anthology pieces are short stories describing the end of our day — school for her and work for me — and the walk we each take to meet at our usual place. It's always a bright spot in the day!

During a back-and-forth email conversation with an editor, hashing out the details of a story he needed yesterday but assigned today, I look at the clock and see that it is nearly three o'clock. I'd better hurry.

I grab my bag and long puffy coat, toss treats to the dog, and skip down the stairs. A rush of cold air hits my face as I push through the front door of my apartment building. It's snowed again, and the banks, already black from the day's traffic, edge from the curb and into the middle of the sidewalk, creating narrow paths that funnel the afternoon bustle into tight lines like ants in a plastic farm.

> "...creating narrow paths that funnel the afternoon bustle into tight lines like ants in a plastic farm."

I turn up Fifth Avenue and pass the record store that somehow survives, the flower shop with lavish splashes of petals crowding the window, and a string of cafés where freelancers linger over cooling cups of coffee. A few blocks later, I arrive at *our* café.

Samori is waiting in our usual spot against the southern exposed brick wall. She looks up, her hands still tapping out a message on her smartphone, and smiles. There is new art on the wall, bright swaths of thick paint on canvas. I feel calm now. Here is at least an hour of writing and laughing, without editors and deadlines (although here, I am the editor and the keeper of deadlines. I wield the power kindly).

We order our drinks — me, apricot tea, her, Boylan's black cherry soda. We both pause to watch her twist off the metal top of the slick glass bottle. It opens with ease, and we laugh. "It came off this time! You're getting stronger."

I blow on my tea and breathe in the tones of fruit and spice. We talk awhile about our respective days. She still hates geometry but her grade is getting better. I still feel worn out from turning in my book but I'm enjoying my free weekends. We open our notebooks. And then we write.

Samori Covington

YEARS AS MENTEE: 1

GRADE: Freshman

HIGH SCHOOL:
  Millennium Brooklyn
  High School

BORN: NY, NY

LIVES: Brooklyn, NY

Working with my mentor has opened me up to trying different types of genres, not just poetry. I notice now that after meeting Brooke I can write more, for longer periods of time, and now I can make my stories flow.

Brooke Borel

YEARS AS MENTOR: 1

OCCUPATION:
  Freelance Writer and
  Journalist

Samori has reminded me what it is like to be a teenager, a time when the world really broadens to a new landscape. We've been discovering new ways to practice our writing together. I think our biggest breakthrough moments have been figuring out which pieces to submit for various deadlines and working hard to edit and polish them.

Paralyzing Sleep

Karilis Cruz

*I was talking to friends about sleep paralysis. The
topic chilled me to the bone and made me curious.
That's when I was inspired to write this short story.*

Staring at the screen
Eyes grown dreary
I think I'm ready for sleep.
My head reaches the pillow.
My eyes slowly shut.
And all is well till my heart starts to race.
Frozen
Stuck
I can't breathe.
My eyes search around me in panic...someone's there...
Beside my bed?
On it?
Beside me.
I sit up but my body still lies down.
Dreams don't exist in my world now, only night terrors accompany me.
When I close my eyes it feels like they're still open. I am fully awake but my body is
still resting.
I can hear them hiss my name into the dark corners of the room. I need to get up, I
need to do something.
Please help me.
Who's going to hear me? Who is going to stop them?
How? No. When?
I can feel them, pressed up against me, they touch me randomly.
My side.
My arm.
My back.
**I feel my body but my body does not feel me, it keeps on dreaming
while I'm inside screaming.**

Imagine a Coal-Dust Fox

Lyndsay Faye

I flipped Karilis's original idea about exploring sleep paralysis and imagined myself as the unseen nightmare.

I am the
  thing
That goes *hissssssss* in the night
    As air from the window's small crack draws cool fingers
  along your cheek, sending a tingle
  like the chime of small bells
  down your spine
Only the wind, you think
    But if only you knew
Unseen, I observe you
    Imagine a nightmare
  imagine
    Imagine a stranger
  here
  beside you
  imagine
    Imagine a dark form lurking with teeth older than the stones
  imagine
    Imagine a lithe predator shaped by the ashes of your hopes
  imagine
Can you imagine?
  You can
Can't you?

But I am not imaginary
  no
    I am the gentle breath of death in your ear
    I am the fox that steals sweet dreams
  clever
  clever
  clever fox

Black as midnight
Come to swish my tail like formless smoke and snatch your rest
Pin you down with knife-nails and phantom-fangs
    Imagine me
    A coal-dust fox
As slowly I sink my tender teeth and you awaken to
    the subtle *crack* of your own bones.

Karilis Cruz

YEARS AS MENTEE: 2

GRADE: Junior

HIGH SCHOOL:
Urban Assembly Media
High School

BORN: NY, NY

LIVES: NY, NY

PUBLICATIONS AND RECOGNITIONS:
Scholastic Art & Writing Awards Honorable mention

'Hazzah!' We have been burning through my writing like there is no tomorrow. Lyndsay has helped a lot; she pushes me to try public speaking and I'm slowly (and hopefully) diminishing my stage fright.

Lyndsay Faye

YEARS AS MENTOR: 2

OCCUPATION:
Author at Amy Einhorn/
Penguin/Putnam

PUBLICATIONS AND RECOGNITIONS:
Seven For A Secret, an international bestseller, was nominated for the Dilys Winn Award from Independent Mystery Booksellers

When I first met Karilis, I wouldn't say she was shy — she was bold and bright and eager to start writing — but she didn't volunteer much at workshops. She preferred to stay out of the spotlight. Now, she's ready to emcee a Girls Write Now CHAPTERS Reading Series! I'm so proud of my unicorn.

Work

Shannon Daniels

This piece was written about the summer after my
freshman year of high school.

> "Our laughter condensed like raindrops on the windshield."

The August air hung, like overripe fruit, over my body until we got the car going. I leaned out the window, and my hair came alive with grease and wind. We beat back miles of New York highway. Dea sang and Andrew cracked jokes. Our laughter condensed like raindrops on the windshield. We let the songs on the radio stream out the windows. We giggled and groaned and leaned back in our seats. We talked about love like it'd just dropped by for a chat one morning — what we had done, how many edges and corners had we seen, every smell, every taste, as if they were things we could keep in jars to hang on a shelf. We wasted summer days on yellow and white lines — hours away from the beaded sarongs and sweet, sweet fudge of Long Beach Island, yet miles away from the carpeted office floors and water coolers of New York — but we wouldn't have had it any other way.

Days like these were a respite from my first summer job: lifting elbow after elbow of rope over a boat's railing, waiting for rusted cages and twine nets to materialize out of the Hudson. On particularly hot and slow days, I reasoned that in some other universe I was captain of the *Lilac*. Instead of fending off blue crabs, the interns and I battled enemy crews. We weren't pulling up nets for population studies but probing for buried treasure. And on the ship, I would stay a lanky, fifteen-year-old girl forever — that part took the most believing.

What I did believe without a doubt was that time took a break from its job to burn change at the arcade with us at Long Beach Island, lick powdered sugar off its oily fingers, and tuck seashell bits into our pockets. The stores, the restaurants, the fudge flavors, the sunshine — these were as immobile as any sidewalk or shore. Andrew, Dea, and I had never seen a sunset on the Island — even now, it's preserved irrevocably this way in my mind, like summer raspberries that still taste good in November. We ate our fudge on the same bench every time. We'd talk about music videos and pranks and groan about summer assignments — "not *again*." Then we'd search, like a scholar for rare documents, for some idea of who we wanted to be five, ten, twenty years from now. Would we still like Billy Joel and sing "My Heart Will Go On" over and over until we got the notes just right? Would we live on opposite ends of the globe? Would we still pretend life hadn't begun so that we could imagine the champagne flutes, fireworks, and contained laughter of adulthood for hours on end?

I thought about work — my work. What I pushed up the hill every day of that summer wasn't a rock like Sisyphus but buckets of seawater. So many people told me that I should get used to work, *real* work like this: day in, day out. A schedule, a to-do list, and bosses. This is what I have been doing ever since. The offices are different and the carpeting under my feet changes every year, but I am becoming slowly, irreversibly 'mature.' I have sacrificed beach days and swing sets and laughter-filled afternoons. I've rethought my wardrobe, attended interviews, and explained in more essays than I can imagine who I am. I have worked hard — but this is only half of it.

The most laborious tasks cannot be spell-checked by Word or alphabetized by Excel. The real work is this — *this* right here. Resurrecting the long-gone — conversations my trio of friends had, dismissed, and brought up again and again. Remembering the taste of air in New York City during one exact summer, on one exact day. Remembering the people I've met and the smells of their homes, the boys who kissed me and the ones who spurned me, the texture of uncertainty in all of its crevices. Recording it all abashedly, unashamedly. Bringing the dead back to life — and bringing life back to life. This is an endless, ravenous duty that I love. This is real work: pulling armfuls of rope out of the water and seeing what treasures live in its murky depths.

... And Out Come the Wolves

Whitney Jacoby

The moment described in the piece was my introduction to music and probably one of the most influential events of my life, shaping a large part of who I am today.

I'm home alone after school, dying to hear the song my dad played the day prior. "Daddy, who sings that song you were playing yesterday in the car?" I ask into the phone. "You know, 'Ruby ruby ruby ruby soho.'" "Rancid," he replies. When we get off the phone, I run to the record collection, grateful the thousands of records are alphabetized, and pull out "... and Out Come the Wolves." The many steps of using the record player are second nature to my 10-year-old self. I pull the record out of its sleeve, making sure I only touch

> "I pull the record out of its sleeve, making sure I only touch the edges."

the edges. "No finger prints!" echoes in my head. I gently place the record player on the turntable and flip its on switch, grabbing the brush and lightly holding it over the spinning record, making sure it's clean. I turn on the preamplifier and switch it to aux. My favorite part comes last: gently dropping the needle onto the exact right spot of the record, which at the time I could only get right one out of 10 times. This always felt like an accomplishment — like pulling a bone out of the cadaver in Operation and not hearing that irritating buzz. When I think about how my life with music and my father began, I remember the painstaking process of using the record player. I remember my dad's Magneplaners, which towered over my child-self like giants, and the boys serenading me, dance breaks between between math problems.

Shannon Daniels

YEARS AS MENTEE: 3

GRADE: Senior

HIGH SCHOOL:
Stuyvesant High School

BORN: NY, NY

LIVES: NY, NY

COLLEGE:
Stanford University

PUBLICATIONS AND RECOGNITIONS:
National Student Poets Program Semifinalist; Scholastic
Art & Writing Awards Gold Medal for Writing Portfolio,
Gold and Silver Medals for Poetry; Poetry Society of
America's Louis Louise/Emily F. Bourne Award Finalist

*From a coup in the Philippines to the marshes of Louisiana,
Whitney and I have traveled around the world in our writing.
Our stories bloomed, spanning continents and generations,
all within the walls of a cupcake shop. All year, we'd said that
a good story breaks out of a writer's comfort zone. Without
Whitney, this would have been impossible for me. I've written
about places around the world from deeply personal places in
my memory. The maps of our lives have intertwined in more
ways than I can count, and even when I'm in California, they'll
still connect us, like constellations.*

Whitney Jacoby

YEARS AS MENTOR: 3

*I walk into The Little Cupcake Bakeshop to see Shannon's back.
Her positioning is perfect for my surprise. I tap her on the
shoulder and greet her with a bouquet of flowers. As usual,
Shannon is surprised by my gift. "You didn't have to!" are the first
words to leave her lips. But of course I had to. The entire year had
built up to this moment — SATs, college essays, long discussions
on the benefits of small colleges versus big universities — and
it's over! Yesterday Shannon committed to attending Stamford
in the fall. Our three years together are coming to an end and if
I could, I would give her all the flowers in the world.*

My Search For Comfort

Paldon Dolma

This writing piece relates to the theme, "Breaking Through," because I have finally been unveiled to comfort and love. I was able to discover the big brother that I had always wanted and find the happiness in life I'd searched for.

He sits in that room as if he's in a retreat, barely making his way out of that door. As I sweep each room, I reach his door. I surreptitiously step in, afraid of intruding on his business. He is nowhere in the room. I heave a sigh of relief. I peer over the scrawl in the notebook. I drop my broom, and imitate his messy cursive in the notebook. *When I grow up I am going to write like this* I assure myself. *I really want to learn how to write like this... so professional.* After some time of simulating his handwriting on the notebook, I felt satisfied and continued my task.

When I lived in India with my uncle's family, I found no connection with anyone. I had really longed for a person who'd listen and care for me but the search was difficult and unprogressive. My brother was the only one I somehow wanted to connect with but he was always locked in his own zone, barely coming out of that room. My brother and I went to the same school as my two cousins who I was living with, but they acted as if I was a stranger in school. In the first few days of the school, I'd really wanted the guidance from them as I was lost and oblivious about everything. My sister (my cousin) would rarely come to seek me. School was the place where we had to act like we had no relations. *Maybe they are ashamed of me since I am like the "FOB" type and such a needless burden,* I had assumed. From second to fourth grade, I gradually found my way in school with my helmet haircut, crimson cheeks and uneven knee high socks. (Tibet is a frigid place and due to the cold weather, most Tibetans originally born in Tibet have rosy, crimson cheeks). In 2007, when my uncle announced that we were going to America to meet his sister and our aunt, I was excited and nervous of what would unfold. After our month long stay in the Bronx in our aunt's house, my aunt decided that my brother and I would stay with her while my uncle and cousins left for India. In a way I felt as if my shrunken wings were lifted. I didn't have any hatred toward my uncle's family but as a thirteen year old, I understood what comfort meant and the decision made me feel an impending sense of love and affection that I'd greatly

"In 2007, when my uncle announced that we were going to America..."

longed for. So in my aunt's house, my brother and I shared a room, which we still do. During the first few months, we would get into countless fights and we were like two opposing parties finding a way to live and breathe in the same space. I didn't want him near me. His presence was a nuisance. We would battle over almost anything and he'd say that I wasn't supposed to "Big mouth" (direct Tibetan translation) or talk back to elders. Partly it was my fault because I believe I was frenzied over finally being able to express my feeling, and thoughts. The bubble in me had burst. However, as some years passed, he grew on me. We became close. He stood by me during my high school triviality, my endless chatters about nonsense things, and my curiosities and infatuations about boys. Now, he has become my best friend, always making sure that I'm on task, keeping up with school and veering off from boys. He is no longer a pest, but a person very dear and important to me. He has grown on me and I hope it's reciprocal.

Terrorists Within
Alice Canick

Not closing myself off to any possible idea has helped shape the piece I wrote. Even though I have been most fortunate in not having political terrorists to deal with, I have focused on whatever has caused problems for me.

They are apolitical atheists, and have attacked or will attack anyone in this room or universe. Their names are not exotic, but rather short, P.C. or Mac. Their colleagues try to sound like family or friends, and are called "Brother" or "H.P." They are partial to writers and prefer to attack before a deadline.

My most recent experience began with a paper jam, when a single piece of paper was kidnapped by a brother, and required an hour and a half of negotiating to obtain its release. Ransom was arranged through the services of a technician, with instructions, which involved dismantling the plastic housing. The memory of this trauma had to be erased from the printer's long-term memory of the experience, but was not so simply removed from my memory.

Like the girl with the curl in the middle of her forehead, when she is good she is very, very good but when she is bad she is horrid. The mastermind behind the evil is known as Microsoft Word. As Words, we are all addicted to it, whether in the form of poetry, fiction, essays or memoir. Our lord and master is Microsoft Word, even though a minor god is called Pages; both can be volatile and vicious. For example, when the copy-and-paste function is selected, the law-abiding writer can highlight selected words and follow up with the paste command.

"Gentle writer, be forewarned, and not surprised..."

Gentle writer, be forewarned, and not surprised, to find double and triple entries of the same text anywhere from five to one hundred pages apart.

The remedy we have been told is to put our faith in the Edit/Find function, which will search to locate the multiple entries. What a perfect opportunity for Find to transform into a temperamental diva. "No, I cannot locate what you seek. I will not."

I have been reduced to a beggar, and say, "Find, I'm looking at the same phrase in two different places. Where are the others hidden?"

The answer, "I've searched and can't find. Leave me alone I have a headache."

My experience with the inanimate necessities of my life has convinced me that I have powerful chemistry coursing through my body into my fingers, which affects my MacBook mysteriously. Yes, misery loves company, and I have compared notes with other writers.

If anyone has a magic formula or incantation to combat the inanimate terrorists, we could patent it and auction it on eBay. Deadlines may never seem as terrorizing again.

Paldon Dolma

YEARS AS MENTEE: 2

GRADE: Senior

HIGH SCHOOL:
Manhattan Hunter
Science High School

BORN: Tibet

LIVES: Bronx, NY

COLLEGE: Hunter College

SCHOLARSHIPS:
Full Scholarship to
Hunter College

PUBLICATIONS AND RECOGNITIONS:
Scholastic Art & Writing Awards Gold Keys

After working with my mentor, I have a better understanding that the similarities and difficulties in a family situation are universal and not limited to nationalities or religions, which was a breakthrough for me.

Alice Canick

YEARS AS MENTOR: 2

OCCUPATION:
Writer

My relationship with my mentee has made it very clear that China has been an enslaving power in relationship to Tibetans and Tibet. The persecution by way of isolation from contact with family in Tibet for Tibetans in the free world is reminiscent of the Germans' treatment of Jews during the Holocaust. It is unacceptable.

You Damn Immigrant

Nakissi Dosso

*Comments that have burned me the most were about
my nationality and the motive behind my parents'
immigration. I developed this sense of a cultural
obligation to stand up for immigration as a whole.*

You damn immigrant
Go back to Africa and go eat with your hands.
Go eat with my hands?
Go eat with your grandmother
Ask about her mother
Ask about the blood running through her veins
Ask about the everlasting pain
Ask about the footsteps in the ocean
Footsteps that trailed a path of desperation
Deep hesitation of the new world they were forced to leap into
Ask about their life full of trials and tribulations
Neither you nor I can ever imagine
Ask why the sweat that drips off her face and trickles down her back never found its way
back into her body
Ask why when the master calls you better respond and not only respond
you must reach deep down into your body down into your soul and pull out your very
existence ball it up place it in your palm and respond
And yet you call me the immigrant me the foreigner me the alien
But boy me and your grandmother's mother are like sisters, brother
You ask what was the worst thing someone said to me
This has to be it because it seems that seemingly our heritage, your culture her family
his knowledge has skipped a generation but boy survival is key and I'm sure your
great grandmother would agree
I walk away from your world of hate
So as not to taint the legacy of my people
give you time to educate
the rotting mind that sits on your head.

War Story

Heidi Overbeck

*This poem was inspired by a podcast on Radiolab
that stayed in my mind for days; the image was of
horses suddenly trapped in ice. It communicated
such desperation to break through.*

On a dark, cold night in the thick of war,
A stable of horses was suddenly surrounded
By a wild fire born of bullets ricocheting
Off of rocks and the helmets of still men.
With the frothing power of sheer terror
The horses broke free from the tinderbox
Of hay and wood and stampeded toward
a nearby lake, a body of such pure water

That it had resisted the temperature's
Insistence to freeze. And so, though the air
Could burn black the hand of a man
From frost or from fire, it was not until

The horses – and the raw earth that clung
To their hooves, and the pungent sweat
Flung from their coats, and the saliva
Expelled by the force of their whinnies –

Rushed headlong over each other and
Into the lake to break free of the flames
That the lake lost its battle and snapped
Shut around the herd of colliding horses.

As the inferno danced higher around
The sculptures of ice, as the snap of gun
Fire gave way to the popping of sap,
And bodies charred in the ruin of woods

The horses watched frozen in horror.

Nakissi Dosso

YEARS AS MENTEE: 2

GRADE: Junior

HIGH SCHOOL:
The Young Women's
Leadership School of
East Harlem

BORN: NY, NY

LIVES: NY, NY

Heidi helped me muster up everything I was feeling. She essentially gave me the confidence I needed to really write about the life changing experiences I went through.

Heidi Overbeck

YEARS AS MENTOR: 2

OCCUPATION:
Vice President,
BerlinRosen Public
Affairs

Nakissi and I come from such different backgrounds and have such different day-to-day lives, but there's an intrinsic way we relate to the world. When we write together, and share these moments from our lives, we create this space where we can find the universal truths in seemingly disparate experiences.

Dumping Pink

Mariah Dwyer

My piece reflects the theme of "Breaking Through."
I had been hiding and making decisions based on
being a girl. Being in Girls Write Now made me
grasp that gender is not a mask or a reflection of self.

When I was younger I was confused about what gender meant. Being raised in a household with two brothers, I believe, can do that to a girl. On Saturdays, we'd go to the nearby park bringing with us super soaker guns and a soccer ball. We'd play soccer — or football as my family calls it — and though my breath would come out short trying to keep up with the ball, and my brothers, I would always try. My dad would encourage me to keep playing, always saying, "One more game!" How could I refuse my father? What I didn't know is that the more I played soccer the more I lost my sense of how gender separated the world. I didn't see anything wrong with these Saturday rituals. After we were finished playing, we drank sodas sitting on green benches looking upon the green grass and noon sky. Saturdays were not the problem, Sundays were.

On Sunday, my mother would do my hair. She'd sit on the black leather couch, watching TV, combing it out. I'd yell out in pain and she'd kiss her teeth telling me to stay still. I'd sit there, face "made up" in anger. After that test, we'd go to church, which meant one thing — dresses. I did not understand who invented the damn things but understood only that I could not run, jump or even fight. What kind of life would I live without being active? I had to actually sit still and for me that was torture. I would fix my dress about thirty times before sitting.

This was one reason that I didn't like school. I was required to wear a navy skirt, yellow shirt and black shoes. I could only wear pants twice a week and we had a recess every day. Along with gym three times a week. The question that overwhelmed my mind was: how do I play soccer in a skirt?

> "I thought by talking to more girls that somehow I would understand what being a girl meant."

In middle school I tried to reinvent myself. I bought truckloads of pink, blue and yellow — even Nike's — in those colors and permed my hair. I thought by talking to more girls that somehow I would understand what being a girl meant. The more female friends I made, the more pink I wore and the less my guy friends wanted to just hang out. I started talking more about Taylor Lautner and less about soccer. We spoke of guys as love interests rather than friends. I did not understand the glamour of having a "The Notebook" romance — even though I never watched the movie.

It took lies and betrayal for me to dump the pink and go back to what I like to wear. It took my friends' realizing that I did not truly understand half of what they spoke about and me hanging out with a guy they hated for them to dump me. Unfortunately, at this point, I did not even know what I liked anymore. My constant agreeing with my "friends" made what they liked what I liked.

During my self-exploration, my mother took me shopping and picked out the usual pink shirt. Instead of taking the shirt, I picked out baggy clothing that fit better on a male's body so that I could mask my shame and the fact that I would never belong. This new clothing made me fade into the background. I did not understand how to be a girl rather than a boy. My baggy look got more looks as it seemed; every girl but me knew what it meant to be a girl.

Throughout high school I hung out with people who would not judge my clothing and instead look at my academic achievements. In my freshmen year I was in a program called, Girls Inc. In this class we learned about how females were perceived by the media and about our body. Even with living in my body for fourteen years I did not understand my body. I wanted to be a boy as bad as I wanted to write. Girls Inc taught me it was okay to be a girl.

It wasn't until this year with Girls Write Now that I had to think about what it means to be a woman. I got to see what many people thought about their identity as a woman. The history of oppressed women has taught me not to take my gender for granted. That I am more than my organs and I don't have to follow what the ideal of a woman is. That regardless of what I wear and what I do, I am still me. I can still love soccer, writing, and other things. I am a female but that doesn't define me.

Hold the Phone

Meg Cassidy

I hadn't yet met Mariah when I had this experience, but I knew she would "get" it. Although our phones are often a conversation starter (watching a video clip, checking in throughout the week via text), our meetings are always a valuable time to disconnect from that part of life and connect to each other.

I often have the thought, walking down the streets of New York, of how strange it would be for a person from the past to happen upon us. What would their reaction be to seeing us all scurrying around with cell phones plastered to our ears? Cords coming out of our jackets? A screen that we rarely tear our eyes away from, even when crossing a busy avenue in the middle of rush hour? It sometimes seems insane, even to me.

It struck me, in a different way, when I was sitting solo at a café in southern Italy one cloudy afternoon last spring. I'd left my book at the hotel and was waiting for my sister to finish class, so instinctively, I of course reached into my bag to busy myself with my phone. Even though it had basically zero service since I was too cheap to fully activate it abroad, I could still take and browse photos, use Viber for messaging my friends back in the States, and...what? Pretend to be otherwise occupied? It's a habit I'm ashamed to have fallen into, especially as a writer, over the past few years.

Now, I'm not scared of strangers. I love people watching and consider eavesdropping a hobby every writer should pick up. When I travelled through Europe as a college student (without any cell phone, period), talking to new people on the train, in restaurants, and at the hostels was the highlight of most days. But in the ten years since then, we've grown so used to plopping down on the subway, avoiding eye contact, and zoning out in front of our little handheld devices, that those exchanges seem to have become a thing of the past. It's become a protective measure, even against making eye contact with others.

So there I was, feeling both silly and uncomfortable at the same time as I put my phone back in my bag, and turned to the older couple sitting next to me. I smiled, and introduced myself. And though we didn't talk about much — the lovely weather, where we were from, where we were headed next — it felt like I'd knocked down a huge wall, and the rest of that trip, I seldom pulled my safety-blanket of a cell phone out to pass the time.

> "Like someone visiting from a bygone era, I'm frequently stunned by how much of a barrier our phones have become..."

Like someone visiting from a bygone era, I'm frequently stunned by how much of a barrier our phones have become to the people and sights right in front of us. It might not always be friendly fellow travelers, or a beautiful vista in Sorrento, but who knows what that next conversation might hold, or what view is right before our eyes?

Mariah Dwyer

YEARS AS MENTEE: 1

GRADE: Senior

HIGH SCHOOL:
Central Park East
High School

BORN: NY, NY

LIVES: Bronx, NY

PUBLICATIONS AND RECOGNITIONS:
Girls Write Now Poetry Ambassador, Poet-Linc Poetry Slam
at Lincoln Center

Something that I learned from my mentor, Meg, is that everything comes in due time. In life, we are handed obstacles and it's up to us to work through them toward what we want. Along with that comes not always knowing what we want — and that can be okay, too. Sometimes, detours happen for a reason and you can't lose faith #wewontstop.

Meg Cassidy

YEARS AS MENTOR: 3

OCCUPATION:
Publicity Manager,
Simon & Schuster

Working with Mariah this year has opened my eyes to the joys of writing fiction. She excels at the same things I struggle with in my own writing: dialogue, fast-paced scenes, moments of magic that make the reader feel like they've been transported to another world. I love how excited she gets about her characters, often "falling in love" with them. She has also reminded me of how fun it can be to talk about works in progress, and how poetry can be a great stress reliever. She's like a wise soul owl #wewontstop.

There's a First For Everything

Leilah Fagan

This piece was inspired by the concept of fate and romance. I love the ideal thought of love at first sight and two people connecting. All I really had to do was sit down, pull out pen and paper, and the rest came easily.

He's more than aware that he's been boring his eyes into her this whole outing. More than aware that she grew more and more fidgety around him the more they met up like this. More than aware that this girl sitting in front of him was never the one to have a destroyed canvas, but just by the way she closed in any openings he found or poked at, he could surely tell it was ripped. She was delicate. Delicate like everything else that accompanied her.

The small hands he'd been trying to get a hold of all night, the tiny lips that tended to wiggle out of his grip every time he offered his hand to help her out of his car earlier that evening, the gentle curve of her plump lips that he was...hoping to get the privilege to taste before the end of their night together.

Everything about this girl screamed sensitivity and fragility. She wasn't his normal chase and he...enjoyed that. Her innocence interested him 'cause he knew he could penetrate that wall she bricked up.

It just took time. And by the way her eyes lit even in the dim lighting of the pizza shop they were in, he was sure he had all the time in the world.

Her first perception of him tasted of "charm" and "suspicion." She knew he was used to getting his way just by the way he carried himself. Such confidence, pride.

His eyes never left hers; bearing into the depths of her soul if she even tried to peek past him. He had no problem making contact or any connection. It was like... it was the only thing he was looking for. She found herself growing hesitant to even move with his softened eyes locking onto her features.

> "His eyes never left hers; bearing into the depths of her soul..."

This was their first date. Yes, their first. It held a vast amount of awkwardness from herself that made him laugh in fits and watch her even more attentively, not even the jingle of the door catching his eyes.

Although her nerves were on high there was that still giant part of her that felt how gentle he was. She couldn't help but get diverted by his irresistible cat-like eyes, his distinct scent and, powerful bone structure. The twists that hung just above his chiseled cheekbones curled at the ends like tiny swirls of ribbon and the snapback propped on top of them, the red of it bringing the glisten out more from his right side. They had sat across from the cooler that held all the soda cans in the shop, making one corner of his face seem more heavenly than the other.

No, that was a lie. The boy was gorgeous...

The Distance Between Two Points Increases Over Time

Jackie Clark

The piece came about through a pair session with Leilah where we both used the same writing prompt as a jumping off point and ended up with two very different pieces, which is one of my favorite things — the way that perceptions and imaginations differ.

Outside especially
Morose calamity
It is time that changes
Migrating down the coast
In spirit
Changing the position of the starting point
Buckets of air spill over in my chest
Enlighten the capillaries
Being older means going first
Precluding the two points
Denying a fixed point
Denying in the waters
Playing guessing games like children
Masking and enterprise

Talk and talk and talk about the road
Overheard love dissipates in space
In New York someone is more accomplished
At home someone is more domestic
Straddling the effort of the balance
Thinking a lot about leisure
The long line of the body
When it is allowed to take up space
Judging space as if authority prevails
What prevails over time
An answer indicated by bloom

Leilah Fagan

YEARS AS MENTEE: 1

GRADE: Junior

HIGH SCHOOL:
Millennium Brooklyn
High School

BORN: Brooklyn, NY

LIVES: Brooklyn, NY

I believe Jackie and I have constant breakthroughs with one another every time we're together. When writing, we notice a lot of differences in our styles; it opens us to new worlds and gives each other a different view of things. I love that. We usually spend about 25 minutes writing and then we talk and have discussions about the things going on in our lives. She's always there when I need help with my writing but also anything that's problematic. Our breakthrough is constant and I appreciate it wholly.

Jackie Clark

YEARS AS MENTOR: 2

OCCUPATION:
Coordinator of Faculty
Affairs at The New School

PUBLICATIONS AND RECOGNITIONS:
Aphoria

One real breakthrough moment that Leilah and I shared was when we went to see preliminaries for the Urban Word Teen Slam Poetry Competition at The Poetry Project. As someone who has been to a lot of poetry readings but never really a poetry slam I was completely blown away not just by the poems (which were incredible) but by the power of recitation and the confidence it takes to recite a poem well. Leilah has often expressed interest in performing herself and I hope this experience opens her up to a new community of teens like her!

My Love Is Mine

Roberta Nin Feliz

I've learned that not everyone in your life is
deserving of the love you are willing to give.

You stroke my aching back
And rub my temple
Up and down the middle of my back
Alternating between circles and spirals at my upper back
Alleviating my worries and pains
I mold myself to fit into the crevices of your arms
Embracing the strong scent of men's Gillete deodorant
That has stalked me throughout
Summer days spent splashing around in the water
Rushing out of the fire hydrant with kids on the block
And heartbreaks on school nights
Stroke my mother's back

My pen grazes along pages of malformed preconceptions of love
And my mom abides in the kitchen
Adobo and cilantro, where her dreams go
She makes you a meal with everything but ego in it
With her brown, burnt, scarred
Wrinkled and trembling hands
She kneels and holds up the plate to you
You look the other way as you eat

You warned me of boys that rob you of
Your heart and innocence
Devouring your dreams
Leaving you with the scraps
To toy with once they've gone to work
You warned me of boys who abuse
Girls and steal them away from their fathers
Only to go off somewhere and bear little girls
Doomed to be stolen once again

I wish you had warned me about men like you

Who drain your life of your aspirations and dreams

And then go live their own elsewhere
Sharing secret kisses with forbidden women
And come home to their daughters
Only to rub their backs
With stomachs full of another woman's food
And colds cured by their tea
Who lie and let your hands be kissed by the hot stove each night
As you drudge trying to make a meal
Hoping that they will finally tell you
That you did something right
Telling you your dreams don't taste good enough
Who glare at grass before they even dare to look up
At the roses and tulips and chrysanthemums
Who utter yearly "you're beautiful"
It never encompasses what it feels like
To be told one is beautiful

Too many tears have been shed for my mother
Kisses she gives me when I cry for her are permanently engraved in my heart
Don't cry for me when I cry for you mami

I fell in love with you again

He stroked my back and rubbed my temple
Listened to me as I spoke about you and my mother
I swore I wouldn't go back when I saw you in him
I did
Like when you struck my mother
Knocking her womanhood out in one swift hit
I forgave you both
For two years, bearing double the burden on my chest

He filled my head with promises to be broken later on
Welcomed me when it was convenient for him
He too, rubbed my pains with the same hands
He used to caress another
As my love grew for him, his eyes grew for other people
My curls and kisses were not enough to satiate
His desire to experience other girls
I believed that he loved me as much as I loved him
But love does not hurt
You do not love my mother and she hurts
I hurt
Failed attempts of sewing him up so that he was not like you

A sweater broken at its seam
As I begged you to put the bottle down
But my hope grew weary, only so much could be accomplished with two hands
Pieces of me I've donated to make you guys whole
Now come back to haunt me
As I slowly convalesce
Neither of you looked up at me crying
Supplicant tears over your heads,
Noticed only once they had fallen

"I never would have imagined that I would have a little girl like you"
You cried tears of joy when I was born
But I spent the next 12 years mourning the loss of naïveté
Back when all my worries consisted of coconuts falling from trees
I am your daughter
I will always love you
Counted the times you've called me pretty on one hand
My beauty exceeds all of the knuckles in the world
I'm ready to love myself
My love is not for you or for him
My love is mine

Variations on 'We Made It'

Jalylah Burrell

*Witnessing Roberta try so many new things —
trying out for her school's basketball team, taking
a philosophy class at CUNY and joining Impact
Repertory Theatre — inspired me to break out of my
creative writing slump.*

'Go off' whispers the haint
Huffing redemption along the arc of lobes
Weak and zircon-laden

The poor have this Gospel
Preached to the unsilvered spots on their bathroom vanities

'Go off' rat tats the co-op
every recoil goes higher, higher

we embrace adversity

Roberta Nin Feliz

YEARS AS MENTEE: 2
GRADE: Sophmore

HIGH SCHOOL:
Manhattan Center for
Science and Mathematics

BORN: NY, NY

LIVES: Bronx, NY

PUBLICATIONS AND RECOGNITIONS:
Girls Write Now Poetry Ambassador; YCteen Magazine

Jalylah and I met when I was on the brink of coming out of my shell and ever since then, she has helped me to rid myself of the shell completely. I've learned that in order to make new discoveries you have to try, even if you fail. She's taught me that just because you can quit, doesn't mean you should and because of that, I've become more committed and dedicated to the things I set out to do.

Jalylah Burrell

YEARS AS MENTOR: 2

OCCUPATION:
P.h.D Candidate,
Departments of
American & African
American Studies,
Yale University

Roberta and her family have been diligently working to secure her permanent immigration status. I no longer take for granted citizenship and I am more attuned to the challenges that the undocumented face. I am in admiration of Roberta and other students who excel despite these stresses and have been encouraged to become more politically engaged on that front.

Inferno Academia

Teamare Gaston

This story was inspired by a school errand. As I
traveled to the copy room, I imagined my world to
be like Dante's "Inferno." It was then I realized that
thinking outside the box makes even the lamest of
tasks adventurous.

Days passed on since my last quest. Before I conquered the dreaded harbors of Pre-Calculia Island, I was sent on a mission by the divine goddess of the Kingdom of Literature. She said, gazing upon me from a throne of classics, "Find the last doppelgänger oracle. Upon seeing him, ask for another Dante and pray that he returns. For it is you, mighty and noble vassal, who is free to travel among the kingdoms of Academia."

I bowed and began my mission. Upon exiting the Haven of Literary Knowledge, I found myself in the Hall of Isolation. My task was simple. Rescue Dante from his ever-duplicating inferno and return him and his brethren clones to the Goddess of Literature.

As I trekked through the barren Halls of Isolation, I began to feel uneasy — as though the atmosphere was putting pressure on my chest and weighing itself as anxiety. "What if," I thought, "Dante has already been cast aside by the Troll that guards the doppelgänger oracle?"

I shook my head. If such were the case, then I would be forced to draw my sword as a means of intimidating the Troll. The thought of having to reveal my weapon of language against such a beast made my stomach turn. What if the monster saw past my sword? Would my syntactic daggers work? Weapons of mass discussion can only get one so far.

I stopped and stood staring down at the spiral cavern. Rubik-like platforms aligned the walls, creating a mighty bridge of downward advances. I peered down; listening closely I could focus on the exchange between the detention bandits. One false move could reveal my position to them. I gripped the metallic rope that kept my balance. "Dante awaits...for Literature. I shall reveal my math homework answers if it means bypassing the bandits."

And with that, I began my descent. Then with a bite of my thumb I yelleth, "YOLO!" as I proceeded to exit my detention hold.

One of the bandits stood amongst his fellows reciprocating the tales of his captivity. "The sorceress of science could not contain me for I am, as I have saideth before, my brethren, a boss."

My further descent went by with ease, for upon seeing my silhouetted figure among the cavern walls, the bandits stood. "If that is the vile sorceress, then let us proceed, my brethren! She will not detain us again!"

> "Fair vassal! Have you traveled three circles for me?"

Through the metal ropes, they clung down and slid away into the sub-cellar. My path was clear once more. I reached the doppelgänger oracle and studied the room before entering. There was no Troll in sight. Dante sat upon the shelves among other paperback warriors. As if hearing my thoughts he chirped, "Fair vassal! Have you traveled three circles for me?"

"Yes, Dante!"

"Who are you talking to?"

I turned to see a fellow Academia knight. "Huh? Me? Oh, no one." I grabbed Dante off of the shelf and put him in my satchel.

"You shouldn't talk to yourself. People will think you're crazy and weird."

I shrugged and smiled. "It's okay to get lost in your imagination. Sometimes, you never know, you may even run your own kingdom in your head if you imagine long enough."

I smiled and made my way out of the room. She looked upon me with judgment-filled corneas, yet I saw no malice. She lacked compassion, and thus passed the torch to me. Again, I stand alone among my own — a knight of dreams, a protector of the unimagined.

Breakdown or Breakthrough

Katherine Nero

This piece was inspired by a conversation about choosing a major.

"Breakdown? Breakthrough?" I remember hearing Tom Cruise say that in *Jerry Maguire* and it has stuck with me ever since. Why is it that every epiphany, wake-up call or "aha" moment occurs in the midst of strife? My most memorable breakdown/breakthrough moment was the night I realized that Chemistry was not the major for me.

I was a college sophomore with delusions of being an orthodontist. Why did I select a vocation for which I had no yearning or burning desire? My primary motivation was m-o-n-e-y. I believed that a career in orthodontics would provide a *safe*, comfortable living. Besides, my fantasies of directing movies seemed too far-fetched to even discuss.

Having survived chemistry and calculus the previous year, I braced myself for a double whammy of organic chemistry ("orgo") and biochemistry. A group of us studied together the night before for the orgo midterm. A friend patiently tried to explain organic synthesis to me. It just wasn't sinking in. Nothing made sense. I grew more and more frustrated.

Suddenly, it hit me that the exam was less than 12 hours away, and I could not grasp the concept that would be a major part of the test. Everything froze at that moment. I realized that I was going to fail not only the exam, but very likely the whole course. Panic set in. Fail? I can't fail. What will I tell my parents? Will I get expelled?

Concerned eyes watched as I completely lost it, crying and laughing simultaneously. As suddenly as it began, the hysterics stopped. A sense of calm came over me. I wiped my tears and gathered up my books. My friends urged me to stay and continue studying. I just wanted to get out of there.

> "...as I completely lost it, crying and laughing simultaneously."

I returned to my dorm room, took a long shower, curled my hair and went to bed. I awoke refreshed and ready to face the world. I figured that if I couldn't pass the exam, I would at least look good taking it.

That experience was the best thing that ever happened to me. It led me to reevaluate my priorities. Instead of choosing a major based on its moneymaking potential, I refocused on subjects that really intrigued me like political science, history and film. I trusted that my interests would lead to a fulfilling career and it has. I love writing and directing movies even though the financial rewards haven't arrived — yet. Using my creative gifts to their fullest brings me a peace of mind that all the money in the world can't buy.

Did I have a breakdown or a breakthrough? Breakthrough!

Teamare Gaston

YEARS AS MENTEE: 3

GRADE: Senior

HIGH SCHOOL:
Central Park East
High School

BORN: NY, NY

LIVES: NY, NY

COLLEGE:
Baruch College

SCHOLARSHIPS:
Pace University
Presidential Scholarship

PUBLICATIONS AND RECOGNITIONS:
Scholastic Art & Writing Awards Silver Key

My relationship with Katherine has been a divine one over the last few years. She has been a best friend to me and like a second mom. Our breakthrough moment would have to be when she helped me realize that thinking outside the box is okay and there is nothing wrong with being confident. I am now ready to go on to college and use the advice Katherine has given me over the years, such as "go where you are celebrated, not just tolerated" and "when the right people come into your life, you'll know."

Katherine Nero

YEARS AS MENTOR: 4

OCCUPATION:
Writer and Director

PUBLICATIONS AND RECOGNITIONS:
For the Cause, Outstanding Film of the Year, African American Arts Alliance of Chicago

Meeting Teamare has been a blessing, a gift that keeps giving. My title of "mentor" is somewhat misleading because I learn so much from her. I admire Teamare. She is a beautiful young lady inside and out who handles herself brilliantly in difficult situations. Teamare does not back away from challenges. Instead, she embraces new possibilities on a daily basis and inspires me to do the same. Teamare also puts my mind at ease knowing that she is our future.

The Absurdly Long and Depressing Life of a Rock

Mennen Gordon

As humans, we are lucky we get to break through
any obstacles in our way. Unfortunately, rocks can't.
It's a real struggle.

I am a rock. Maybe I fell off a mountain (it must be hard to keep your consciousness as you fall, so good thing I don't have one). I may have fallen into the ocean. It must be hard to hold your breath for long, so it's a good thing I don't have to breathe but it's a bad thing I'm being cast out of the ocean because now who will tuck me in when I want to go to sleep?

But, anyway. I feel a little bit smaller. And anyway I don't like being skipped back into the ocean just to be spit out again; pick a fucking place you want me to be I can't be everywhere at once. I can't do anything at once.

I feel a little bit smaller.

It's like every time I get picked out of the ocean I lose my roughness around the edges. And the smaller and more pocket-sized I am, the more people think it's okay to fuck with me, and the more they think I fell off a mountain just so I can hold down the corners of their picnic blankets. And then I get tossed back into the ocean and get cast out once again. And the smaller I get.

> **"I wonder why I had to fall off a mountain in the first place..."**

And the more insignificant I become.

I am now just a piece of sand.

And the more I wonder why I had to fall off a mountain in the first place, and why no one wants me at a picnic, and why the ocean doesn't want me either. And now there are all these pieces of me floating around the universe. And you'd think I'd like that everyone can have a piece of me now, but now they just track me into their homes, and wash me from their ears, and you'd think it's nice everyone can have a piece of me.

But I don't even know what I'm doing, I just want to be whole.

Plastic Flowers

Natasha Naayem

Reading the poems of Russell Edson inspired
Mennen and I to do a series of exercises exploring
the life of inanimate things. We were surprised by
how fraught these unconscious objects were with
human sentiment once we were able to stretch our
imaginations to accommodate them.

Nobody offers us as gifts.
We do not act as symbols
Of love, celebration or forgiveness.
We are born deceivers.
On a good day, when our job is done well,
We can get a person to gently lean in his face
(Though we will not feel its warmth – we never feel)
To smell the perfume we do not produce.
But we cannot get him to return, and cannot help but disappoint him.
We promise you eternity, in return for no care.
And though our physical shape will remain
In the spot you have placed us
To light up the room, our impression fades
To the habitual observer.
But we are never missed.

Mennen Gordon

YEARS AS MENTEE: 3

GRADE: Junior

HIGH SCHOOL:
Institute for Collaborative
Education

BORN: Brooklyn, NY

LIVES: Bronx, NY

PUBLICATIONS AND RECOGNITIONS:
Scholastic Art & Writing Awards Silver Key Honorable
Mention

*Natasha and I were in a café and read a beautiful poem,
"Counting Sheep" by Russell Edson. The narrator was fixated
on these tiny sheep in a test tube, and what to do with them.
Natasha said we should pick something; what would be in our
test tube? I drew a short comic about a galaxy in a bell jar, and
later we did it again, about a rock. Natasha and I always wind
up writing something amazing whenever we meet, even if it just
looks like scribble on a page or a lightly drawn comic.*

Natasha Naayem

YEARS AS MENTOR: 1

OCCUPATION:
MFA Candidate,
Columbia University

*The first thing I noticed about Mennen was how rich her imagi-
nation was and how quickly it flowed onto the page. When we
sit down to write, she gets right to it while I twirl my pen in
hand, waiting for my brain to warm up. Mennen's creative in-
hibition was even a bit intimidating at first. But it quickly became a source of inspiration. Through our work together, my
initial love of writing, which had become buried under the demands of graduate school, has resurfaced.*

I Have a Voice

Priscilla Guo

*Four years ago, I joined Girls Write Now as a
mentee in the program. Since then, I have learned
new genres and processes of writing. One of those
genres — spoken word — has allowed me to break
through and find my voice.*

"No matter what language I use. I speak. You listen. And you understand with your heart: She has a voice." I practiced these words over and over in my head as my lungs swelled with deep breaths. I pinched myself for a reality check: I was performing in the first ever — and *my first ever* — Poetry Slam at Lincoln Center.

Even as a native New Yorker, I never had the chance to go to Lincoln Center, much less perform there. I felt a heightened sense of awareness as I looked around the hall. I was awkward in these new surroundings. I saw eyes darting between the stage and me, trying to reconcile the two. Their thoughts about where I *should* be and what I *should* be doing were deafening.

Their assumptions engulfed me until the emcee announced: "Everyone give a big round of applause for our next performer, Priscilla Guo!" I swallowed the last bit of doubt that I had in myself, and as I stood up, I felt myself tear apart from the crowd. Now, I was representing Girls Write Now as a poetry ambassador. As a performer, I was supposed to change their minds with my poetry.

> **"Each stride across the stage to the center made me feel stronger."**

Each stride across the stage to the center made me feel stronger. I adjusted the mike stand to my height but just as I was about to start, it wobbled, nearly falling from its stand — an auspicious start. In the silence, I thrived. I stopped the microphone from tipping over and held it firm to my lips. The words began to flow up and out of me — words that stood not only as a testament to their content but to my continuity to thrive. They carried with them, the rhythm of my life.

I delivered three poems, my confidence rising with each. For my last poem, I started by clicking my tongue against the roof of my mouth. The audience stared back at me in confusion.

I had written the poem nearly a month after Malala Yousafzai's attack. The contorted faces of the audience began to smooth as they realized the singular sound symbolized the push of a finger on a gun that had threatened a young girl's life. As a spark, I wanted to inspire other girls to be change-makers. Clicks aren't commonplace at poetry slams but neither was I. I will move and shake the world.

"Ode to the voice that has left me with choices. I rejoice. I rejoice. For I have a voice."

Applause greeted me from all sides of the atrium hall. And before me, I could see the future audiences that will look back at me and hear my words — a strong, everlasting expression of my story. I have a voice and the world is listening.

Karaoke Dreams
Traci Carpenter

The stage is the place where I allow myself to break through the shyness and just sing.

My first karaoke solo was to Alanis Morissette's "You Oughta Know," the classic angry-girl-anthem, which I would quickly learn does not make boys want to go out with you. In fact, it actively terrifies them. But I wasn't looking for a date or for approval. And that was good, because by the time I stepped up on to that stage at the Chuck E. Cheese pizzeria my sophomore year of high school, I already knew that I was a terrible singer. I just didn't care.

The elementary school music teachers tried to let me down gently, casting me as the goose in *Charlotte's Web* or the rabbit from *Alice in Wonderland* in a Disney medley, when I had auditioned for the leads. My parents weren't much better, refusing to hire the voice coach who guaranteed he could get me on *Star Search* (think *America's Got Talent* with Ed McMahon), because they knew it was a scam.

> "I've never heard anyone sing so confidently, and so painfully out of tune."

Instead they bought me a karaoke machine with a tape of early-'90s hits (at the time known simply as "hits"). It included "I Will Always Love You" — Whitney Houston, not Dolly — and against all good advice, I sang it in front of the entire fifth-grade class at the talent show. A year later, a girl in homeroom would recall the performance with a compliment and a critique. "I've never heard anyone sing so confidently, and so painfully out of tune."

I didn't let the rejections keep me from the stage. I sang at high school graduation without knowing the microphone was turned off. I sang Journey at a highway bar outside of my college town after a terrible bathtub dye job. And, most recently, I grabbed the mic at my boyfriend's dad's 60th birthday party and belted out Jon Bon Jovi's "Dead or Alive."

I eventually took my parents' advice and traded my dreams of stardom for a notebook and focused on building a career in something I was actually good at: writing.

But some days, if you listen closely outside my office with a cup to the door – first of all, stop doing that, it's creepy, just come in – you can almost hear me singing the female vocals to the B52's "Love Shack," quietly to myself.

Priscilla Guo

YEARS AS MENTEE: 4

GRADE: Senior

HIGH SCHOOL:
Hunter College
High School

BORN: NY, NY

LIVES: Queens, NY

COLLEGE:
Harvard College

PUBLICATIONS AND RECOGNITIONS:
United States Senate Youth Program; Scholastic Art & Writing Awards Gold Keys in Poetry, Short Story; Young Playwrights NYC Finalist

There couldn't have been more agreements and exclamations of mutual understanding in our first meeting than in a year on the Congressional docket. It was our love of politics and writing that bound us together. Our exploration of the word "feminist" pushed us to break through.

Traci Carpenter

YEARS AS MENTOR: 1

OCCUPATION:
Speechwriter, The Rockefeller Foundation

A Midwesterner and a New Yorker walk into the Grand Central Oyster Bar. Not the beginning of a joke, but a celebration of college acceptances hard earned. It's not our usual meeting spot – my office, or a brunch spot in Queens where servers give our computers the side eye. But, Priscilla needs to love lobster rolls if she's moving to Boston. We talk about our shared interests – women, politics, women in politics, television. She urges me to try slam poetry. I make a face. I make her try an oyster. She makes a face. But major breakthroughs will take time, and we have all year.

Awfully Beautiful

Shirleyka Hector

This is one of the most personal pieces I have
written. After writing it, I felt like I had broken
through so much. I have made a lot of progress in
my writing and in my personal life.

When I look into my looking-glass self,
I smile, seeing that I am very blessed.
I think about where I came from.
I think about what I have been through.
Life can be sweeter than pure honey sometimes
And be as bitter as quinine in a cinchona tree at times.
Life can be a mountainous chain of roads
And it can be a silky chain of roads.

I keep a smile on my face whether joy or sorrow is flowing through my body.
In my perspective, life is a race full of hurdles
Those hurdles try to keep me from accomplishing
My goals. Instead of complaining about those hurdles,
I save my breath and jump over each one in the pursuit of happiness.
I know what I want in life,
That's why I do not let anything or anyone put me down.

Everything that comes my way,
Does not frighten me because I know I can break through.
I am a female warrior, I will be victorious, I will be a champion.
I know for a fact that challenges are meant
To make me stronger. They are meant to shape me
into a better person. Just as a tailor cuts fabric to make them into beautiful dresses,
challenges break me into pieces
And then shape me into greatness.

I made an oath to myself, promising myself to let nothing
Jeopardize me from reaching the top of the lofty mountain.
I keep fighting and breaking through with strength and courage.
With all my might, I'll continue breaking through until the very end. Life is a bitter-
sweet marathon but
I still put on a happy face because I know that
When the storm is over, the sun will rise and shine
as if nothing ever happened.

Breaking Through by Letting Go

Anne Heltzel

I was inspired to write about a time I faced a challenge and how that changed the way I make decisions.

I am, and always have been, a planner. Plans make me feel secure; they give me goals to strive toward. My former marriage is an example of a time when I managed to perfectly execute a plan with catastrophic results. My ex-husband was great on paper: successful, seemingly stable, kind, handsome. Yet in hindsight, enduring love — the most crucial aspect of the relationship and the only one that couldn't be planned — just wasn't there.

"Sometimes the most direct, least complicated advice is enough to change a person."

Around the time my marriage ended, the youngest of my three older brothers gave me some very simple advice: "Follow your heart." Sometimes the most direct, least complicated advice is enough to change a person. Those simple words brought me back to the basics. I realized for the first time in a long time that I'd been so worried about guaranteeing my future security that I'd begun neglecting my heart.

When it comes to work, my heart has always aligned with my career aspirations. Writing is part of my identity; and thus I'm emotionally invested in my writing pursuits. After college, I eschewed plans for law school at the last minute and followed my heart to an MFA program in New York. As a direct result of that program, I got my first job in publishing — which almost certainly put me on the path to becoming an author. A few years later, when I took the chance to move to India, my first published book was born. But at some point along the way, I stopped listening to my gut, in particular when it came to my personal life. I began relying on plans to wrap themselves around me like a security blanket. Maybe it's because the older you get, the harder it is to leap (or fall, as the case may be).

Recently though, I recognized one more opportunity to follow my heart. I left my job as a book editor at a prominent New York City publishing house and moved to France. I'd received a part-time job offer that would allow me more time to write while covering my basic living expenses. For the first time ever, I had, decidedly, no long-term plan. Living abroad didn't go as expected; but from it came friendships, work successes, and relationships that I value today. The experience brought me past the need for control that I used to feel, and has landed me in very uncertain — yet happy — territory. It took two overseas moves to figure it out, but now I know: deciding what you want doesn't mean you're going to get it the way you think, or even that it's good for you. And, breaking through means letting go.

Shirleyka Hector

YEARS AS MENTEE: 1

GRADE: Sophomore

HIGH SCHOOL:
The International High
School at Lafayette

BORN:
Port-au-Prince, Haiti

LIVES: Brooklyn, NY

PUBLICATIONS AND RECOGNITIONS:
Scholastic Art & Writing Awards Honorable Mention

Each time we meet, Anne and I discover a new thing about each other. The more time we spend together, the more we find out that we have so much in common. I love writing in different genres more everyday as I explore this year's theme, "Breaking Through." I only used to write poetry, but Anne has helped me push myself. I got to know her when I did. She is constantly challenging me to try new things and to break through my set patterns. I absolutely love her for that.

Anne Heltzel

YEARS AS MENTOR: 1

OCCUPATION:
Novelist and
freelance editor

PUBLICATIONS AND RECOGNITIONS:
Circle Nine; The Ruining; Feuds; Charlie, Presumed Dead; Torn

Shirleyka and I meet at a little coffee shop on Wyckoff Avenue in Bushwick, where she always greets me with a smile and a hug. She is ever thoughtful, texting me on birthdays and holidays or just to say hello. Our mentor relationship has developed into a friendship. She has shared bits and pieces of her life story and the obstacles she's overcome. Her strength of character blows me away. Each week, through her writing and our conversations, we swap stories about our lives. I leave our coffee shop with valuable lessons about strength and resilience.

Every Little Thing

Calayah Heron

This piece was a breakthrough experience for me.
I've rarely spoken about my past, much less written
about it to share. It was also liberating.

It was back in the early 2000s, when everything seemed so simple; I was six or seven at the time, and my mother was still in her twenties. When I'd come home from school, she would be there in our small kitchen, still in her clothes from the night before, making rice and corned beef while talking on the phone. Bob Marley's "Buffalo Soldier" would be playing absently in the background, and the *sizzle sizzle* of meat cooking slowly in oil would accompany the mellow music. My stomach would growl vehemently when the smell of it hit my nose, and my mother would give me that knowing smile of hers when she heard it. Before settling down, we would greet each other with a hug and a kiss, and then I'd go into the living room to put my stuff away; the weight of the day would be shed with every outer layer of clothing I took off.

As I'd make my way back into the kitchen, I'd watch my mother continue to make our dinner and talk on the phone at the same time. I'd laugh at her silly antics of flailing her hands in wild gestures, trying to make a point to someone who couldn't even see her. Her high pitched laugh always infected me with its cheeriness, even if I couldn't fully understand whatever joke was being told. Just the sound of her mirth gave me reason to smile. After she finished with what was to be our dinner, and her conversation had conveniently ended, we'd make our way into the bedroom to eat.

> "…I swayed to the rhythm of the bass guitar, the sound of the islands moving through me."

Once the door opened, the music would become louder in our ears, pumping from the speakers on the little radio that sat in the corner of the room. As I'd sit on the bed with my plate of food, my head would unconsciously rock back and forth, bringing my whole upper body with it as I swayed to the rhythm of the bass guitar, the sound of the islands moving through me.

There wouldn't be any conversation yet, just the King of Reggae filling our ears with his singing of war and survival. My childish mind couldn't really comprehend the true meaning behind the words, of course, so I'd just hum along to the lyrics, singing the words I knew. My mother would sing along with me, but somehow with more power behind her voice, and I'd be able to hear her heart.

It was when she would finish her food, and I'd hurry up to finish mine, that we'd go put away the dishes, and lay down on the mattress-made-futon. My mother would stroke my hair, fingers raking my scalp in a soothing manner, and hum a tune similar to the smooth melodies of *whoy yoy yoy* surrounding us. She'd ask me about school from time to time, pausing in her humming to speak up whenever a question struck her mind. With my belly being full and my hair being petted, I would close my eyes and answer just as softly. My mother would then get up and walk over to the radio, momentarily leaving me cold under the warm covers. The radio was always on her favorite reggae station; I liked to call it the oldies station because the songs that played were the songs she grew up with, and the feeling of nostalgia would engulf me whenever I heard them. She would turn down the volume until the music was just a low buzz in the background that had a nice, slow rhythm. She'd then get back on the bed, lift the covers, and wiggle back next to me before laying down on her back with her arms stretched on either side. I'd lay my head on one of her arms, usually the left one, and grab her other arm to wrap around my waist; by then I'd just be able to make out the words *Dreadlock Rasta, in the heart of America...*

My mind would start to think of everything and nothing as she went back to massaging my head. Thoughts would start to drift at such a fast pace, but I could hear them clearly as if they were being read to me slowly. Why were we in such a small apartment? Why couldn't my little sister be with us when she was just across the hall with her father? Why was he so mean? Why couldn't my mother kick *him* out? Didn't she wonder about these things too?

Said he was a buffalo soldier win the war for America;
Buffalo Soldier, Dreadlock Rasta,
Fighting on arrival, fighting for survival;
Driven from the mainland to the heart of the Caribbean.

I would always think on those nights, maybe if my mother was a little stronger, or if my sister's father was a little nicer, then we'd be able to get my sister back and then she could listen to the oldies station, too. Instead, I was able to hear her father's new soundtrack blaring from next door on some nights. I felt as though my sister didn't really care for his music, but she was only a baby, so she couldn't pick sides. It wasn't fair that her father got to choose for her, and my mother had no say. My mother didn't find that fair either, it seemed.

Troddin' through San Juan in the arms of America;
Troddin' through Jamaica, a buffalo soldier
Fighting on arrival, fighting for survival:
Buffalo Soldier, Dreadlock Rasta.

These thoughts that always lodged themselves into my brain, thoughts that usually made my eyes burn and my throat tighten, never took hold of me during that time, though, or any other time before or after. Just before my heart could clench and my stomach could drop as reality had started to creep up on me, the harsh reality of what was truly wrong with the picture that was our lives, my mother would wrap both arms around me and squeeze real tight, lifting her chin so I could fit my head into the crook of her neck. It was those moments when I liked to breathe in her scent. She always smelled of Johnson's Baby Oil because she loved their products and the way they left her skin feeling smooth. I liked it, too. The sound of her soft humming along to the music, and the secure feeling of her warm arms wrapped around me, always managed to put me to sleep. Reality would wait another day as I dream.

Woy yoy yoy, woy yoy-yoy yoy,
Woy yoy yoy yoy, yoy yoy-yoy yoy!

Ladies and Gentlemen: The Beatles

Joann Smith

This story was inspired by Girls Write Now's Music Memoir workshop. It was at this workshop that Calayah and I first shared our writing. I was so impressed with the sensuality of her memoir — the smells, the tastes, the touch — that I revised my piece to create a more visceral experience.

> "...my sisters and I stand behind it wearing our plastic Beatles wigs..."

A clean white sheet is hung on the clothesline on the roof, and my sisters and I stand behind it wearing our plastic Beatles wigs and holding our cardboard cut-out guitars. Gus, the long-legged cop, and his wife who live on our floor are there. They don't have children yet. Elsie Stewerwald is there, smoking and smiling, as she always smokes and smiles. Her dyed red hair is pinned up but not in the tight way some women pin theirs. I have never seen her husband, though I hear him every night, wheezing with emphysema; the sound comes through my bedroom wall. His breath scratches its way into his mouth, into his lungs, into my room. But it is not so unpleasant. It is like the smell of the sun-heated tar on the roof — familiar, a part of everything.

My father stands in front of the sheet greeting the audience. My father is white-haired. It means he is old. Even though he can lift and flip me and slide me down his back, he's old. Even though he laughs much more than my mother does and runs with me in the park, where my mother never runs, I know that my father is old, and I worry that he will die. I worried the day before my birthday — I didn't want my party ruined. I worried the night before Father's Day. I worried last night. I didn't want him to die in his sleep because then the show would have to be cancelled. And we had practiced so hard.

He peeks around the side of the sheet. "Ready?" he asks, smiling.

"I'm sorry," I whisper.

"What, honey?"

"I love you."

He sees that I'm about to cry. "Don't be nervous, Jo. You'll be great." He kisses me.

I say a quick prayer, thanking God for not making him die last night, asking him not to let him die tonight, either.

"Ready?" he asks, again.

"Ready."

He yanks the sheet from the clothesline and announces, "Ladies and gentlemen, The Beatles."

Calayah Heron

YEARS AS MENTEE: 1

GRADE: Junior

HIGH SCHOOL:
Cardinal Spellman
High School

BORN: Bronx, NY

LIVES: Bronx, NY

I feel a breakthrough with every pair session and workshop I have with Joann. The way she encourages me always gives me that little push that I need when we're writing something new. My favorite was the slam poetry, though. It was funny because in the beginning we were so skeptical. But when the speakers presented their pieces to us, and we were both like, "Whoa, that was so powerful I don't know whether to snap or bawl my eyes out." And when we broke off to write our own, it was amazing how engrossed we were. Greatest breakthrough ever.

Joann Smith

YEARS AS MENTOR: 1

OCCUPATION:
Writer, Editor, Instructor

PUBLICATIONS AND RECOGNITIONS:
Serving House Journal and *Chagrin River Review*

I believe Calayah and I shared a breakthrough moment at the Poetry Slam workshop. Neither of us had thought of slam poetry as our favorite genre; I had never thought of writing or performing poetry that way. But after that workshop, we were both very excited about trying to express our experiences as women in that form. Calayah was especially successful.

Who I Am

Martia Johnson

I am a secret of what was left abandoned.

I am forbidden.
Cast out to the netherlands of her kingdom.
I am refused the treatment of acceptance.
I cry tears that are void of life.
I am a daughter.
A niece.
A cousin.
A friend.
But mostly,
I am a granddaughter.
I am her granddaughter.
I am their niece.
And they are not my cousins.
But no,
I am poison.
I am a secret of what was left abandoned,
A product of misfortune.
I am broken, without repair.
I am scared,
Though no longer am I lost.
I see the reality left for me.
I am the seam that is coming apart,
Slowly.
I am who she could never be:
I am loving,
I am kind,
I am selfless;
I am compassion.
Yet I am still her:
I am the height,
I am the nose,
I am the dimple.
I am made of her skin,
Her flesh,

Her blood.

I am a granddaughter,

A friend,

A cousin,

A niece;

A daughter.

I am the treasure buried under my family tree.

I am acceptance.

I am pride.

I am fear.

No longer will I be meek.

I am ready to know who I am.

To digest the truth.

I am a stepchild.

I am in need of something that is apart of what should be.

I am who I thought I could never be.

Who I am,

Is the daughter of my grandmother's illegitimate daughter.

Martia Johnson

YEARS AS MENTEE: 1

GRADE: Sophomore

HIGH SCHOOL:
Academy for Young
Writers

BORN: NY, NY

LIVES: Brooklyn, NY

I'd like to thank Allison for just being a cool person. She's really easy to get along with and she helps me learn new ways of writing. My favorite thing is that she takes the time out to look up prompts that we can work on. Allison is a completely awesome person, who is honest and kind. I thank Allison for being understanding and relaxed.

Allison Yarrow

YEARS AS MENTOR: 3

OCCUPATION:
Journalist

Working with Martia is always fun and surprising. Whether we're reading short stories, watching YouTube videos of spoken word poetry, or writing ourselves, I'm always eager to hear her thoughts and reactions to art. She knows even more than she knows. I'm perpetually wowed by the emotional honesty in her writing. We've shared many breakthroughs, most recently one about writing about expectations and family.

Halcyon:
A Collection of Poems about the Purity of Nature

Kiara Joseph

So frequently, we are imprisoned by the technology around us. We need to break through this barrier that shelters us from the true beauty that is nature.

Ombré petals glued to a ball of life
There, they lay
In an unbounded sea of emerald,
with ribbons of jade.
Oblivious to the developing world around them,
untouched by the ignorant hand,
hidden by a God-given shield of serenity.
Alas!
A place that remains innocent!

Sol
Striking us with its radiance,
glowing,
shining,
illuminating.

Oh Great One!
How nice of you to grace this place,
with your continuous presence.

Your promise to come remains a blessing.
Providing,
creating,
crafting.

Oh Great One!
You provide life where you go,
a miracle that never fails to astonish.

You continue to give without return,
as if living is a one-sided bargain.
Your giving is not in vain,
your perfection is cherished.

Apparatus
Indeed, I shall put it down.
It won't be easy,
but it must be done.
I shall break this addiction to machines.
To live a life through devices,
is not a life at all.
We ignore the world around us,
and surround ourselves,
with that which is excessive and unnecessary,
instead of connecting with the one thing
that has always provided.
Earth is an enticing being,
magnificent,
alluring,
delightful.
Providing fruit for our indulgence,
and marvels for all to see.

I Hate

Rachel Krantz

I wrote this piece after getting catcalled on the street.

i hate
that i feel like i shouldn't use the word hate.

the idea to write a hate poem comes to me
while i'm crossing the street
and a man stops in the crosswalk to catcall
(i hate the word catcall)

as he passes me

he's a caricature in my periphery
just another man on the street
making a stereotype of me and himself
muttering words i don't need to hear to understand

it's not that i hate the come-ons
some days
(i hate to admit)
i feel downright grateful for them.
no.
what i hate

is how i always look down.

can't help but smile politely
with tight white-lady lips
shoulders hunched
sorry for the imposition of my body
and the embarrassment it's caused both of us.

sometimes, in anticipation of a group of men
i'll tell myself
don't look down this time
don't look down!

and then,
fuck.

i look down.

bad posture made even worse
i smile curtly
then somehow feel guilty about the fact
that i expect these men to do
exactly what they end up doing.

look down, hunch shoulders, smile.

when else am i so polite?

when i was a teenager
i started noticing men checking out my ass
soon i found myself assessing other women's asses
looking at how they went with their jeans
and feeling an aesthetic, sometimes sexual appreciation
but mostly
(what i hate)
a judgment

as to whether or not these women
no — these *asses* — were successful.

i hate

that sometimes
when a man i'm expecting to harass me on the street
doesn't look at me at all
i'm disappointed, worried even
that i've lost a certain mirror i could rely on

like that man who told me
what a beautiful waist you have!
that August afternoon when i was feeling fat.

what i hate most:
i sometimes avoid my body in the mirror
as if it were the man on the street.

i look down
sorry for the imposition
the embarrassment it's caused both of us
only difference is, i don't bother to smile.

i hate
how often
i measure productivity
in gluten, sugar, coffee spoons

i hate
that i can't *just enjoy*
this free chai latte with honey-foam swirls
without some voice telling me this is a lapse
a lapse of some important judgment
and another voice, just as strong
telling me to drink it
drink it all right now.

how could i expect myself to write about anything else?
to form full sentences

when my body informs everything
from my walk here
to how it feels to simply *sit and exist*
and drink some tea?

a woman with a room of her own
is neutered by the fact

that she does not occupy her own body.

(what would it look like if we set up camp
and protested *that*?
we are the shoulders-hunched-look-down-smile-i-feel-fat-today percent)

i hate
i hate
i hate

that i've come to the end here
and I still can't feel hatred
for anything i can't take the blame for.

what i don't hate:

sometimes
i have nights
when i manage to check myself out:

chest thrust forward, eyes fixed
a wide internal grin
i pass myself
and force myself to stare, take my beauty in.

i don't look down.
i see it all.
i occupy myself.

and i can see it clearly.

in those moments
i can feel
what those men who make me hunch
must only glimpse a shadow of.

and i'm sure.

if they saw what i can feel
they wouldn't find words.

Kiara Joseph

YEARS AS MENTEE: 2

GRADE: Junior

HIGH SCHOOL:
NYC iSchool

BORN: Brooklyn, NY

LIVES: Brooklyn, NY

PUBLICATIONS AND RECOGNITIONS:
Scholastic Art and Writing Awards Silver Key

Sixteen Handles needs to reserve a booth for Rachel and I, because when we go there, nothing can stop our minds from exploring, experimenting, and creating. It is easy to stick to one genre, or topic, but Rachel constantly pushes me to try new things. Having Rachel as a mentor has helped me break through the walls of conformity. We don't just write or talk about what pertains to girls. We touch on all topics, which I will always appreciate and value.

Rachel Krantz

YEARS AS MENTOR: 2

OCCUPATION:
Editor, *Bustle*

This year, I saw Kiara break through in so many ways. Over the summer, she transformed as a writer and a young woman, displaying a new confidence and maturity I hadn't seen before. Sometimes, she was disarmingly wise when it came to answering the questions that seemed impossible to tackle. I can't wait to see where she goes next year, both in her writing and in her preparation to move on to college.

Second Smallest

Kiara Kerina-Rendina

I wanted to address the theme "Breaking Through"
by exploring my transition from childhood to
young adulthood. I have been wondering when I
underwent the metamorphosis of growing up, and
how it happened so fast.

I was second smallest in my class and hardly tall enough to place my feet solidly on the floor when I sat in my chair. Instead, the tips of my toes flirted with the cool floor. When I sat in my chair, my feet swished and kicked like I was trying to make myself fly higher on the swing, because when you are small everything is a jungle gym.

Hard-pressed callouses popped up on my curly palms. Sometimes I picked at them because they were blisters first, and it would sting when I pressed my fingertips into the baby skin underneath, but I did it anyway. I liked that I felt strong enough to endure the salty ocean that pressed itself into my rawness.

Sometimes I jumped off of the swing because it was such a rush. I only flew for seconds, but since I was hardly tall enough to put my feet on the floor when I sat in my chair, it seemed like years before I would try to make the sand absorb my shock. It also seemed like years to pull air back into my lungs when I fell too hard.

Everything I see swoosh by me is close enough to grab but my now-smooth hands cannot seem to grip and hold on tight. I am slippery and my palms have not curled in a long while. I have often hoped I would shrink into myself, small enough to not have to bend my legs when I want to lurch myself forward, handle-by-handle on the jungle gym.

> "...when the sun touches your eyelashes and you can see rainbow diamonds..."

I have almost forgotten what it feels like when the sun touches your eyelashes and you can see rainbow diamonds at the tips of them.

I flew into my adolescence, but instead of flying off of a swing and landing chest first into a sandpit, I was impatient, bought a one way ticket there and landed turbulently, bumping along down a short runway.

My four-footed days are over, left behind on the seat of the airplane with confused flight attendant parents wondering where they can put them. I left them at baggage claim, and they have been spinning around and around on the carousel ever since. They lie dormant in the trunk of a suitcase that we buried with the rest of the boxes, because it just would not fit anywhere else.

Diners Like This

Rory Satran

*As I looked around the midtown coffee shop where
I meet with my mentee, Rory, I felt a wave of
nostalgia that led me to write this fragment.*

I used to come to diners like this when I was your age. Diners out in the valley, with dusty cigarette machines in the vestibule and cherry pie behind glass. We would order a plate of fries to split and spend hours talking: "Do you like him?" "But do you like-like him?" We would conjure endless scenarios while drinking fountain diet cokes out of plastic amber-colored cups. This was before cell phones. We would just hope our friends would show up. This boy I liked played Jewel on the jukebox and I blushed because it felt beyond embarrassing and corny. "What?" he said. "I like this song."

> "This was before
> cell phones."

Kiara Kerina-Rendina

YEARS AS MENTEE: 2

GRADE: Junior

HIGH SCHOOL:
Frank Sinatra School
of the Arts

BORN: NY, NY

LIVES: NY, NY

Everything we do makes me want to push myself further out of my shell and break free. We have conquered poetry and stretched ourselves across a world of outstanding literature. We have woven ourselves across nations, experience by experience. We are growing empires, libraries of culture and know-how, pushing our boundaries with every line we read and every line we write. Our curiosity knows no bounds, and I am so glad that Rory has taught me that there are none.

Rory Satran

YEARS AS MENTOR: 3

OCCUPATION:
Creative Digital Director
i-D magazine

Every meeting with Kiara involves some type of breakthrough, whether it's listening to e.e.cummings read his work on my iPhone or debating the merits of a Dunkin Donuts location. Breaking through (to one another) is the essence of great communication, and Kiara and I have carried on an amazing conversation for the last two years. We just keep writing. And talking. And listening.

Lost and Found

Karla Kim

*This piece comes out of an exercise Sherry and I did:
"Write about something you've lost." The vignettes
are from stories I've heard, Humans of New York
photos, the old man outside my train station...*

She tried to backtrack, pinpoint exactly when it started becoming different. She could've sworn only a month ago she wasn't digging through her head to rediscover the sweetest memories, afraid to lose that feeling she got at his slightest touch. He used to be so afraid of losing *her* that every day he would tell her a new secret, as if planting more and more seeds so that the vines and leaves would entrap her. So how the heck did she end up here, watching his hands draw unending circles around another girl's back? It was as if chance was laughing at her, as she sat in the café across from him with her unwieldy purple cello occupying the seat beside her. She had to pretend that they had no past together, as if she was unaffected. But for the first time in her life, she was unable to use her skill — the art of seeming indifferent.

"I can't live without you," he whispered. She looked at his tired face and out-stretched her fingers to grab onto his calloused hands. But for some reason, she saw the door. And the door was just there. So instead of caressing his enraged face with her hands, she ran. The door was a better lover. It had always been a better lover and it was only now that she fully realized that fact. "I'm going to kill myself if you leave me!" he cried. She almost felt the weight of her heel beckoning her back. Pictures flew across her eyes of their late nights on the balcony watching the city lights, of their first tears shed together. Maybe. But she saw the door, and how it seduced her, and so she ran. The next month, she saw him walking down the train station platform. He wasn't dead.

"Sir, you must leave the rink."

"Just a little longer," he said. He was tracing her neckline onto the rough surface of the ice, the way her lips curled inwards. It was 2 a.m. No one was supposed to be here, but he couldn't stop. It wasn't the fact that she was gone. It was the fact that she had left without giving him what he needed. She had left without ever telling him what he meant to her, what these past years meant to her, how one mistake could unravel the trust they had built for over a decade. It still didn't make sense to him. The longer he thought about it, the more he couldn't stop skating, retracing every corner. With each stroke, he was back to square one — clue-less, confused, and lost. He was lost with her and without her, and this was what

> "...she had left
> without giving him
> what he needed."

scared him the most.

A loud clang rang throughout the house as the porcelain bowl fell to the ground. "Mom, I see them again!" he said. She hurried back to the kitchen, where she saw her 15-year-old son cupping his face into his hands. "Sh...sweetie, don't worry. It was nothing." "But they were crawling all over!" "They're not there. Look? See?" She grabbed the porcelain bowl, little droplets of milk and cereal still on the bowl's edges, and motioned to her son. "They're gone!" He peeked through the slits between his fingers, and in a sudden movement, smacked the bowl away from her again. "It's there!" She pinched herself. *You cannot cry, don't let him know your hopelessness.* It pained her to see her son like this, always seeing things in his empty cereal bowl. She wished she could see everything for him.

He hated the eyes. The way they stared at him made his blood boil even as inches of snow fell on top of him. "We would help you, but we can't," those eyes seemed to say. They didn't know that it was he who saved his niece from drowning that summer night, or that it was he who received all the sick and the poor back in his village. They didn't know that it was he who broke his back trying to lift a 400-pound broken piece of a tank off his comrade's legs. So what was it to them if he was now here in the streets? The way they grabbed the newspapers away from his hands as he recited, "AM New York." Who did they think they were? For him, this was a challenge. He would never outstretch his arms or walk over to pedestrians. No, they needed something from him, this rolled-up paper. Try, try and take this from me. But once in a while, there would be a starry-eyed 13-year-old who came around the curb. Each time they locked eyes, she would hesitate. That was when all his defenses melted, when he saw that a 13-year-old was suffused with both empathy and fear as she saw his frail body. She saw *him*.

All Heart

Sherry Amatenstein

This story is about the age-old conflict between an
adult child and a mother.

"Warning: Do not get married to please another person. If your heart isn't joyously going, 'Yes, yes, yes, this is the match of the century. I can't wait to make it official,' then pull back and take another look at your motives for taking one of the most important steps of your life." — Rachel Stern, *Single No More If You Follow My Advice*

"I know what your thinking. I had this heart attack to make you feel guilty enough to hurry up and get married before I die."

Since it's not sporting to get angry with a sick person, I hold my fire. Besides, how awful would I look screaming at my mother while she's lying, defenseless, in a hospital bed? Even though she didn't actually, thank God, have a heart attack.

"Ma," I say, careful not to look below her neck. I don't want to see that frail, pitiful body hooked up to machines and swimming in a voluminous green and blue checked gown. "I love you but let's not exaggerate. You had an angioplasty. There was an artery blockage so they put in a balloon. Everything went great."

Tears burn inside my eyes; tears I refuse to let fall. I don't want her to know how petrifying it was to get the call from dad late last night: "Rachelshee, your mother's leaving me. Come quick."

Once I got over the speed bump of thinking she was kicking him out of the house, as I rushed to North Shore Hospital I faced the elephant in the room: my mother is mortal. Ta ta to the vague 'she's in her seventies, she can't stay healthy forever' mindset from days of yore. I've drizzled down to the incontrovertible down and dirty, clock is ticking, time passes whether or not you're ready for it truth that I can lose her at any moment.

There's no time to continue playing life as wait and see; I have to make my future happen. Or not only will my mother miss it, *I* might!

A tear manages to slip out. I brush it away. Taking mom's wrinkled hand, I'm careful not to touch the tape covering the IV needle. "I'm doing my best to make you happy, Ma. I hope you know that."

> "A tear manages to slip out. I brush it away."

"Betty?" The saw-like snoring in the next bed has stopped. "Is this your daughter with the published books?"

Mom's neighbor, silver-haired Gladys Something Something "checked in" an hour ago as dad and I were heading out — him home for a nap and me to grab a cup of lukewarm caféteria coffee.

"Yuh," mom says. "This is Rachel, my daughter that makes me so proud."

She's proud but also deeply anxious. Has her worry over my single state helped land her here? Guilt, guilt, guilt. Where's a spouse where you need him? Is that orderly mopping the hallway single?

"So Rachel, your mom said you write about relationships but you can't make one work yourself?"

Great – another shrunken person lying helpless in a bed now has the power to upset me.

Karla Kim

YEARS AS MENTEE: 2

GRADE: Senior

HIGH SCHOOL:
Hunter College
High School

BORN: NY, NY

LIVES: Queens, NY

COLLEGE: University
of Pennsylvania

SCHOLARSHIPS:
National Merit Scholarship

PUBLICATIONS AND RECOGNITIONS:
Scholastic Art & Writing Awards Gold (2), Silver Keys, Honorable Mention

Whether it's sharing old stories or opening envelopes with college decisions together, Sherry has supported me through our breakthrough moments. This year especially, she's encouraged me to explore new boundaries, creative ideas, and new genres, so that I can grow as a writer. With Sherry, I've always felt as if I could be something different and new. Even though it is my final year with Girls Write Now, I will always share my breakthrough moments with Sherry.

Sherry Amatenstein

YEARS AS MENTOR: 2

OCCUPATION:
Therapist/Author

PUBLICATIONS AND RECOGNITIONS:
Brides, USA Weekend

It has been a joy working with Karla these last two years. Helping her discover herself as a writer has reawakened my joy of the craft and together we have explored various genres including poetry and fiction. I am excited to see where this amazing girl's future takes her!

February 28th

Kirby-Estar Laguerre

*My piece is dear to my heart as it signifies my growth
from a child to a young woman. While writing, I felt
a whirlwind of emotion — reflecting happily on one
chapter of my life and anticipating a new journey
with some trepidation. This is my story so far.*

Looking at myself
Applying coats and coats of Tarte mascara
To my curly eyelashes.
Admiring the rich, plum color
of M.A.C's "Rebel" lipstick
Against my deep chocolate skin.
Hearing my mother say
From the foot of the door
To my carnation pink room,
When did you learn to do your makeup so well?
Putting on the black, fitted dress
With the heart shaped cut-out.
Feeling strange in my body.
My mother smiling,
I like the way it looks on you.
I can't tell if she is sad
Or happy or both.
Hearing my iPhone buzz
And reading Kayla's text:
I remember when this was me last month, Kirby,
I felt so old and I still do.
Reading the hundreds of college emails
Flooding my mailbox:
You're a student who is poised for success,
and because of it, you've caught my attention

Mr. Wotypka seriously asking
What would you like to major in?
And Mr. Deutsch slyly wishing me a
Happy Friday.

Balloons and gifts,
Locker decorations.
Being the basketball team's lucky charm.
Not knowing what to do
When the waiters at Applebee's
And my entire chem class
Sing to me.

Judging my little cousins
Riley and Sydney and Gabby
As they dance for our family.
No longer being a contestant.
Feeling the heat rise from the candles,
The flashing lights,
The laughter as everyone chants:
Are you 14, are you 15,
ARE
YOU 16?
My cheeks swelling up,
Blowing out the fire in one shot.
Crazy! You got them all at once!
Did you make a wish?
Realizing I forgot.
Uncle Peter relights my candles,
All 17 of them — one for good luck.
I close my eyes,
Take a deep breath:
Please let me stay 16 forever.

In the Dark

Avra Wing

A suggestion in the Slam Poetry workshop was
to start each line of writing with "I remember."
I thought of my grandmother, who died when I
was nine. When that happened, I broke through to
adulthood: it was my first experience with death
and with seeing my mother vulnerable.

I remember my grandmother hissing, *The fool!*
Did she think I didn't know she was there because I couldn't see her?
I was eight, with my grandmother
in the courtyard of our apartment house.
A neighbor lady passed by and didn't say hello.

I remember my grandmother waking in the dark
not being able to tell if it was day or night.
I remember that's when I knew she was blind.
I remember her pale wood cane topped by the head of an ivory swan
with glassy yellow eyes.

I remember the Pond's cold cream jar on her dresser,
and how she would move her finger from the tip of her nose
to her scalp so she knew where to part her hair.

I remember sitting with my grandmother in the evening, watching
her open the enormous Lighthouse phonograph,
lifting the 78, centering it on the turntable, feeling for the record's edge
and setting down the needle. I remember listening
to the voices on her "talking books." I remember the records
came in flat, brown cases tied with straps like sad presents.

I remember my grandmother went to visit my aunt
and my aunt calling our house and my mother wailing, *Mama!*
And when I asked what was wrong my mother told me a lie and I knew
it was a lie. And when she told me the truth,
that my grandmother was dead, she said I shouldn't cry
because my grandmother wouldn't have wanted me to.

I remember thinking, *You're wrong! You're wrong!*
But I hid my tears
so no one but Grandma could see.

Kirby-Estar Laguerre

YEARS AS MENTEE: 1

GRADE: Sophomore

HIGH SCHOOL:
  Leon M. Goldstein High
  School for the Sciences

BORN: NY, NY

LIVES: Brooklyn, NY

Friday afternoons at a small wooden table in the crowded café in the library is serenity for Avra and me. Whether laughing about extravagant sweet 16 parties, being curious about a new pie shop, or just talking about our week, there is never a dull moment during our meetings. Through observation and paying close attention to detail, I am having the time of my life discovering how to write about others and not just about myself. Now, on the bus coming home from school, at the library with Avra, or just about anywhere, I find my hands itching to write.

Avra Wing

YEARS AS MENTOR: 1

OCCUPATION:
  Writer

PUBLICATIONS AND RECOGNITIONS:
After Isaac, Finalist for Foreword Reviews Book of the Year in YA fiction; IndieBRAG Medallion winner; Moonbeam Children's Books Gold Medal Award for YA fiction. *Brain, Child, 2014 Jewish Currents Anthology.*

It has been a delight getting to know Kirby — her warmth, wry humor, energy. We are both somewhat reserved, but, over time, have broken through to become friends. She is a role model for me. She works so hard in school and yet finds time to write. In trying to help her develop creatively, I am challenged to think about the essentials of good writing and try to come up with useful, if sometimes crazy, prompts for both of us. And she always takes them to imaginative places I didn't foresee — and that opens up more possibilities for me. Thanks, Kirby!

vii

Jennifer Lee

*This piece is a breakthrough for me; I was able
to really experiment with language to further its
emotional expression.*

i. we send beetles to heaven

We meet when I am seven; you are 17.

You lead me to the bathroom with your beetles and white candles; I follow. You lock the door behind me and rummage in the drawers for scissors and tweezers (*shh; it's all safe*). You trisect the beetles and hold them over the flame so they shrivel like raisins but crackle like leaves and fall like ashes to the tiled floor.

I drown in the smoke of crushed legs and heads and hearts — do beetles have hearts? — but then you kiss my ear and warn me not to scream (I didn't know boys and girls are different).

ii. our bodies press close and you tell me not to tell

Afterwards, my father is too drunk to notice that my eyes are red and my fingers quivering, or that I am limping beneath the sweat-stained air. When we go home, I scrub myself until the blood and tears are gone, and the water icy-cold. I shiver, teeth chattering, until my mother tells me to get out because she needs the shower.

That's when it starts — the wrongness inside me. I scratch at my arms, my wrists, my legs; beetles are gnawing at me, trying to find *outoutout* so I let them bleed out with my blood.

I know their larvae still fester within me, but at least I'm a little bit cleaner.

iii. i purge myself

My bones go hollow, the beetles are dying, and I cough up acid and crushed wings.

I am 14, and my skin is pink from scrubbing as walls close in around me. Sometimes I think I see you in the hallways or around corners, and I stop walking, only to shiver under cold water until somebody says it's their turn to shower.

I want to go to heaven, but there is no heaven for murderers.

iv. there is nothing for murderers

I am 15, and a boy kisses me. He is 15, too.

My hands shiver; I cannot breathe. I know I'm dying, but I don't want to go to hell.

He tells me to relax (*it's just me*), and I remember (*shh; it's all safe*). I know there is no easy death for killers, so I shake my head as pupae ooze from my pores. I push him away and run, afraid my beetles will devour him, too.

When my math teacher asks to talk to me after class, I freeze. All I can think is that I have an "A"; what does he want,

what does he want,

what does he want?

until I am trembling again, realizing that it's just the two of us together in the room. He says "Sit," but I can't sit; I can feel you in my veins, boiling, snapping, and condemning, until the whole world is consumed by black abdomens and thoraces and elytra until I am on the ground with him kneeling beside me, asking me if I am okay. My nails scrape my arms, saying, No, *don't touch me; nobody touches me but you.* I can feel them (you) hollowing me. I need to get you out, and I cannot obey the command of Stop, Stop, Stop before my teacher leaves to get the nurse.

When he leaves, I can breathe. When I return to class a week later, he says nothing.

v. the dead have no place in the world of the living; the dead do not speak

The shrink pulls me from class to talk (spider fingers, wasp eyes). She asks how I am, and I say "Fine." She asks me about what happened, and I don't tell her about the beetles.

"I want to fall like ashes; I want to feel your love." When she asks me how often I eat, I lick my lips and tell her I eat too much. She blinks, saying "You're Too Skinny," and I tell her that I know. I know I'm skinny; I know I'm breaking, but I cannot feed your beetles; I cannot feed your love.

She asks me if I want to be thinner, prettier, and I say "No:" I know I'm ugly; I know I'm just a husk; I want to fall like ashes; I want to feel your love.

vi. i miss your love

You are the only one who loved me.

I am 17; you are 27. I don't know where you are, but I live with your beetles and they are my blood (or a symbol of your love).

My mother is dead; your mother was dead, and my father is my father is my father (not all men are created; not all men are created equal). I light a candle and my fingertips graze the flame; the beetles shrivel like raisins but crackle like leaves and fall like ashes to the tiled floor.

I am the millions of beetles that live within me. I want to rise like smoke, but killers don't go to heaven. Now I know: I have sent so many beetles to heaven — just kill them, just kill them, just kill them.

vii. i will send myself to heaven.

Bisexual Culture Is No 'Fiction'

Alex Berg

This past year has been one defined by 'breaking through' from the personal to the public for me. I started writing about being an LGBTQ person, with the intent to create more visibility so that others could live their lives in a happy, healthy and visible way.

Bisexuals are "slutty." We're "men in denial about their homosexuality." Most of us are closet cases. We're "not a legitimate sexual orientation," in the eyes of 15 percent of heterosexual people. We're undermined by the "mysterious" female sexuality. We're "something you simply do," devoid of any parallel to gay culture. Sometimes, we're even "en vogue" because, you know, bisexuality is "the new black."

At least this is what the mainstream media would have you believe about us.

Recently, *The New York Times Magazine* featured a story by Benoit Denizet-Lewis called "The Scientific Quest to Prove Bisexuality Exists." The story profiled the research of the American Institute of Bisexuality, which is responsible for funding much of the scientific research around our orientation. Though the piece didn't overtly question the very existence of bisexuality itself (*The New York Times* already did that in 2005), it focused largely on experiments that measure pupil dilation and genital arousal in search of concrete evidence of male bisexuality. Coupled with personal stories from mostly white, bisexual cisgender people (those whose gender identity matches the sex they were assigned at birth), the research presented by Denizet-Lewis served as a reminder of the ease in which bisexual lived experiences are reduced to the offensive — and untrue — platitudes listed above.

Yet, while *The New York Times* story was imperfect for its failure to present diverse bisexual identities, a response to the piece on *Slate* titled "Is Bisexual Identity a Useful Fiction?'" posited whether bisexuality is more than "something you simply do" in part because "it's nearly impossible to imagine a developed bisexual culture at this point in time," according to writer Mark Joseph Stern. Stern, for his part, ultimately affirms the existence of bisexuality in men and women, but condemns the modern bisexual movement for failing culturally "...to articulate a coherent platform beyond its initial goals of recognition."

Even if these writers concede — with hesitation of course — that we bisexuals exist, how do we do so without a cultural identity?

This might as well be the same as questioning our very existence — it certainly translates into real-life experiences that do. At its best, it's when I'm viewed as little more than sexual meat by couples propositioning me on OkCupid, or when I'm accused of being too afraid to come out as gay. At its worst, it's precious media space devoted to how I'm perceived as "dirty," instead of exploring why 45 percent of bisexual women have contemplated or attempted suicide, why we're twice as likely to have an eating disorder compared to our lesbian counterparts and why, compared with straight women and lesbians, we have the highest rates of alcohol abuse.

But, I don't have to look to *Slate* or any other online magazine to know that when I tell people I identify as bisexual, it holds less cultural currency than when I say I'm simply "queer." Given that the term has been recently reclaimed from its pejorative roots, the political undertones are more obvious. Remove the word "bisexual" from my vocabulary, and I'm instantly more accepted in the lesbian scene; considered more dateable and trustworthy, even. So, when in October, bisexual writer and editor Anna Pulley gave some compelling reasons in *Salon* why we ought to consider putting "the word to bed," it was hard to look away.

After all, "bisexual" is marked by strong negative connotations that perhaps a new term would present a re-birth for those of us with fluid identities. "I think people's attitudes toward bisexuals comprise the bigger obstacle to acceptance....We're *Girls Gone Wild* or giving you HIV or closet-cases taking advantage of straight privilege or stealing your boyfriend. These are hard stereotypes to fight because they're so pervasive and culturally ingrained, even among bisexuals ourselves," Pulley wrote me in an email last year. Then, the term is criticized within the queer community for being too binary. Pulley wrote in an email that "If you're involved with a person who's genderqueer, trans, or intersex, for instance, 'bisexual' doesn't really cut it."

"Given that "bisexual" triggers the world's-worst-dirty sex taboo, I wonder..."

Given that "bisexual" triggers the world's-worst-dirty sex taboo, I wonder: Has this connotation, perpetuated by places like *The New York Times* and *Slate,* become so unshakable that it's time to replace the term? Absolutely not.

Bisexuality should, for once and for all, be publicly understood under activist Robyn Ochs' definition: "I call myself bisexual because I acknowledge that I have in myself the potential to be attracted — romantically and/or sexually — to people of more than one sex and/or gender, not necessarily at the same time, not necessarily in the same way, and not necessarily to the same degree." While this definition itself encompasses all the identities of the LGBTQ community, in *Slate*, Stern wonders: "Is bisexuality even an identity, in the way that homosexuality is?"

My bisexual identity is one that is defined by my proudly challenging assumptions about sexuality altogether. Outsiders frequently judge my sexuality based on the gender of the person I'm with; in coming out to them as bisexual, through my capacity to love, I immediately challenge their notion of what makes a person LGBT. Faith Cheltenham, President of BiNet USA, put it this way in a phone call this week, "People think one thing about bi people and the reality is different. That's what we talk about when we use bi-culture, how people see us being different than who we are." Equally as profound is the word's rich cultural and political legacy. Just look to last year's bisexual White House summit, which helped inspire Bisexual Health Awareness Month, and the many publications, musicians, manifestos and organizations dedicated to documenting the experiences of bisexual people. If these don't constitute a "coherent platform," what does?

Perhaps most proudly, bisexual culture represents intersectionality at its core. We are cisgender and trans people alike, among all of the other identities we intersect as 50 percent of the LGBT community. Cheltenham wrote me in an email last year that for her, "Bisexuality is not who I am, it is a component of my identity. As a black woman I have other aspects of my identity that will consistently affect my life. As a black American I am more likely to have poor health outcomes. As a woman I am more likely to be affected by sexism." So, when Stern insisted in *Slate* that it's time for the bisexual "movement to stop substantiating its own existence and start trying to give that existence the cultural substance it craves," it made me wish I could. In fact, I'd be more than happy to stop — as soon as the media stop looking to scientific studies to prove we exist.

Jennifer Lee

YEARS AS MENTEE: 1

GRADE: Sophomore

HIGH SCHOOL:
Hunter College
High School

BORN: New Haven, CT

LIVES: Queens, NY

PUBLICATIONS AND RECOGNITIONS:
Scholastic Art & Writing Awards Gold Keys in Poetry, Short Story, and Personal Essay/Memoir

I've realized that having a writing mentor isn't just about having a writing mentor. It's also about having a Cool Wise Person to talk to and laugh with, and that has been a break through in my relationship with Alex.

Alex Berg

YEARS AS MENTOR: 3

OCCUPATION:
Associate Producer at
HuffPost Live

PUBLICATIONS AND RECOGNITIONS:
Nominated for a 2014 GLAAD Media Award, *HuffPost Live, live.huffingtonpost.com, The Huffington Post's Gay Voices*

Developing a new mentoring relationship is rich with break through moments as you get to know each other. Jenny has opened me up to new experiences through her use of varied genres and topics in her writing. But perhaps our greatest breakthrough moment as a pair was when we stopped writing and started talking. There have been a few sessions where we've just chatted, and those have been as valuable as when we spend our time writing.

Living in the Moment

Rumer LeGendre

*This is my first time writing honestly about how I feel
about going to college. I've always dreamed of what
it would be like for me. The way I look forward to my
college graduation is not something I ever shared,
because I know many people look at college differently.*

Whenever I think of going to college, all I envision is my graduation ceremony. I glaze over the four years of studying and classes and go straight to that last shining moment. I see myself among thousands, completely joyous, sitting with the class of 2019 as we listen to several long, inspiring, and boring speeches. Then the most exciting moment of all — I throw my cap into the air and attempt to catch it as it sails down from the sea of caps above.

It's not as if I haven't given thought to what I might study. I definitely have. Maybe Law, or History, or Sociology. I'm just not sure about that right now. The only thing I'm positive of is the type of graduation I want to be part of.

I've always had this dream, but it wasn't until my sister's graduation from Baruch last May that I realized something so spectacular could actually be possible for me. I picture myself five years from now, filing into the stadium from the wings. My sister is sitting with my parents, wondering how she's going to see me when there are so many graduates.

> "I picture myself five years from now, filing into the stadium..."

Five years from now, my sister will be the one asking my parents what school I'm in, as she begins to realize that each school of the university comes out together. When my parents say they don't know, my sister will text me. "Look now!" she'll shout when she hears my school announced, so they don't miss me. The three of them will see my smiling face on the big projector screen, waving as I walk by in my cap and gown. Minutes later, I'll text them, just as my sister texted me last May: "Did you guys see me?"

The way I look at it, college has only two important moments. The first is getting in. The second is graduating. There's nothing in between. I work hard to get in, and then I enjoy the graduation I've always wanted.

Now that I'm a junior, my whole life is geared toward the first step: getting in. I'm starting to think about which teachers I have a good relationship with and can ask for recommendations. I've also applied to so many programs — writing, arts, technology, history, and even joined my school's bowling team that more than half my school didn't know existed — that at one point I couldn't remember what one was about when I got an email wanting to schedule an interview.

I try to put things in perspective and focus on what's in front of me right now, that being the most intimidating and important test of my high school career, the SAT. This test is not the make-it or break-it of getting into college, but it's still a big deal. I'll also be taking the AP literature exam, and I'm trying to maintain my 3.3 GPA or get it higher. I don't want any low scores on my transcript. All this means sleepless nights, tons of homework, harder classes, lots of studying, and hours researching colleges — how are you going to pay, are you going to get a scholarship, and many questions about life after high school that keep me up in the night.

My advisor said to start a list of schools I'm interested in, what they're offering, what they're looking for. I actually started my own list last summer. It includes Syracuse, Stony Brook, Baruch, Genesco, Hunter, and others. In my mind, I thought that in order to have the graduation I've always dreamed of, I need to be in a large school. But if I went to a small college, I would be fine because I've gone to small schools my whole life, and that's actually where I'm most comfortable. My desire to be in a large school is only so I can be part of the huge graduating class.

At my sister's graduation, I didn't know what she was studying, but it didn't matter. What mattered was seeing my sister be part of this huge organism, just being there on the day-of. All those people. Family. Friends.

Five years from now, it will be my turn. All my hard work of getting into college will have paid off when I am standing among my fellow classmates at graduation. My cap will be decorated with rainbow glitter and gold sequins, and I'll smile as it falls down into my hand.

Beethoven's Fifth

Vivian Conan

*When Rumer was envisioning her college
graduation, we talked about my upcoming 50th
reunion, when I will don a gold cap and gown to
march with the class of 2014. (Yes, I graduated in
1964.) This is about the morning vitamin shot that
got me through scary courses, like calculus.*

I turn up the volume on the hi-fi, set Beethoven's Fifth on top of the spindle, and hurry to the mirror before the record drops — just in time to raise my arms and bring in the orchestra. *Da-Da-Da-Daaah!* They're right with me. Crisp. Precise. Forceful. Pencil-baton in hand, I turn my body to cue in the strings, the winds, the brass, as they playfully toss *Da-Da-Da-Daaahs* back and forth before uniting in one so loud the apartment walls quiver.

This is my time: weekday mornings. My parents have gone to work, and my brother leaves for class before me. I conduct the entire 32- minute symphony — little wrist flicks in the delicate parts, more elbow in the louder ones, full shoulder for the giant swells, but always with the clear beat I learned in conducting class at music camp. I make eye contact with myself in the mirror, but it's the orchestra members' eyes that look back at me. We move and breathe as one through every crescendo, diminuendo, staccato, and fermata. The air vibrates. My muscles and bones vibrate. The hole in the center of my chest fills with majesty. And power. The orchestra is making this glorious sound under *my* direction.

> "The hole in the center of my chest fills with majesty."

We sneak up to the finale over a bridge from the scherzo. I hunch down, arms close to my body, to keep the tympani soft as it tolls in the background. The strings, so quiet I can barely hear them, begin their upward spiral. Like a slow-moving wave, they gather strength and swell to a sudden crescendo, following me as I unfold. I keep them on the crest a few seconds, feeling the audience holding its breath, before I let them spill over into the first strident chord of the finale.

The full orchestra is off now, on a relentless forward march. The strings and winds break away a few times to frolic with scales that scamper up and tumble down in curlicues, but they always fall into step again. My insides fill with the booming sound. Now the fake ending, the wind-up chords that suddenly decide it's not time to wind up and step aside to let the winds sneak back in. The whole orchestra follows, and we're marching again, ever onward. Now the coda. The orchestra doubles its pace. I keep my beat strong, to hold them in check without breaking their spirit as we race toward the real ending. This one is drawn out, chord after resounding chord — we need so many to slow us down after such speed. I hold the final chord for a few seconds, feeling the vibrations in my bones, then cut it off with a flick of my wrist. But I keep my arms raised another moment, loath to drop them and relinquish my power.

The silence in the apartment is different from before, alive with energy. I feel full, satisfied, ready to ride my bike the three miles to Brooklyn College.

Rumer LeGendre

YEARS AS MENTEE: 2

GRADE: Junior

HIGH SCHOOL:
NYC iSchool

BORN: NY, NY

LIVES: NY, NY

Talking. Laughing. Writing. These are the words that sum up my meetings with my mentor. Vivian has helped me discover what I really feel through probing questions and fast typing. I'm most proud of the poem about my grandmother. It truly came from the heart. Vivian helped me realize it was the perfect piece to develop and share with others. She has encouraged me to voice my opinion as much as I want in my writing. She has also pushed me to step out of my comfort zone and do what to me seemed impossible — to get inside the mind of a cat.

Vivian Conan

YEARS AS MENTOR: 2

OCCUPATION:
Librarian, Westchester
Library System

Rumer, I love watching you blossom and become sure of yourself. A special moment for me this year was seeing you suddenly view yourself as a woman. Your poem just bursts out of you. I love our weekly sessions, where sometimes you know what you want to write, and other times I ask questions and listen to your tone of voice to gauge whether I'm on the right track. Then, I type your answers. When we zero in on what's important, it's as if we've discovered it together.

A Letter to My Friends and Family

Xiao Shan Liu

*Many of my friends and family back in China have
overstated assumptions about my life in New York.
The purpose for me to write this letter is to make a
clarification that I am in fact, living in a normal life.*

To My Friends and Family Back in China:

Over the years, many of you have been very curious about my life in New York. You've asked me about school, food, friends, and everything that happens around me, with all kinds of assumptions due to the overly exaggerated American TV shows. I think I know what you imagine:

1. You think my parents make a big fortune in America and we own a big house and car.

2. You think there are no Chinese people here, no traditional foods, and no one speaks our language.

3. You think I automatically get good grades and will attend an Ivy League college because that is what Asians do here.

4. You think I am dating an American guy, of course.

5. You think I always eat fast food just like the Americans do.

Well, friends, you're not too far off. Here's a typical day in my American life:

Every morning, I wake up in my bed, wearing my blue pajamas, made in the USA with 100% cotton. I brush my teeth with an electric toothbrush (my toothpaste, shampoo, and lotion are all made in the USA too, you know). After I finish blow drying my hair, I put on my red and white American Eagle coat and blue American Apparel pants. When I take the subway to my school, sometimes, I feel lonely and miss home, because I'm the only Chinese person around. When I get to International High School (obviously, it's famous and beautiful with green grass and a huge parking lot, since "international" means glamorous and high class, right?), I find my tall, blond, handsome American boyfriend in the hallway and we kiss in front of everyone. Then we head to McDonald's or Burger King for lunch — I've gained some weight since I got to America, since there's no Chinese food and we eat cheeseburgers and french fries every day. Next year, I'll be off to Harvard without a doubt!

"Just kidding! My
life is very different
from the stereotypes
you see..."

Just kidding! My life is very different from the stereotypes you see on American television. I know that American pop culture creates confusion for many Chinese people and makes it seem like America is a completely different world, but it is not true. We actually share some similarities in our daily lives and my life and community are not as different as you think.

Here is how I actually live:

Although it has been five years since we immigrated to America, my parents didn't make a big fortune out of it. Both of them are working class: my mother is a health aide and my father just lost his job. We rent a basement apartment in Brooklyn. We have two bedrooms, a living room with open kitchen and a bathroom. It is not a big apartment but we are satisfied with it. Before, my family lived in a small bedroom in our relatives' apartment. Even though it was crowded and we were glad to move out after a year, living with my aunt's family helped me a lot to fit into New York and get used to the new lifestyle.

I attend International High School at Union Square. I know in China, "international" makes a school sound very famous and elite, but in our school, it means we have students coming from different countries, and, of course, that includes Chinese students, too. I have friends who came from Guangzhong, Fuzhou and even Beijing — and I also have friends who came from Mexico, Yemen and Senegal. In school, I have worked very hard to become a straight-A student and joined many outside programs to try to boost my grades and college application. But none of this guarantees that I will get into an Ivy League college. In the U.S., there are many kinds of colleges other than the big famous schools. I want to attend a school that is suitable for me and that I like, not just because it has a famous reputation in the world.

When I have free time, I like to hang out with my friends and my boyfriend, also a Chinese immigrant, in Chinatown. I know many of you are shocked that there is a Chinatown in New York, but in fact, the Chinese have a long history of immigrating to America, and many Americans admire our culture and have welcomed "Chinatowns" in their cities. In ours in New York, there are a lot of delicious Chinese restaurants, though I will admit it can't compete with the pure taste in China. I miss the Tanghulu (candied gourd) in China and how the hawker always lets me pick the largest one on the bamboo stick. But other than that, when I see and hear people talking in different dialects and inhale the smell of the fish market, it is almost like I am back in China again. After all, life isn't that different here in New York.

The Farthest I've Ever Been from Home

Alyssa Vine

This short prose reflects on my experience in the mountainous Guangxi region of China, which might be the most foreign and far away place I've ever been.

There's a gentle haunting here. The mountains are stacked against each other, echoing in the mist like holograms. It just doesn't look real. For the first time since childhood days drenched in sand and salt and summer vacation, it occurs to me to wonder where, exactly, I'd pop out if I dug straight through the earth to the other side? If I were at home, could it be here, somewhere in this lush, foggy piece of southern China? The origins of these deep green humps of earth must have a lovely story, maybe a giant who leaps easily across them like stones, criss-crossing rivers to deliver a message to his love. Maybe his message is written in flourishing expressive strokes that I cannot, for the life of me, discern from one another. Maybe he speaks in the language that flows and trips around me. But who knows? I've touched this corner of the earth so tentatively, without recognition or understanding, but its ghostly grandeur will travel home with me.

> "...his message is written in flourishing expressive strokes..."

Xiao Shan Liu

YEARS AS MENTEE: 2

GRADE: Senior

HIGH SCHOOL:
International High School at Union Square

BORN: Shenzhen, China

LIVES: Brooklyn, NY

PUBLICATIONS AND RECOGNITIONS:
Scholastic Art & Writing Awards Gold Key

This is my second year with Alyssa in Girls Write Now. This year, we worked together to challenge ourselves and try new writing styles. We know more about each other through writing and it has made us closer. With Alyssa's help, I wrote a fictional story that gained recognition from the Scholastic Art & Writing Awards, and became one of the Gold Key holders.

Alyssa Vine

YEARS AS MENTOR: 2

OCCUPATION:
Director of Media Relations, Barnard College

PUBLICATIONS AND RECOGNITIONS:
Trop, tropmag.com

In the time I've known Xiao Shan, she's taught me a lot about her home country. Through her writing, she's introduced me to all kinds of Chinese phrases and ideas that are deeply rooted in the way that she sees the world and expresses herself. Recently, I traveled to China for work. Before I left, we studied the map and talked about the challenges of exploring a new place (and the local cuisine I should sample!). While I was there, I felt like she was with me in spirit, helping me experience her country with the same enthusiasm and sense of purpose that she shows every day.

The Connection That We Had

Janae Lowe

*I was inspired to write this piece because of the death
of my grandma. Through knowing my grandma and
remembering the times we spent together, I am now
able to see the world in a different way.*

My grandmother and I had a close connection. Her name is Janie Mae Lowe. My grandmother was so beautiful; she could have been a supermodel. My grandmother had a lot of adventurous moments when she traveled to places like Aruba, Africa, and the Caribbean Islands. Before she became ill we went on three family cruises — she was always the life of the party! My family shares stories about 'home' where my grandparents gave parties every weekend. Grandma and Papa always said that they loved dancing. When I look at family pictures I can tell that she was having the time of her life.

I remember staying with my grandmother and Papa in South Carolina one summer, especially the times when she and I walked around the park after dinner. I especially recall the time when I was wearing flip-flops and one of the shoes broke and we were laughing hysterically and because on that day we walked instead of rode in the car, I had to walk back home with only one good flip-flop. My grandma tried calling my grandpa but he said he was cleaning the pool and didn't hear the phone. Grandma then thought of the funniest thing to do — she and I switched shoes every five minutes! When we finally got back to the house we told my grandpa about it and he hollered with laughter!

I wish she could see all of the things that my family and I are going to be doing in our lives now. I wish she didn't pass away. Without her, nothing feels the same. I am very thankful that I got to meet her and that I knew her for so long. Since the day my grandmother died, I see the sky differently. I realize that everything around me is not evil — it's like I am in a whole new world.

> "Since the day my grandmother died, I see the sky differently."

After Grandma passed, I have been able to let go of all the things that have been breaking me down — like boys, for instance. I am going to treat boys as friends for now because I have experienced heartache and depression. When I become angry at bullies who bully other people, I am going to think about my grandmother. I have decided to hang out with friends and join more clubs and participate in sports at school, like tennis and flag football because interacting will be good for me.

Some of my best memories are of my grandmother and I spending time together. I will never forget the things that we did. Now it is time for me to teach my cousin all the things my grandmother taught me and do the things that we did together with my cousin. Since the day my grandma died, my life has become easier and better than I expected. I am proud of my heritage and I am happy to follow her legacy.

A Poem for My Father, Jerry Lee Crooks, Jr., III

Ave Maria Cross

Being a mentor at Girls Write Now and witnessing girls opening up their hearts and expressing their feelings through their writing has given me the impetus to break through and tell my stories.

Daddy jazz piano played Saturday morning bebop tunes//
as he emulated baaad ass jazz piano playin' heroes/
consecrating Eubie Blake, Count Basie, Duke Ellington, and Fats Waller/
whose music did *not* fall on deaf ears.//

Our mouths full of 'colored' folk stone soul picnic/
fried chicken, black-eye peas with white rice and brown gravy/
'mess' of collard greens, macaroni and cheese//drinking
Ice cold real lemonade/watermelon, cornbread,/
peach cobbler, sweet potato pie/down home soul food rapture!

When his brown piano fingers with round pink nail beds/
peeping pearly white half moons/
played his version of *the boogie woogie* on the out-of-tune piano/
He jazz piano played my childhood memories with razzmatazz/
so elegant as you taught us how to 'soft shoe dance'//
and march like you did as an American soldier.//

My father never played the 'blues' although I now know that/

his South Carolina suppressed memories of life oppressed/
took its toll //and how his third grade education in a segregated clapboard 'colored'
school/failed him as did America//time and time again//
while walking through back doors/in his World War II uniform//still//

He taught us through his refined actions/without distraction//
that we were something//
So ex/tra/or/di/nar/i/ly special//'til we walked around/
as if we were actually all that and he was right!//
all little girls are special//like//
My father only bought 'colored' dolls for me and sis//his Black princesses.

Janae Lowe

YEARS AS MENTEE: 1

GRADE: Freshman

HIGH SCHOOL:
The High School of
Economics and Finance

BORN: Greensboro, NC

LIVES: Bronx, NY

My mentor, Ave Maria Cross, has given me an amazing book, called "Choosing Glee," by Jenna Ushkowitz and Sheryl Berk. One sentence in the book that stands out for me is, "The only real path to joy and happiness is truth." When I read that I thought it was my grandma speaking to me and I felt as if I was a child again in the summer. Grandma and I had so much fun together — she made me feel special. We had quiet 'secret' talks and she taught me so much! I can share what I learned from her.

Ave Maria Cross

YEARS AS MENTOR: 1

OCCUPATION:
CEO of Godmother
Productions. Freelance
Creative Writer, Poet and
Playwright

PUBLICATIONS AND RECOGNITIONS:
NYC Department of Cultural Affairs, Greater NY Arts Development Fund Grant Award through the Bronx Council of the Arts. Artists Summer Institute-Lower Manhattan Cultural Council/Creative Capital's 'Professional Development Program award. My play 'Peanut Butter and Yam Bread (an educational 'comedy' about Booker T. Washington and George Washington Carver) was produced with a grant from The NYC Department of Cultural Affairs, at Bronx House

Janae writes about her memories of South Carolina and her family there — my family is from South Carolina, as well! I was inspired by my mentee to write about family, which is something I wanted to do for a long time. I am now breaking through and writing about trials, tribulations and triumph!

Finding Inner Strength

Rayhana Maarouf

Participating in Girls Write Now for the past two years has given me the security and confidence to write about a very painful time in my life. That was a true breakthrough!

On October 28, 2010, my world as I knew it blew apart. The events of that day — and the year that followed — are forever seared in my memory. I was in the eighth grade, and I was waiting for my dad to pick me up from school. We were planning to go out for pizza and to come back for a parent-teacher conference. But my dad, who was always super-reliable, never showed up. I didn't know it yet, but what turned into a real-life nightmare had begun.

After dismissal I waited and waited, but there was no sign of my dad. At first, I figured he was running late. But, after twenty minutes or so, I began to worry. I kept dialing my dad's number until I finally reached him. He just said he was held up at my brother Mohammed's school.

The parent-teacher conference started. Still no dad. Just then, my phone rang. It was my mom, and the tone in her voice really scared me. She told me to meet her at Mohammed's school and to get there fast. When I asked her where my dad was, she didn't answer me. That's when the first tear rolled down my cheek. I grabbed my belongings and rushed to Mohammed's school.

I cried the whole way there. I had no idea what was happening. The only thing I knew is that my dad didn't show up and that something had to be seriously wrong. My dad always kept his word. Always. I don't remember what was running through my mind, but I remember not being able to control my tears as if it all happened yesterday.

I found my mom and two brothers sitting in a car outside Mohammed's school, along with two people who were strangers to me. I got into the car, and we all drove to an ACS Office in Jamaica, Queens. ACS stands for Administration for Children's Services and is the agency responsible for the welfare of children in New York City.

On the previous day my father and Mohammed had had a terrible argument. It had gotten physical and my father had struck Mohammed over his eye, leaving a bruise. When Mohammed got to school the next day, someone called ACS and reported my dad for assaulting Mohammed.

After we arrived at the ACS office my brothers, my mom, and I were separately questioned about the fight between my dad and Mohammed. The rest of the time, we sat in the waiting room trying to stay calm. I found out later that my dad had been arrested and was in jail. I was in a state of shock.

We finally were allowed to go home. We ate dinner in silence and went to bed. My dad wasn't there to tuck me in. The next morning the ACS agent and the police showed up at our house and took me and my brothers to a foster care center where we spent three miserable days and nights. It was the first time I had ever been away from my parents. I felt so alone, but I couldn't fall apart because I had to be strong for my brothers.

> "I felt so alone, but I couldn't fall apart because I had to be strong for my brothers."

We came home on a Monday afternoon and were reunited with my mom. A judge had released my dad from jail but said that my dad was not allowed to return to our family and that we could only see him during supervised visits. I saw my dad at the ACS office two weeks later. I cried the whole time. I cried on the way there, I cried when I was with him, and I cried when I had to say goodbye. I hated saying goodbye.

Court dates happened every eight weeks. Each time we thought my dad would be allowed to come home. We would decorate the house with "Welcome Back" banners, balloons, and party streamers. We would go to the courthouse smiling with hearts full of hope. We would wait for hours for the verdict, and time and again our hopes were crushed. We would cry and take the train back home with tear-stained cheeks. We would take down the party decorations and store them until the next court date.

My dad came back a year later when I was in the ninth grade. It was hard at first. My dad wasn't used to a lot of noise, and we had gotten used to him not being there. It felt like he was a piece of china, so fragile you had to handle it carefully so it wouldn't break.

But over time, we became a family again, and that made me very happy. During that year my mom and I grew much closer, and I learned a lot about myself. I learned that I was a resilient, optimistic person who could continue to function during really tough times. I am hopeful that the inner strength I discovered will help me overcome future challenges with the same kind of courage and determination.

A Very Different World

Anne Feigus

Facing the aging process has been a challenge for me recently. I decided to write this light-hearted piece in an effort to push past that anxiety.

I recently attended a memorial service for Barbara Goodwin, a dear friend who died at the age of 94. She was a gifted artist, and two of her luminous paintings grace the living room of my home. A number of people gave moving tributes about an exceptional woman who had touched many lives. But, my friend Betty Diamond's remarks stood out from the rest because they were both eloquent and thought-provoking. Noting how much the world had changed during Barbara's lifetime, Betty remarked, "Ever since I read how Laura Ingalls Wilder began her life traveling West in a Conestoga wagon and ended it taking a jet plane to Vietnam, I have been struck by the transformations each of us experiences over a lifetime and how different a world we inhabit now from one, two — or even eight decades ago." That observation really resonated with me as I rapidly close in on age 67. So, I began to think back on the world as it existed in the 1940s, 50s and 60s during my childhood and teenage years in the small Appalachian town of Uniontown, Pennsylvania. Here are some fun facts that bring a smile to my face,

> "I began to think back on the world as it existed in the 1940s, 50s and 60s..."

especially when I compare that world to the social-media saturated, iPhone, iPad, Facebook, Twitter, computerized world of the Girls Write Now mentees.

The hospital bill for my birth in 1947 was $99.

Postage stamps for a letter cost 3 cents.

Milk was delivered in glass bottles.

The telephone was a "party line" shared by more than one family.

If you had a television there were only a couple of channels, and the programs were in black and white. A treat at age three was going to my grandparents' house to watch "Captain Video and His Video Rangers," which ran from 1949-1955.

The hottest spot for a date was the drive-in movie.

I had to type my papers in high school and college on a portable typewriter.

The innovations I have witnessed since then truly boggle my mind, and I often feel "technologically challenged." But, one thing is certain, I hope to be around for a long time to witness many more astounding discoveries that the future holds.

Rayhana Maarouf

YEARS AS MENTEE: 2

GRADE: Junior

HIGH SCHOOL:
Aviation High School

BORN: NY, NY

LIVES: Queens, NY

PUBLICATIONS AND RECOGNITIONS:
Scholastic Art & Writing Awards Gold Key in Personal
Essay/Memoir

Anne and I meet for our pair sessions at a cozy café on Seventh Avenue in Manhattan. It is a special time when I can forget all my other responsibilities and focus on becoming a better writer. Last year, I was hesitant to express my deepest feelings in writing. This year, with Anne's support, I'm able to set my fears aside and to write a very personal piece for the Girls Write Now Anthology. I am very proud of myself for accomplishing that breakthrough!

Anne Feigus

YEARS AS MENTOR: 2

OCCUPATION:
Former Appellate
Attorney

This year Rayhana and I hit the ground running! A wonderful hallmark of her personality and her writing is her great good humor, with which she approaches all aspects of life. She displays grace under pressure and is an impressive problem solver. Rayhana's biggest breakthrough thus far has been her ability to write movingly about a very painful period in her life from which she emerged more exuberant and resilient than ever. It has been a privilege to be her mentor and to become her friend.

A Writer Like Me

Brianna Marini

I looked at what I think a writer is, versus what a
writer actually is, only to find out that the definitions
may not be as similar as I think.

What is a writer? Is a writer a specific type of person? Can anyone be a writer?

I'd gone a while without thinking about it until one of my best friends wrote a piece on the subject.

"We are the most vulnerable; we bear our deepest darkest secrets to the world. But it's never at our expense, we share just enough to tell a story but we conceal just enough to be lying."

I asked Kayla, the author, what those lines meant.

She shrugged. "You should know what they mean, they were inspired by you."

Inspired by me? I wanted to laugh. I didn't think I could inspire anyone, even myself nine days out of ten. Senior year has sapped all of the energy out of me, stolen the desire to write like someone stealing bread to feed the family — quickly, desperately, and with no intention of returning what had been stolen.

I hadn't even thought of writing memoirs until my second year at Girls Write Now, for the thought of writing about my life scared me. But writing memoir has been a breakthrough for me, and part of how I've become a writer.

So, I could understand what Kayla's line meant, but in the moment I was still reeling from the fact that I had caused a friend of mine, one of the best writers I know, to draw from me for a line in one of her pieces.

When I think of a writer, I think of my mentor Kristen, my friend Kayla, or J.K. Rowling, who I wish I could be when I grow up. I think of all of these extremely talented people who I think write so much better than I do, who can thread words onto paper like a seamstress threading a needle before starting to work on a new sweater.

Senior year, however, has taught me a lot of things. When you apply to a college, you have to sell yourself. You have to put your best foot forward, raise your head high, shake someone's hand, and go, "Hi, my name's Brianna Marini, let me tell you all about the wonderful things I've done." Even if I don't think I've done anything wonderful. Being genuine can be hard sometimes, especially when you look around a room of people applying for the same colleges and who you assume think are so much better qualified than you.

"I love to write," I've said. "I want to be an English major. I want to write for the newspaper, submit pieces for the literary magazine." *I want to be a writer.* I've said it a thousand different ways, wormed my way around the word, found synonyms that passed for the same thing. I've ignored the pit in my stomach because I didn't think I was worthy of being called a writer, despite having written creatively since I could hold a pen and spell enough words to string a sentence together properly. When I think about being a "writer," my skin itches. I feel uncomfortable. I worry that I have no right to say it.

To be a writer, you need to have a passion for writing. A writer sits in front of a piece of paper with a pen, in front of a laptop with fingers on the home row, on a train with a notepad open on an iPhone, and stresses over the right words. They open thesauruses and wrack their brains for the right word to describe exactly what they want to write. They get writer's block, cry in frustration over words that won't come out, that itch at the walls of their mind, cry at the words that do come out because sometimes it hurts to tell the whole truth, even if you have no intention of sharing it. They finish pieces minutes before deadlines, hand them in to editors with cheeky yet exhausted grins, and then go home to sleep off the effort they exerted in trying to make up for lost time.

"...all you know is that you want to write a thousand words about that butterfly sitting on that leaf..."

"Although it is a skill that can be close to but never perfected, anyone can write but not everyone can be a writer." There's never been a truer statement. Not everyone can take the crazy hours, the desire to write at the oddest times, the weird things that can inspire you when you have no idea why you're inspired; all you know is that you want to write a thousand words about that butterfly sitting on that leaf in that tree a few feet from you and you want to do it *now*.

But if you put up with all of these weird aspects of the creative process, and you type the word "by" under a piece after you've struggled to finally finish it, then you are a writer.

Like me.

Ink-Stained Fingers

Kristen Demaline

*After four years as a Girls Write Now mentor, I've been
reflecting on my time in the program as a writer and
mentor — on, moreover, what it means to be a writer.*

Does being a writer mean having ink-stained sheets, pants, fingers? Scribbling an idea born at 3 a.m. in one of the notebooks always by my side? You bet. I believe you can be a writer without making your living at it. Indeed, you may not make enough money to do much besides get a Persian cat or two.

I'm not sure when I stopped being self-conscious about identifying myself as a writer. I didn't entirely believe I deserved that title when I was my mentee's age, and it's a thrill to realize how far I've come. I was immeasurably helped in my writing life by mentors — honoring that help largely motivated my journey to join Girls Write Now.

My mentors gave me plenty of gifts (including the work of Virginia Woolf) along the way, some modeled, some discussed, some assigned. Practice. Take risks. Ask tough questions that make you uncomfortable. Write every day. (Yes, you will notice a difference.) Know when to stop, but always keep going; one and a half pages into your freewrite is when the magic will happen. Not until then. Bank on it. Read. Watch.

Listen. Be inspired by your fellow creators. Don't hide. Make yourself heard. These stories of ours really can help change the world, whether they're in a memoir or on screen. Writing matters. Your voice matters.

> "Don't hide. Make
> yourself heard.
> These stories of ours
> really can help change
> the world..."

Five years ago, a friend who was a Girls Write Now mentor invited me to a CHAPTERS Reading Series, and I was hooked. I couldn't believe the talent, the passion and the feeling in that room. In a moment, I knew I wanted to be a part of it. We need more groups like ours and rooms like ours. In a world where women are still a huge minority in editorial pages, in writers' rooms and on screenwriting Oscar shortlists, we still need to model possibility for each other, mentor and mentee alike.

This is a community that has each other's backs and pushes each other to leap. We encourage 30-year-old journalists to try slam poetry. We celebrate 16-year-olds discovering their talents for dialogue and character and science writing. We cheer on forty-something novelists trying a bit of memoir. We all do creative trapeze work here. This is a gift — our room, white paper and a group who will support your growth. That's what makes the experience. We've found a way to create this room of our own (thanks, donors!) and this special community.

I've been inspired during every workshop by our mentees. I am so proud of the collective bodaciousness, grace, courage, strength and wisdom of their words. I look forward to reading them for years to come.

As well as nagging mine via text message to take a breath and keep writing.

Brianna Marini

YEARS AS MENTEE: 3

GRADE: Senior

HIGH SCHOOL:
Young Women's Leadership School of Queens

BORN: Bronx, NY

LIVES: Queens, NY

COLLEGE: Dominican University of California

SCHOLARSHIPS:
Dean's Scholarship, Dominican University of California; Dean's Scholarship, Eckerd College; Godman Scholarship, Ohio Wesleyan University

PUBLICATIONS AND RECOGNITIONS:
Scholastic Art & Writing Awards Silver Key for Personal Essay/Memoir, Honorable Mention in Journalism, Honorable Mention in Writing Portfolio

Kristen and I have had one major breakthrough moment this year — the college application process. With Kristen's help, I was able to not only ship things off on time, but I was able to realize that I could get to where I wanted to next year. This year had a lot of moments when I was forced to self-evaluate and, throughout everything, Kristen was always there to help me through it and become a better person because of it.

Kristen Demaline

YEARS AS MENTOR: 4

OCCUPATION:
Communications Manager, GRACE Communications Foundation

Brianna and I have both dealt with a lot of challenges during our final year at Girls Write Now, but we've relied on our senses of humor and determination to keep going. I'm mainly struck with the overall journey Brianna allowed me to share these past three years as a mentor. Meeting a high school sophomore, you really can't tell who the young woman you're meeting will become, and one of the great joys of this experience has been watching her grow and change. I can't wait to see what comes next!

Breather

Shanille Martin

*This piece is about an organized girl who gets
trapped in an elevator. She begins to freak out,
thinking that death is headed her way. She has
to break through her fears and stay strong in a
daunting situation.*

"Do you have an appointment?" the woman at the front desk asks. I nod nervously
and show her the paper. "Yes, I'm here for an internship, 18th floor." She smiles and
points ahead. "Take the elevator right up."

I check my watch: five minutes late. I was never on time for anything. I got that
from my mom. She always jokes and says she'd probably be late for her own funeral.
The building wasn't hard to find, seeing as it's the tallest skyscraper on Wall Street. I
slip into the elevator. There's no one else in there, which is weird. I would expect these
buildings to constantly be packed with people moving from floor to floor.

"Hello, I'm Hanna McAllister. It would be my pleasure to begin interning here," I
say to myself, and then laugh at how ridiculous I must look. *You'll be fine*, I think. *It's
just filing papers, no biggie.*

The elevator is slow. Slower than most of the others I had been on before. I take a
deep breath. The elevator goes dark for a second and the lights slowly flicker back
on. I stop moving. The elevator is planted between the 16th and 17th floors. My heart
begins beating faster. So fast it seems to be pushing its way out of my chest. I take
another deep breath and close my eyes. *Stop panicking, Hanna*, I think to myself,
you'll be fine. You're going to be fine.

I'm going to die. They're going to forget I'm in here. I'll starve.

I laugh. I'm losing it. Being closed up in a small space is something I'm never comfortable with. It's just been like that for as long as I can remember.

"I won't ever see my parents again, or my little brother," I say aloud, pacing. What
am I saying? I bet they're fixing the problem.

*I won't have my first kiss. How pitiful. I've never been kissed. No epic kiss in the
rain. No skydiving or surfing the California waves. They'll remember me only for
being boring. I can see it now: My mom at my funeral saying her daughter was no
fun, just this boring over-organized girl who never knew how to let go.*

I could call my dad if I hadn't forgotten that stupid phone on my nightstand. I figured it wouldn't be a big deal. The elevator shutting down is something I just didn't
see coming.

The only thing in my bag to eat is mint gum. Three left from the pack I bought yesterday. And my journal will have to be my only means of entertainment (I read what I write in it later on and it does sound a lot like a soap opera).

First sign of madness is talking in your own head — J.K Rowling. I'm losing it. I'm going to die a mad woman. Yet no one considers me a woman, just a lost little girl. *A waste of space is what I'll be remembered as. I'll die a nothing!*

Well, at least my SAT scores were really good.

> "The day before the test, I finally crashed."

I spent six weeks prepping, drinking at least two cups of coffee per day. The day before the test, I finally crashed. I couldn't move the whole day. I was ready to give up my chances of ever going to college. Then my mom gave me this special tea and within minutes I was good as new.

Why was my brain focusing on everything other than the fact that I was stuck in an elevator?

"Stop!" I shout. "I need to get out of here!"

"Hanna."

I spin around. "...God?"

"Are you alright Hanna?" he asks. His voice is calm and soothing.

I'm dead. It's official, I'm dead. I'm talking to God inside a broken down elevator. I must be dead.

"I'm not sure. I'm not in pain...but I'm scared," I say, staring into space.

"There's nothing to be scared about. The elevator will be moving in a matter of seconds."

I nod and wipe the tears rolling down my cheek. "Thank you."

I didn't get to say goodbye. The elevator will start moving and I'll be gone. I'll disappear into forever. And God was right: within seconds the elevator begins to move again. There's a loud ding as we reach the eighteenth floor and the doors open.

"I'm Vince, the building manager. Sorry for the inconvenience. We had a mild power outage."

I stare at the man standing in front of me in disbelief.

"You started freaking out really fast. You didn't give me time to explain."

I continue staring at the man.

"Are you okay?" he asks.

All I could do was laugh. "I thought you were God. You didn't say you weren't."

"Hanna," he says, reaching out to me.

But I walk away from the man and the elevator quickly, hoping I've left some of my insanity behind.

Winter Blues

Amanda Krupman

*The protagonist, Hannah, deals with an oncoming
panic attack.*

Hannah wrapped her arms around her waist. The buzzing was happening: the crowded cell of caustic words and unwrapped worry. She planted her sweating, bare feet onto the kitchen linoleum, breathed: one, two — deeper — three. You've gained the *power of blindness. Your thoughts are deafening. Build a wall. Sleep for an instant.* Four. Five.

She closed her eyes and first dealt with the remainder of the material world's imprint, outlined in short-term memory and given fuzzy shape through light that penetrated the thin skin of her lids. She summoned colors for her kingdom. Blue was a good choice, green fine. She called on both and they didn't flood her mind — that was not what she wanted. They pooled, they dappled, they ribboned and pocked like oil paint poured into a water glass, spreading with fluid mystique. She let them dance and dissolve within one another. It cooled her, prepared her for the blank page.

Your body oppresses, it brainwashes. Flee the body, free the ego.

Hannah unwrapped her arms from her torso and let them hang at her sides, going limp. Her knees buckled and she fell down onto them, sat back on her heels, bowed her head. The breath, the breath. Lifting the sea foam veil to stinging whiteness. Ringing, crowded voices, clutter piling, rain falling, June crying, Marcus eating, a soft towel she'd stolen from the honeymoon motel, an enormous towel, plush, warm, around her, over her, wiping it clean. Reverberating quiet. Quiet that has presence. Quiet waving goodbye.

"Ringing, crowded
voices, clutter piling,
rain falling,
June crying..."

White. Black. Black.

It wasn't like coming out of the tank. And it wasn't like waking from a nap, except that she could not immediately know how long she had been gone. She was instantly stunned with sensation. She was nauseous, she was dizzy; her feet were asleep.

Not quite right, but better. Eventually, she'd be getting better.

Shanille Martin

YEARS AS MENTEE: 1

GRADE: Sophomore

HIGH SCHOOL:
Academy for Young
Writers

BORN: Kingston, Jamaica

LIVES: Brooklyn, NY

Being Amanda's mentee has been nothing but amazing. I've learned to break through the barriers that would keep me from succeeding. I've matured into a strong independent person. Amanda and I talk about writing and our lives. I tell her if there's something on my mind and she'll give me advice. I've grown to trust her and appreciate everything she has to say. When I told her I never had a taco, she took me to a great taco place and I had my very first one. It was an incredible experience.

Amanda Krupman

YEARS AS MENTOR: 1

OCCUPATION:
Fiction writer, Writer and
Editor at City College of
New York

I was delighted to be paired with Shanille, a recognizable member of the writing tribe. She is observant and hungry for new experiences. She's ambitious and dedicated and fills pages of her notebooks with new stories and her next plotlines and characters. She has a gift for plot structure, which I envy!

A Postcard to Heaven

Karina Martinez

This story embodies the theme "Breaking Through"
because it's about a girl who had the courage to
discover who she was, while breaking away from
the expectations of others. She wants to be happy in
life and follow her own path.

I want to go home,
to the place where I can feel the sunlight
on my skin and no longer feel afraid.
Not where I grew up,
not where I had my first kiss,
but where I can hear the melody of the song of silence and run away.
And I know that I shouldn't stray from what I know,
but sometimes the sun shines too bright and it blinds me.

Don't tell me the answer is in me.
Don't tell me to follow my heart.
Don't tell me I already know the truth
because I haven't gotten that far.
I don't understand how we find where we belong.
I don't understand how we know what we're doing wrong,
and I don't want to.
The questions don't mean a thing.
The words just don't come to me,
so don't you dare ask what my favorite color is
because I don't understand how you can choose just one.

Let me learn that fire will burn me.
Let me learn that love will hurt me.
Let me learn that this world is too big for wide-eyed girls like me
and maybe I'll come back.
Until then I'll write you and I'll tell you all my stories.
I'll send you a postcard, it'll go straight up,
and then you'll see that I didn't run;

I've been running all my life.
I've only just found a place to stop
and finally learn how to walk.

Eve

Jillian Gallagher

The theme, "Breaking Through," sounds like it should
be, or must be, something bigger than yourself.
I think the biggest breakthrough of all is diving,
however bravely or cautiously, into what's inside
and too easily avoided. Also, picking up memories,
no matter how sharp their edges might still be.

It smells like butter and cigarette smoke and melting, melted yard.
Like beer and honey liquor and sauerkraut and why don't you have a glass.
It smells like the leather of handbags piled in a bedroom.
And like the wet wool of snowed-on coats.
It smells like an unforeseen ending six months out of reach.

It looks like chaos, like din, like steam on windows.
Like flushed cheeks, like family.
It looks like couples on the cusp.
Like a folding card table that's seen better days, and an artificial tree that hasn't.

It sounds like decades have passed. Like minutes. Like moments, too.
It sounds like the compromise between mirth and melancholy.
Like bells and whines and damp good cheer.
It sounds like the clink of cared-for glasses. The hiss of the radiator.
Like ice cubes melting in a plastic cup of wine.

It tastes like winter air. Like sugar, syrupy.
It tastes like food that never saw a measuring cup.
Like garlic, like sausage, like vinegar.
It tastes like last year.
And the one before.
And all the others that passed before.

It feels like the pressure of a single bathroom.

And the anxiety of watching a door without a lock.

It feels like the shock of a soaked sock.

Like happy and sad run through a blender to bittersweet.

Like the ticking tally of what's been lost and what's been gained and, most elusively, what's held steady.

It feels fuzzier, the tape breaking down further with every viewing.

The good, the glorious.

The bad and the breaking.

The cozy and the comfort.

The here and the now.

The eve of what was. And the eve of what will be.

Karina Martinez

YEARS AS MENTEE: 1

GRADE: Freshman

HIGH SCHOOL:
The Bronx High School
of Science

BORN: NY, NY

LIVES: Bronx, NY

Our odd conversations, revolving around topics such as life after death or even serial killer Jeffrey Dahmer, would probably scare off most people, but not for Jillian and me. It lets us ask questions and start conversations about the subjects we would typically avoid. This year, I realized that being introverted and shy isn't a bad thing and that I should learn to speak up. Jillian helped me do that by allowing me to delve into the world of Spoken Word poetry. I realized that I could pierce through the veil covering people's minds and cause a breakthrough in someone else.

Jillian Gallagher

YEARS AS MENTOR: 3

OCCUPATION:
Senior Writer,
FutureBrand

For an hour and a half each week, nothing is off the table. To me — and I hope for Karina, too — this is living the dream: to be able to speak aloud, thoughts funny or sad, scary, any place in-between. I used to think writing needed to only concern the exceptional or the unusual or heroic or dramatic. But in my time with Karina, I've seen that writing can be smaller, but no less universal. The inspiration can come through the simplest phrase, "how's your week?" The stories can be our own. The wider world can be as close as the thoughts repeating in our minds. And yet the words are no less beautiful for it.

Weather Veins

Katherine Martinez

This poem is about someone coming to terms with
self-awareness and wanting to break old patterns.

i have always had a really
bad habit of making my
home in others.
of carving a space out for myself
in them
without them even knowing.
i tend to attach my limbs to their hearts and hold on real
tight, terrified if i unclench
for even one second they'll let me go.

this bad habit began
somewhere in first grade and
i've still yet to learn how
to stop myself.
the pattern is:
meet, latch, cling.
repeat.

i do this over and over,
time after time and every
single time i am
left there, bloody
and sad with cuts i don't even
remember receiving and
it took me a while to realize i was
pretty easy to leave behind. pretty
easy to let go of.

Stuck

Amy Flyntz

I wrote this in hopes of being able to break
through self-doubt.

I stare at the computer screen, my middle finger rolling lazily back and forth across the wheel of my mouse. I'm reading a tribute to Gloria Steinem, who turned 80 this year. One of the greatest faces of feminism, still radiant with life. With purpose. With passion. I sigh and drag the mouse back and forth along the smooth wood of my desk, my eyes following the random trajectory of the cursor. It's always been like this, of course. Me, on the outside, looking in. Passively looking at. Looking upon.

> "Me, on the outside, looking in. Passively looking at..."

When I turned 15, my friends surprised me with a birthday party at McDonald's. I'd always had my birthday parties at home and had mentioned that just once, I'd love a ridiculous party with a birthday cake that bore my name in sloppy cursive gel and balloons made of colored red, blue and yellow sugar. I was shocked when I walked in to see them sitting there, their gangly limbs too long to be at the kids' table but overjoyed by the silliness of pulling it off.

Later, I stood inside and watched them on the playscape: ducking under the giant metal Grimace and peeking out through the bars on Hamburgler's hat. I felt mildly dizzy with displacement, like a tourist looking at an upside down map of my own life.

I'm a long way from 15 but I still feel like I'm grappling with that same map. Everything seems off-kilter. I journal. I talk with friends. I call my family. Still, I'm left wondering if perhaps I was born without an internal compass. Something to point me in the direction of here is where you're meant to be.

Biologically, I'm an adult. I wish the rest of me would get the memo. Mind, body, spirit each headed in a different direction — seemingly on the same path to nowhere. I wonder if Gloria ever had moments, days, years where she felt like she was floundering. I can't imagine the face of feminism waiting for her real life to begin.

Katherine Martinez

YEARS AS MENTEE: 1

GRADE: Senior

HIGH SCHOOL:
Aquinas High School

BORN: NY, NY

LIVES: Bronx, NY

COLLEGE:
University of Rochester

Amy and I are at the point in our relationship where nothing we say is surprising to the other. We've grown so comfortable with each other and so at ease that time flies when we're together. I know I can count on her 100 percent and I am so grateful that I got to know her when I did. She is constantly challenging me to try new things and to break through my set patterns. I absolutely love her for that.

Amy Flyntz

YEARS AS MENTOR: 2

OCCUPATION:
Copywriter

Katherine and I have a connection that I cherish. I am constantly inspired by her passion for writing, her tenacity, her work ethic and her sense of humor. She's introduced me to the world of fan fiction, and reminds me why I fell in love with words all those years ago. She's encouraged me to break through with my writing. I'm so lucky to have shared her senior year with her. I will miss Katherine terribly, but cannot wait to see her soar!

Shock Radiates

Amanda Day McCullough

*It took five months and twelve drafts to write
and polish this story. What you are reading is my
breakthrough.*

Tuck, somersault, explode.

These motions govern my life in the pool and on the page.

Tuck. I brought my knees and head to my chest, watching the bubbles stream from my nostrils. We only trailed Stuyvesant High School by four points, which meant my race was critical. Yet, I went through the flip-turn's motions without thinking. Twelve feet below me, at the bottom of the pool, I imagined my family's disapproving faces. I wanted to look away but I didn't dare look up; if I did, the tuck would be disrupted. I trusted that my body knew what to do.

The crisis started weeks before, with the first sentence: "Repetition numbs." That was the tuck. I typed without thinking, my eyes glued to the keyboard. I wanted to see my words materialize on the computer screen but I didn't dare look up. If I did, I would see my family's disapproving faces in every word. I would stop writing. I trusted that my fingers knew what to do.

Somersault. As I turned through the water, every sore muscle in my body burned. My need for air tore my abdomen apart. I was upside down. In that moment, I was hyperaware of my emotional pain and knew that my memoir had humiliated my family. My throat constricted; I was almost out of air, but I wasn't done somersaulting.

I cried when I wrote it. The memoir was about the deterioration of my relationships with two of my closest family members. A burning sensation radiated through me as I typed. I was writing the memoir with the intention of sharing it at a public reading. My parents were going to hear it. Was it ethical to reveal private family moments for the sake of my own catharsis and writing career? I didn't know the answer, but I plunged into the memoir anyway. I was upside down. Recounting the painful memories tore my gut apart. Physically and emotionally drained, I couldn't take a breath. I was still somersaulting.

> **"I was upside down. Recounting the painful memories tore my gut apart."**

Explode. BAM. I am reading my memoir aloud in front of two hundred people. I didn't warn my parents. When I see my mother's hurt face in the crowd, I choke on my words. Her expression cuts into my skin. I exploded too soon, without considering the consequences.

Audience members begin to whisper. I continue reading. When I leave the stage, my family's disappointment and rage greet me. From then on, my ethical dilemma plagues my consciousness. My parents weren't ready for this story to be released into the world. But how can I be a memoirist if I stifle my voice to protect their feelings?

I stop mid-turn and my feet hit the wall. Shock radiates from my ankles upward and my feet slip. The world is a frenzy of bubbles and blueness and I choke on the chlorinated water. Muffled shrieks reach my ears as I struggle to orient myself. The plastic lane line rips the skin from my left shoulder but I keep swimming, ignoring the tears filling my goggles. I can see my opponents ahead of me and I know that my disastrous flip-turn will cost me the race. My team might lose the meet because I wasn't concentrating. When I climb out of the pool, I am facing another disappointed family.

Tuck, somersault, explode. Writing and swimming are not individual acts. I would not be a swimmer or a captain without my team, just like I would not be a memoirist without my family. There is no such thing as an individual act.

Everything I do has a ripple effect.

Graveyard

Samantha Carlin

The line "the world is a frenzy" in my mentee,
Amanda's memoir inspired this poem.

The world is a frenzy
where umbrellas, discarded
after storms
lie broken on sidewalks — metal frames splintered, fabric ripped —
I see fractured bones, torn skin.
To me, the umbrellas are lined up tombstones, commemorating the New Yorkers
caught in the rain.

I imagine the umbrellas snapping back — *WHACK* — in their faces,
as they hurry to one or another
important place.
Drenched now, dripping now, I imagine their voices
cursing the weather, and their arms
flinging the umbrellas — *SMACK* — on the concrete.

A woman sprints down subway stairs.

Below ground, she laments her dead umbrella,
her once blown-dry hair now pasted to her face in soppy tangles,
her new suede boots ruined, since this particular storm was unexpected.
She sighs; she'll have to go through it all again soon, when she reaches her stop.

Deep down, I imagine she's not really distraught with the umbrella —
she can buy a new umbrella, after all —
but instead it's her helplessness:
the stone-cold fact that being human
means that all the things she brings with her
to shield her from storms
will litter the streets in the end.

Amanda Day McCullough

YEARS AS MENTEE: 3

GRADE: Senior

HIGH SCHOOL:
Hunter College
High School

BORN: NY, NY

LIVES: Queens, NY

COLLEGE:
Pomona College

PUBLICATIONS AND RECOGNITIONS:
Scholastic Art & Writing Awards Silver Keys in Memoir and Flash Fiction

"This has to be the last draft," I thought, drumming my fingers on my Starbucks coffee cup while Samantha X-rayed my piece. She read with her hands; strokes of black pen danced across the page as she cut words and identified weak passages. "It's great," she said, placing my piece on the table between us. Yes! "Only a few more revisions and then we're good to go!" ...Crap. "Look at the piece again. How can you improve it?" The piece whose perfection I had been convinced of mere minutes ago was not the piece I was looking at now. I saw clunky sentences that needed rewording and paragraphs that needed reordering. Samantha pushed me to challenge myself and make breakthroughs in my writing. Samantha didn't just open my eyes to my mistakes — she opened my eyes to my potential.

Samantha Carlin

YEARS AS MENTOR: 3

OCCUPATION:
Project Associate,
Walnut Ridge Strategic
Management Company

When Amanda asked me to participate in Suzanne Lacy's "Between the Door and the Street" with her and Girls Write Now, the subject line "Participatory Art Performance" made my stomach constrict. Apt to stage fright, I avoid "performing." But Amanda's email was rich with enthusiasm, and the art piece's subject — contemporary feminism— was consistently a topic of our one-on-one conversations. I introduced Amanda to feminism when she was a sophomore. Now, two and a half years later, as a senior, she was the one pushing me to break through my fear so we could utilize our pair talks to impact the world.

A Walk Through My Life

Lauren Melendez

A few weeks after I wrote this piece, my family and I
moved to a new apartment.

You open the dark brown door, all busted up,
Walk through a lobby with dirty, worn-out walls,
Black floor...dried gum, sticky footprints,
Five floors, no elevators,
Just stairs.

We sign in twice a day at the homeless shelter.
Every Tuesday they do apartment inspections
To make sure we're actually living there.
Just me, my mom, my twin sister and my brother —
No extras or you get kicked out.

Cameras on the first two floors
Watch for bad neighbors doing drugs and weed,
Grinning in dark hoodies and torn jeans;
Suspicious sounds: arguing, yelling,
Gunshots in the park.

Sometimes clanking radiators sizzle
But sometimes they don't give us heat.
When there's no heat, there's no hot water,
Just the smell of wet paint and weed, and
I can't take a shower.

I don't know why we got bed bugs
They came out of nowhere and
It took forever to get them exterminated.
We flipped our beds, they sprayed;
We stayed with my grandparents.

Soon we'll get out of that hellhole,
Start a new chapter, get stuff out of storage,
Mom will have her spices and
She'll make brownies again,
Just because she can.

The Girl in the Picture

Nancy Hooper

Working with Lauren has had me thinking about my childhood, which triggered memories about a mysterious photo taken when I was about four.

My family doesn't save photographs, so I'm remembering a black and white one, taken when I was about four. I'm standing in the small backyard of the house where I grew up in Minnesota. There's a flagpole behind me, no flag. Because of all the gray tones, the picture has a wintry feel to it, but for all I know it might have been taken in summer because I'm standing on grass. I'm holding a garden hose with my bare hands, and water is spewing out of the hose in an arc, as if I'm watering a portion of the lawn. I'm wearing a plaid scarf, tied in a big knot under my chin. My outfit is unremarkable: a dark, boxy jacket and light-colored pants. I remember studying the photo when I was in my twenties, after I found it at the back of a drawer. I'd never seen the picture before, or didn't remember seeing it, but of course I knew it was of me. I think I felt sorry for the little girl who was wearing an oversized, wool babushka that made her look, vaguely, like a refugee from the Ukraine. Her eyes seemed to be squinting at the camera. Was she grimacing? Wincing in pain? Was she being punished for something bad? If so, was this the punishment? If it was winter, why hadn't someone remembered to put gloves on her? If summer, why the heavy scarf? What was the real truth behind the picture? Now I'm in my sixties, imagining that photo again. Time has healed perceived hurts and imagined slights, and the picture looks clear and crisp. I think there's a pretty good chance my big sister dressed me up to look like an orphan or an urchin. Love the costume — was that Nanna's old babushka? The garden hose was probably a simple prop — until Sis turned the water on full blast so I looked like a dopey kid flooding the lawn for no good reason. Maybe I wasn't wincing; perhaps the sun made me squint, or I was hiding a bashful smile — just a kid trying to please her Big Sister. Now the girl in the photo looks like a cute four-year-old who was willing to pose for a staged snapshot in exchange for a pat on the head or a candy bar.

> "Time has healed perceived hurts and imagined slights..."

Lauren Melendez

YEARS AS MENTEE: 1

GRADE: Sophomore

HIGH SCHOOL:
Marta Valle High School

BORN: NY, NY

LIVES: Brooklyn, NY

I always have fun hanging out with Nancy, just talking and writing. I've told her about my old boyfriend Luis and my new boyfriend Yovany. I showed her pictures of my friend Sharnae and my medal from The National Honor Society. I've tried to write romantic fiction, but it's not me! We've also brainstormed about Beatles songs, the homeless shelter, and my twin sister — we were born nine minutes apart!

Nancy Hooper

YEARS AS MENTOR: 4

OCCUPATION:
Freelance Writer

Lauren and I meet at Starbucks every week. We talk about boyfriends — hers! Our routine: I always drink two Venti black iced teas, and Lauren always has a vanilla bean Frappucino (with whipped cream). We argue about who is picking up the tab, but since I'm the mentor, I usually win. Then we write, and Lauren shows me the latest pictures on her phone. Now I know what a "selfie" is!

The Image I See

Julia Mercado

This piece is a way for me to look at my imperfections in a different way.

There's a mirror in the bathroom of my school and in it, I see a monster that I recognize. She is made of my worst image. She is a ghost that haunts me when I look and refuses to ever leave me. She points out my acne and the scars that follow along with the mysterious mustache that seems to get darker every day. The lighting in this room must hate me as well. It highlights these imperfections and probably attracts the eyes of the other girls in the room. It seems content with the fact that I cannot stand the image of myself. It laughs and taunts louder the longer I look into this mirror. It makes me want to hide my face. Like I'll always look like this and there's nothing I can do about it.

I hate my reflection in this mirror because she's who I think I am and I don't want to accept that. As I keep looking into this mirror, I tell myself that she's not real because this is a part of life, there's no need to dwell on the image. *Why be afraid?* is the question I keep asking myself. *You're not ugly, just still going through changes...* If I'm just going through changes, then why is this mirror not showing me them?

A friend of mine once said that if there was a way for someone to see themselves in person, they wouldn't recognize their own image. They would be another stranger; someone to judge. Would I see my monster? Would she greet me even in someone else? I can only imagine a girl that looks better than me but with my name. She smiles and recognizes me instead, almost saying, *I remember you, the one with the personal monster. Good luck to ya!* I can imagine myself responding with, *That's it?* and I never get a response back — she would just keep walking.

At times, I think she would appear in the mirror for just a second and my mood would brighten. She would smile with me and I can see my best qualities in just that smile. The smile would show my care and my enthusiasm for anything. They say smiling keeps you happy in general, but who can keep their smile on all day? Your face would start to hurt and the smile would begin to feel like a mask. It then becomes clear that you may be hiding something, no matter what it is.

> "They say smiling keeps you happy in general, but who can keep their smile on all day?"

My smile falters at the thought of this and I no longer see the perfect girl. The insecure one has returned and she doesn't believe in smiling. She looks closely in the mirror with big, sad eyes and they are the only things that I can focus on. There's something beautiful in these sad eyes though. They express more than just negativity. They have hope in the thought that I am better than I perceive. They express the curiosity, creativity and kindness that I've always had.

It then makes me think of the person that I am going to be in the future. She'll no longer be the teenager who worries about her appearance. She will never have to see this mirror again. She'll be a confident woman who knows that the mirror is a lie. It's just a piece of old beat up glass showing, what is at best, a funhouse-type reflection of myself. For now, it shows only one image, the one I had when I first encountered this mirror. It shows the negative perception that can be changed.

If I can turn my mind just like I can turn my head... just change the angle, the perception... there.

I can see the confident woman in this mirror. She looks at me and is willing to walk out of here with that smile on her face. I smile with her and I feel better than when I first walked into the room. I can take those steps I need towards the door and say goodbye to that mirror.

The monster will always be there tucked into the darkest crevices of my mind and may come back at times. We can't rid ourselves of our monsters completely, but we can control them, let them know that we are better than they say. I know I can say the opposite, just change my perception to minimize my flaws and I can overcome my insecurities and see who I aim to be.

Julia Mercado

YEARS AS MENTEE: 1

GRADE: Sophomore

HIGH SCHOOL:
Manhattan Village
Academy

BORN: NY, NY

LIVES: Queens, NY

Creative writing allows me to explore myself and everything else around me. I came into the program midyear, but it showed me something I had never seen before. There aren't many people I know who share this passion with me, so as soon as I got to experience the Girls Write Now program, my mind was blown. At the workshops, I saw that same passion in everyone else that I met. Being a part of the Girls Write Now program is a great experience that I think every aspiring female writer should have.

Aarti Monteiro

YEARS WITH GWN: 1

OCCUPATION:
Girls Write Now
Program Coordinator

Julia joined the Girls Write Now community partway through the year, but it feels like she has been a mentee for a long time. She jumped right into the TV Sitcom Writing workshop, playfully acting in an original sitcom pilot she wrote with other mentees. Whether she's writing about interactions on the bus or addressing body image, Julia's work is perceptive. Although her mentor wasn't able to continue in the program, Julia continues to write and be an active member of our community. She is thoughtful and mature, and I look forward to seeing what is next for her.

Prescription Normality

Marquisele Mercedes

*Some of the best work is usually some of the most
personal, so I wrote about a moment when I noticed
change in myself.*

There's a plastic stopper in my medication that keeps me from getting too many pills.
Abilify is tricky. It makes me feel alive. "It makes me feel safer..."

I tell this to my psychiatrist who nods in his complacent way. His shiny black hair
always moves with his head and it reminds me of the ocean. I've always feared drowning.
He's become such a fixture in my life that it almost seems as if I can tell him things.

Just not too much.

Mostly we talk about anger issues that have arisen because of my hypomanic episodes,
but I don't have the kind of anger issues he's telling me how to deal with — there's
nothing to count to 10 over. I know which battles are worth fighting, and usually it
amounts to none or two. If I do express my anger, I regret I let out the aggressor, so
I lock her back up again as she huffs and puffs. I stoke
the furnace for when she drops down to try and eat what
is left of me alive and whole, chewing the bones for the
marrow and then using them to clean her teeth.

> "...or else I would
> have to divulge that
> there is nothing to
> divulge at all."

I'm sure Dr. Ghumman wonders why I sit on his
couch, probably wonders if my kind-eyed mom is an alcoholic or if my dad abused
me. Thank goodness my mother's insurance covers these visits or else I would have to
divulge that there is nothing to divulge at all.

I guess that's why it's so troubling that there is something, genuinely and majorly,
wrong with me. My sister has had her worst dreams realized with these visits of mine.
She's devastated the whispers in her mind that have said "Something's off about
Mikey" are right.

"Safer, how?"

Oh, I don't know, Doc. Safer from me, from you, from them, and her. Safer from
people without faces and myself. You see, Doc, I'm scared of myself and the things I'll
do. When I'm on the train with too many people, it feels like my synapses are Christmas lights that I've gotten out of the closet once again and they're in a huge knot and
the only way to get these Christmas lights ready is if I swallow the Abilify you're paid
to endorse and I remember my Effexor and Wellbutrin in the mornings and I just
deal, but I can't because all the signals are going to the wrong places and my hands

are going up when they should be going down.

"I just feel more secure. That's what I meant to say."

"Okay, good progress this session, Marquisele. I'll see you in two weeks."

I step out into the quenching cool of the late winter and I almost feel brand new as I walk to the subway at Morris Park. The leather sleeves of my jacket stick to my arms with sweat.

"Marquisele! Marquisele! Hey, wait up!"

I recognize your voice. It's you. And I keep walking with the knowledge that I could very well spontaneously combust if I see someone from school.

Your hand grasps my shoulder and suddenly I am spinning through time and space.

"Do I know you?" I ask with a questioning look on my face. I'm a liar. I've come to terms with the fact I'm good at lying and I don't mind it.

You have a leather jacket on, too, and you've gotten taller. You just got a haircut I suppose and your hand feels big on my shoulder. It slides off in the slowness that comes with confusion.

You're not sure it's me now. I've gained a little weight and dyed my hair copper and put on some hipster glasses. I have no makeup on and I'm wearing jeans.

You've never seen me in jeans. Your memory of me has faded and I can see the gears turning in your head and the embarrassment rising in your cheeks.

You're apologetic and you turn around to walk away.

The next thing I know, I'm riding the subway, staring at my reflection in the window across from my shining bench seat. My face is there and gone and there and gone as the tile of the subway stations alternate between a grungy beige and black. I have lights for eyes, white and blue and red and yellow and gum and graffiti for hair and I fall into the city's rhythm, indiscernible as anything but another person to someone walking along the black peppered floor used in MTA trains.

Your calls and your face flow through my mind like a bad tune. I feel the need, the want to spit and talk and spit again — spit shine your memory and rub away the filth and grime that has built over the time I've been gone.

You were completely unrecognizable under the thin veil of superficial familiarity, like a song you grew up to playing on the radio one day and knowing the rhythm but not the words. And so was I, unrecognizable that is.

Looking in my reflection once again, I reason that I can't really recognize myself either.

Watch Duckworth Exuding Drug

Judith Roland

Sometimes the biggest breakthrough a writer can
make is just getting started.

He never thought he would sign up for a drug trial, but Duckworth was that desperate. Nothing his doctor had prescribed seemed to control the pink crusty scabs that covered his face. It was a rare skin condition called rozacrustateous dermatitis with no known cause or cure.

> "...three times a day a technician entered, set a stopwatch for 10 seconds, and..."

To control for all external variables, he was kept in a sterile room in the hospital where three times a day a technician entered, set a stopwatch for 10 seconds, and administered a shot behind his left ear.

First day, nothing. Second day the same. But by the third day his face had started to clear and by day four, to his delight and amazement, the scabs had finally fallen off, leaving behind a healthy sheen.

Day five produced an unanticipated result, as his face began exuding a distinctly sweet rose-like smell, an apparent side effect of the drug.

Marquisele Mercedes

YEARS AS MENTEE: 1

GRADE: Junior

HIGH SCHOOL:
DeWitt Clinton
High School

BORN: NY, NY

LIVES: Bronx, NY

PUBLICATIONS AND RECOGNITIONS:
Scholastic Art & Writing Awards Honorable Mention

Easy breezy lemon peezy. That's what springs to mind when I sit across from Judy in the café, Juan Valdez. She takes a sip of her latte, says something, and I soak it up like a sponge. She has so many things to tell, like anecdotes from her childhood, trips and friends. I would sit back and just listen to her talk if we didn't have things to do. She's made a burrow in my being and I think that I've done the same. Two people from two different generations have clicked through words and story.

Judith Roland

YEARS AS MENTOR: 2

OCCUPATION:
President, Roland
Communications

I am fortunate and honored to call Mikey my friend. Our meetings were so comfortable, right from the start, and our immediate connection made it so easy to dive into the writing, take risks, be silly, be ourselves. We share our innermost thoughts and talk and write about the people who are most important in our lives. An outsider might see vast differences between us — age, culture, upbringing — but all we see are the things we have in common... a love of writing, really good makeup, and Doc Martens (although hers are black and mine are flowered)!

Happiness in Compensations

Bushra Miah

Tears began rolling down my cheeks; I could no longer handle the topic, in fear that talking about it would emotionally flatten me for days. And with this, I knew I had to write about it.

Before writing this piece, I met with my therapist and we spoke about the topic that lives deep in my soul, clouds my world, and secretly serves as the motive behind any major decisions I make. Within seconds of our conversation, tears began rolling down my cheeks and I could no longer handle the topic, in fear that talking about it would emotionally flatten me. And with this, I knew I had to write.

I was sitting at the dinner table, silently chewing my food, while my father sat to my left, speaking about his latest experience on the A train. Observing my nearly empty plate, he reached over, as though on cue, and placed more curry onto my plate, urging me to take second servings. Looking at him, I shook my head. But when he didn't notice, I raised my hand up slightly in protest, saying "No, no...no."

"You have to eat and become *big*," he said, widening his eyes playfully to emphasize the word. "How else are you going to be a doctor?" Although he was giggling, I knew he was pretty serious. Everyone in my family is pretty serious about me becoming an anesthesiologist, a surgeon or a doctor, at the least...everyone except me.

"The pain exists, but is always hidden." Behind the unceasing smile and the sweet words, my father is aged, lives a colorless life, and is strained in every way due to interminable anxiety. The pain exists, but is always hidden. He may not know, but just a glance in his direction, and I can tell. The only thing remaining on his bucket list is to be able to pay off my college loans and see me a happily graduated doctor — or in any position really, as long as it is a prosperous position in the medical field. This is his "light at the end of the tunnel;" his happiness lies in my successful future. And in short, my happiness lies in his happiness.

I half-smiled back at him and continued to chew the rest of the food. With it, I chewed down the desires I had for myself. I chuckled in my head and pushed aside all the hopes I had of becoming an educator, a writer, or a non-profit entrepreneur. Throughout the rest of dinner, my father spoke about all kinds of things, but I quickly lost interest and found myself drifting away with thoughts of my future.

"Where did I want to be in ten years? Would I even be able to become a doctor?

And if by a miracle I did, would I truly be happy?" I questioned myself. After we finished eating, I took on the job of washing the dishes. As I scrubbed grease off of plates and played with lukewarm water, I allowed myself to think of and compare two different lifestyles: one of a doctor and the other of the woman I wanted to be. I already knew the answer, but for the sake of reconsidering, I asked myself again, "Which would make me happier?"

I didn't want to reconsider. I wanted to go with my gut feeling and blindly decide. I wanted to live my life by doing the things I love and feel passionate about. But if I do, my father will be hurt for eternity. He'll never show it or speak of it, but he is my hero, and I know this would break his heart. I am everything he has. I am his dream, his "prize child." If I don't fulfill his dreams, who will?

As any parent, he has expectations and hopes for me. And who was I to break them like this? *I* would never be happy if I did.

After all, whatever I think my passions are, they aren't nearly as valuable as the passion I have to see my father's smile — one filled with sincere glee and pride. The day I see this, I will have achieved my happiness.

Failure

Gillian Reagan

I wrote this piece after returning from a surfing
trip to Costa Rica, an experience in which I broke
through mentally, emotionally and physically.

Surfing is a lesson in failure. The waves, born off the coasts of Antarctica or New Zealand, navigate through silky blue landscapes, and arrive grumpy from travel. They are powerful, churning, and resentful of the rising sand beneath them, forcing them high so they can crash down. I am in the water with them, fighting them. As the white ruffle of the wave approaches, I hop on my board, belly down, the wax sticky under my thighs, and paddle toward the shore. Chest up! Shoulders back! I feel the wave shove the back of my board. I lift myself up, crunch my legs up toward my chest. Before I can land both feet, the wave spits me up and out. I fall. Over and over again.

"...the white ruffle of the wave approaches, I hop on my board..."

My instructor, a lean blonde Brit named Helen — or "Hell's Bells" when she's ripping a wave — tells me surfers need the strength of a sumo wrestler and the grace of a ballerina. I have the strength of a New Yorker with a stressful desk job and the grace of a big-hipped Irish girl. "Popping up" on the board, with both feet in perfect skate-board stance, my arms floating in curved warrior position, my neck straight and high, is not an easy feat. I fail, again and again. "I can't do this."

Helen tells me surfing is a hard sport for cerebral, brainy types. You have very little control over the waves, the conditions, and, as I discovered, even your own temperament, if you're too much in your head. You have to learn to trust — not only the wave, the ocean, the board — but also yourself. You have to trust that you're going to land on both feet.

Helen is in the water with me, coaching me through each wave, telling me exactly what I did wrong — why I couldn't get my feet on the board. "You looked down." Flop. "You're too far back on the board." Flop. "You're not finding your balance." Flop. Flop. Flop. I don't like hearing about all the ways I am failing.

Finally, Helen finds the right thing to say to me. As I hop on the board, the wave approaching, she whispers in my ear, "Just look at the trees." The trees along the shoreline are lush and tall palm trees. They don't look like the ones from home. But they were cousins of the ancient pines that kept me company during lonely childhood walks in the woods, and sisters of my reading partners whom I leaned on in New York City parks when I first moved there by myself. They are there for me and I trust them. They help me trust myself.

"Just look at the trees," Helen says. And I catch my first wave.

Bushra Miah

YEARS AS MENTEE: 2

GRADE: Junior

HIGH SCHOOL:
Vanguard High School

BORN: NY, NY

LIVES: NY, NY

Two years ago, when I first met Gillian, I had no idea our mentoring relationship would patch together into the beautiful mosaic it is now. Gillian is not just my mentor, she is my inspiration; she brings out my creativity. This year, both of us have broken through by accepting change and writing about things we're scared to say out loud. We are learning to turn negative events into positive life experiences.

Gillian Reagan

YEARS AS MENTOR: 3

OCCUPATION:
Managing Editor, Capital
New York

Bushra and I have been growing together as writers, women, and friends for the past two years. I have watched her blossom from a shy young person to a beautiful writer, poet, novelist, and memoirist. She has so much talent that she is willing to show the world. We have taken on challenges in our lives together, through the loss of jobs, family tragedies, and moving from childhood homes. We broke through by writing, talking to each other, and opening our hearts, ideas, and minds. We shared experiences from going to readings at Bluestockings in the Lower East Side, to writing vulnerable pieces about our fathers, to eating peanut butter pie together. I'm so grateful to have been Bushra's mentor. We still have so much to learn from each other.

Cognitive Instrumental

Bre'Ann Newsome

This poem came about by delving into my mind to
see what really goes on inside it.

What is it about my mind?
That produces self-destructive thoughts
Self-detonating time bombs
That infect my neurons
Like a dark plague

3,
2, 1

And a brain vessel pops
And spews the life liquid of negativity
All over my confidence

It produces a weight so great
I become knee level with the concrete
And my feet dangle through the ceiling of the train station
Waiting for collision

My conscience is suicidal
Plotting on ways to kill itself
Without leaving evidence

This is down
No one is prepared for the out

The train comes
A woman screams
And the train misses
The conductor's tracks change
So all I feel is a gush of metallic air
That leaves my legs dangling awry

Until I drop
Start running on the third rail
Chasing the metal bullet
That dodged me

Come back!
I scream
Come back...
I beg

I slow down
The train dissipates into nothing but,
Red eyes lodging itself further into its man-made cavern

Maestro cue the music

Now this is instrumental
My thoughts are instrumental
My mind is a mental instrument

In need of being plucked
But has no strings
A wood wind
With no reed
A vessel that does not bleed
A fruit that is not sweet
A rhythm that does not have a beat

Maestro let me hear the string section

Let me feel the rhythm of their fingers
Let me feel this song of the mile
While I wait for the next train
Let me catch the next grenade
So I can watch it detonate
In the palms of my rough hands

This is art to the psychotic
This is fireworks to a child
This is braille to the blind
This is fluency with a stutter

This is a cognitive instrumental

Collateral: This Backless Dress

K.T. Billey

*This piece was inspired by conversations with
Bre'Ann — we often get to talking about beauty,
gender, expectations and double standards. I was
surprised at the 'break through' of humor at the end
of this poem, and wonder if that's from Bre'Ann, too.
I admire the way she uses humor in conversation to
deal with, respond to, and question tough realities in
the world. Though her poems are generally serious,
in person she reminds me how complicated, and
essential, a good-natured grin can be.*

aka: the closest I can come to understanding the shackle,
the shoulder blade in the soil, my hilt studding his field
for a change. Not knowing how to barter, I choose to strip

the pillory for parts, a promise to tide them over: I'll go home
when I learn how raptors hunt, how girl nails grow into status symbol
before curling handicap. And who files the ones who can't fasten

anything? If hawk strategies are concentric, in terms of temperature
and fuel economy, my biomimicry is a study in circles, the edges that skirt
the rim of my alarm. As we try to achieve the great migration

inward, to steal third, that trinity of give and take we talk
so much about, I tell him yes I did wake up like this, hungry
and halter topped. I'm ready for date night, throwing a grin in the bargain.

Bre'Ann Newsome

YEARS AS MENTEE: 3

GRADE: Junior

HIGH SCHOOL:
Bronx Studio School for
Writers and Artists

BORN: Bronx, NY

LIVES: Bronx, NY

PUBLICATIONS AND RECOGNITIONS:
Scholastic Art & Writing Awards Honor Roll; performed an original poem at the New York Women Foundation's Starlit Evening; performed in Poets Out Loud Workshop Series

In adolescence, being surrounded by people with enough care and patience to help you discover yourself, is amazing on its own. It is even more amazing to have a consistent and hands-on mentor like I have found in Kara; she is there to assist and uplift. Through our pair sessions, emailing, texting, and work-shops I have become grateful for Kara's personality, advice, and experience. It is for all of these reasons why I sincerely look forward to another year of brainstorming with her.

K.T. Billey

YEARS AS MENTOR: 1

OCCUPATION:
MFA Candidate in
Creative Writing,
Columbia University

PUBLICATIONS AND RECOGNITIONS:
Columbia's Undergraduate Teaching Fellowship, *Phantom Limb, The New Orleans Review, Prick of the Spindle,* and *Ghost Proposal*

Getting to know Bre'Ann has given me a greater appreciation not only for writing, but for the power of performance. Watching the rhythm of her words lift off the page and hearing them empower her voice inspires me to speak up — in written work and in general. She's taught me about growing up in a city like New York, reminded me how intense it is to be teen-age, and pushed me to be more vulnerable and open in my own work.

You and Me

Elshaima Omran

When I wrote this poem, I was mad at a friend. I
couldn't do anything except tell my mom and write
this poem. Every word came from my heart.

You and me
We used to be together.
Everyday together.
I really feel
That I'm losing my best friend.
I couldn't believe this is the end.
I'm tired of everything you have done.
Ignoring me
And forgetting about me
When I did nothing wrong.
All I did was be myself.
So this is it? We ignore each other
And pretend the other doesn't even exist.
Friendship means
Understanding not agreement
Forgiveness not forgetting.
The memories last, even though we've lost each other.
It's sad when you walk right past me
Like you never were a big part in my life.
How we used to be able to talk for hours.
How now you can barely even look at me.
Ask me once, just once, say you want me back
You want to be my friend again but you wouldn't because
You only love yourself, just yourself.
You said "Never lose a friend because of a small misunderstanding."
You left and never talked.
You believed them and never asked.
You were wrong, not me.
If you were a best friend you would have come and asked me.
I believed you once but I will never again.
You wanted? I needed.
You forgot? I remembered.

You promised? I kept it.

You stopped? I started.

You were done? I was trying.

You said you are my best friend? Stop lying.

You never knew who I am.

You were nice and you said, "I am really different from the others."

But I think you are the same.

Don't worry when I fight you,

Worry when I stop because it means there is nothing left to fight for.

Friendship means

Understanding not agreement

Forgiveness not forgetting.

Friendship is a name of hope.

But with it was hopelessness.

It's a door of understanding not lack of understanding.

Life changes every minute of every day.

You lose friends. You gain friends.

You realize your best friend wasn't your friend.

Know I am saying goodbye forever.

Know I always remember the bad things you have done to me.

This is because you didn't leave me a chance to remember the good things and memories we have.

You said, "Never lose a friend because of a small misunderstanding."

You left and never told me the reason.

Even though I can't forget you, I will try, my best friend.

Slipping Through Both Hands

Stacie Evans

This is an excerpt from a longer memoir, about losing someone.

The Nigerian proverb "Hold a true friend with both hands" makes me think of Rachel. We met our first day of college, timid, fish-out-of-water dorm mates. We attached, and the attachment grew. We were friends through loves and heartbreaks, travels, deaths, grad school, her marriage, the birth of her first child, the start of my attempt to have a child ... and then the friendship ended.

While I was focused on baby-making, Rachel decided I wasn't being a good friend — wasn't keeping up with her, supporting her, giving her what she had come to expect from friendship with me.

And that's fair. I *couldn't* have been a good friend. I was hormone sick and heartsick, sicker with each treatment, each miscarriage, a walking definition of "misery." It's believable that people who knew me then didn't like me much. I have some redeeming qualities, but there are plenty of reasons to not like me, plenty of ways I'm not a great friend that have nothing to do with hormones and childlessness. There are ways in which I am a *wonderful* friend ... but I'm human, and I don't always get it right.

I don't think any of my un-fabulousness justifies turning away from me when I'm at my lowest. It's hard to see how Rachel could let that brief period negate 25 years.

I read a blog post by Megan Nyberg about time and loss, friends and friendship bracelets. Nyberg wonders how we can be so desperately close to our girlfriends and yet lose them so easily, often without immediately noticing the loss. We wear our friendships on our wrists and toss them when the party-colored floss frays. We *don't* hold each other with both hands, even when we think we're doing exactly that.

> **"We wear our friendships on our wrists and toss them when the party-colored floss frays."**

It's seven years. I miss Rachel, am reminded of her almost daily — but I've also been angry with her unwillingness to value my stress and pain, to know that I needed her understanding, not her petulance and anger.

Another friend emailed to say Rachel would like to hear from me, but I'm not sure I'm willing to trust her. Yes, it would only be an email, not my heart, open and bleeding in my chest, but really: it's my heart, open and bleeding in my chest.

It's still hard to believe we aren't friends. I thought this friendship would last my life. Rachel was as close as a sister, closer than any other friend. How could either of us have let the other go without a fight?

Elshaima Omran

YEARS AS MENTEE: 1

GRADE: Sophomore

HIGH SCHOOL:
International High School
at Lafayette

BORN: Alexandria, Egypt

LIVES: Brooklyn, NY

Since I started meeting Stacie, a lot of things have changed in my life. One of the most important has been making a friend who is older than me. I prefer calling her "best friend" than "mentor." I trust her with my problems. She gives me advice, and it helps. One of my writing goals was to compose a poem. In the beginning, it was hard. Stacie kept inspiring me to write until I finally wrote a poem. Stacie said, "Wow, I love your poem. You can really find your voice by writing poetry."

Stacie Evans

YEARS AS MENTOR: 1

OCCUPATION:
Director of Cross-Sector
Initiatives, Lutheran
Family Health Centers

When Shaima and I get together, there's always a lot of laughing and talking about what's gone on since our last conversation, how is school going, how are our families, what new writing have we done. Getting to know Shaima and writing and sharing our work has been a pleasure. I love how smart, funny, compassionate and focused she is. Beyond that specialness is the surprise of finding my own breakthrough this year: owning myself as "A Writer." Sharing myself as a writer has forced me to drop my habitual self-deprecation and fully embrace this truth of who I am.

Journal Entry

Katherine Ortiz

This piece relates to breaking through because I've significantly altered my form in writing and found my voice.

Lux. Lux means "lights" in Latin.

That was her name, though and she didn't glimmer the way light does. She was born in November, a month everyone manages to overlook, the way she was. Her hair was brown, the shade of bark, her eyes mirroring the silk strands of her hair.

She liked the sound of classical music but didn't enjoy it. She didn't love her father and hardly cared for her mother. Sometimes she'd hope her parents would ask her about the time she spent away from home or why her clothes smelled of nicotine. Her hair covered her eyes which were dull of emotion. She had friends who wore far too much eyeliner, and mascara clung to their eyelashes desperately. She didn't listen to My Chemical Romance and found herself listening to the soft voices of Ed Sheeran and Nina Nesbitt. Her front teeth were crooked and sometimes she'd hope her parents cared enough to purchase braces.

> "Her hair covered her eyes which were dull of emotion."

She hated snow because the day Luca Rogers broke her heart it had been snowing. She also hated snow because her father couldn't shovel the driveway anymore, and she was an only child. Lux hated shoveling because her hands became raw, and the winds whipped against her face violently.

Lux loved spring because she liked the sound of rain against the asphalt when she awoke and the way the streets glittered in the dim lighting. She loved to see the cherry blossoms bloom along her street or the smell of dew in the morning. Her mother often said that spring was the season of lovers, because flowers bloomed and rain fell. Her father often said spring was the reason for beauty rather than love.

Lux didn't care what spring symbolized, she only cared for the rain and the mist against the caramel of her skin. Lux's mother was Native American and her father was from the state of Montana; they now lived in North Dakota on Crescent Hill, south of Dalton's Coffee House.

She hated coffee because it was bitter and her mother told her that her teeth would tint yellow. She didn't know what she wanted to do once she was older, and maybe she knew she didn't want to do anything at all.

Consciousness & Voice Breakthrough

Y. Joy Harris-Smith

I originally wrote this while studying abroad in Senegal, West Africa during my senior year of college. It represents my coming of age.

February 24, 1999 @ 9:25 a.m.
Dakar, Senegal

I've been fighting for a long time
The voice inside which screams "Mine!"

My throat, my lips say
"Let me out"
"Those belong to me"
"I want to speak"

But I put a lid on it and shut it.
Why? I ask myself. "Why don't I let my voice ring out and shine?"

Maybe I'm not ready. No, that's not it.
Maybe they're not ready. No, that's not it.

You've been taught by the society in which you live that your voice doesn't count — it's not as important as the rest.

Putting a lid on the voice that screams to be let out is the internal oppression you commit against yourself...

It is your reaction to being put down.
You have been taught so well those against you no longer have to stand over you because you carry out the job of keeping silent on your own.

But I no longer can keep silent. My voice won't let me. She's screaming and pounding on the lid, which is my throat and it Hurts!

Help me! Help me! HELP ME! Pleaseeeeee...
It's cold and dark inside, and I am hungry.
I need to devour the words, which exist at the table of our mind.

Breathe in and out. Breathe in and out.

"Mangi fi rek" which in Wolof means

"I am here."

Katherine Ortiz

YEARS AS MENTEE: 1

GRADE: Sophomore

HIGH SCHOOL:
Metropolitan Expeditionary
Learning School

BORN: Azua, Dominican
Republic

LIVES: Queens, NY

Yvette has become not only my mentor in my writing but a mentor in my own life as well. She's educated me on nearly everything I am curious about and provides me with insight. She's helped me find my voice within my writing and for that I am truly grateful.

Y. Joy Harris-Smith

YEARS AS MENTOR: 1

OCCUPATION:
Professor, Howard
University

Katherine looks nothing like me but yet we are so similar. She could almost be my twin. She reminds me of myself when I was her age. I admire her intelligence, strength and thoughtfulness. Katherine is a great writer. My weekly meetings at Odradeks Coffee House with Katherine are like being with the little sister I never had. Katherine's love of fiction and fantasy help me to remember that it's okay to dream while being awake.

My Stories

Adhelia Peña

I realize poetry is a genre I truly enjoy writing.
This poem represents that.

My stories are the Fairy tales I wish to live.
They represent the life that I once lived.
My stories are feelings that I can never express.
Thoughts that I'll never confess.
My stories are memories I wish to desperately share.
But I have no one who would care.
My stories are who I am
and who I want to be.
My stories are my sadness and happiness.
My stories are my past and my future.
They are the time that I wish to consume.
My stories are the love that I never got
And I once got, it slipped out the palm of my hand.
Then it turned into ink and began.
My stories are me.

Mi Querido Viejo

Perla Rodriguez

This poem became a writing and personal break-
through as I struggled with a subject very dear to me.

Papi shuffles across the room.
Our song has begun. Everyone turns towards the dance floor.

Es un buen tipo mi Viejo,
que anda solo y esperando,
tiene la tristeza larga

de tanto venir andando

He stands with me.
I know he smiles behind his mask. His eyes tell me so.
We share the same smile, same dark eyes.

yo lo miro desde lejos pero somos tan distintos

He bows, extends his trembling hand.
I blush, adjust my dress, grip his hand, try to make it
stop.
We both try to straighten up,
but we're pushed down by a third invisible dance partner we don't want around.
My vanilla poofy dress gets in the way. We falter. But continue on.
So many eyes on us.

viejo mi querido viejo
ahora ya camina lerdo
como perdonando el viento

He grips my hand. My fingers crushing.
He stops short. His legs freeze and start up again.
Freeze and start up again.
Freeze and start up again.
I hold him tight.
Balance on heels.
Push back tears.
Swallow hard and smile.
We reach the center. Cameras flash.
Heavy anticipation. Crazy expectations.

yo soy tu sangre mi viejo
yo, soy tu silencio y tu tiempo

Papi lets go and jumps, raises his rigid fists. Ali ready to rumble.
Everyone laughs.
Laughter juxtaposing with the melancholy of the song.
With the melancholy we hide.

El tiene los ojos buenos
y una figura pesada;

We look at each other.
Take a deep breath.
It's my day. It's our day.

la edad se le vino encima
sin carnaval ni comparsa.

Yo tengo los años nuevos
y el hombre los años viejos;

We sway. The three of us.
Papi, me and Parkinson's.

el dolor los lleva dentro y tiene historia sin tiempo

We sway some more.
It's almost done. We're almost done.

Viejo mi querido viejo,
ahora ya camina lerdo
como perdonando al viento;
yo soy tu sangre mi Viejo,
yo, soy tu silencio y tu tiempo.

We did it. We made it.
Perfectly timed. No more, no less.
I walk him back.
Eyes finally look away.
He sits and sighs
lightly.
His shoulders descend
comfortably;
the corner of his lip rises
triumphantly.

I kiss his hand, still in mine, and
I bow to my old man.

Adhelia Peña

YEARS AS MENTEE: 1

GRADE: Sophomore

HIGH SCHOOL:
Manhattan Village
High School

BORN: Bronx, NY

LIVES: Bronx, NY

PUBLICATIONS AND RECOGNITIONS:
Scholastic Art & Writing Awards Honorable Mention

I was told I was a strong writer, but I never believed it, until I met Perla. She showed me that there is more to writing than just a few topics, like love and one specific culture. I have canceled and been late, but Perla never blew up at me. I may have seemed cold and nonchalant, but Perla put up with it. I have a hard time writing my feelings down. Thanks to Perla, I grew as a person and a writer and I really appreciate it.

Perla Rodriguez

YEARS AS MENTOR: 1

OCCUPATION:
Writer and Writing
Instructor at The College
of Mount Saint Vincent

PUBLICATIONS AND RECOGNITIONS:
The New School's 2013 Chapbook Award

"I wanted to try something new. Isn't that what writing is about?" Adhelia said one day as I hesitated before her poem. "Yes, yes it is!" I responded. How else can I respond to the truth? To a wise revelation on life and writing? To a clear invitation to deal with my own insecurities? An earnest request to have a breakthrough? A breakthrough in both of us. And so we did. And we wrote poetry.

Speaking Out

Angel Pizarro

This piece is about my writing breakthrough and find-
ing my voice. I feel that this was an important turning
point in my life and the most meaningful to share.

isolated, anti-social little girl
not able to stand up to the world
afraid to think, afraid to speak
in silence she began to sink
so many thoughts in her mind
but the right words she couldn't find
all the books she quietly read
put a thought in her head
she could write what she wanted to say
that would be speaking up in a way
and so she wrote her words down

I am the little girl in the poem. One of the most difficult transitions in my life was
becoming a teenager. I went through many hardships in middle school and even now
in high school. I felt like I couldn't speak to anyone so I kept everything bottled in.
Even friends were clueless of how I felt. I didn't engage in many after-school activities
or have the same interests as other kids. Instead, I read many books. Reading helped
me in many ways. The more I read the more I wanted to speak my thoughts. I decided
to write down what was on my mind. I wrote everything — journal entries, poetry,
short stories and more. I felt more like myself when I wrote. I felt like it was the solution
to everything.

people saw and gave her looks
"you silly girl with your words and books"
writing lifted that weight off her chest
it gave her mind time to rest
as she wrote, people saw and said
"you silly girl. keep it in your head"
writing gave her the words she wanted to say
it gave her strength day by day
writing was like her red bull and wings
but people saw and said

I read and wrote most of the time. People thought I wasn't social enough. They didn't know what it felt like to be transported to another world through books, or taken back to an important moment in time through writing. I didn't share my writing often. In fact, I was a bit protective when it came to my writing. I was afraid people would judge me for my ideas and opinions. That's exactly what happened. Someone found a journal entry of mine, which eventually was read by several others. They weren't fond of what I wrote and I had to rip up my paper. It shouldn't have been seen by anyone. It wasn't meant for critique and judgment. It wasn't meant for shame. I was told not to write things like that. I was told to stay quiet and be a "good girl." It felt like I was moving backwards instead of forwards. It was as if a mute person had gotten her voice back only to be taken away again.

she stood quiet and felt herself slipping
she was sent right back to the beginning
but she stood up and said
"wait a minute, why should I hide?
what matters is what's on the inside"
so she spoke up loud and clear
for the whole world to hear

I enjoyed writing too much to let it go so easily. Soon I found the courage to stand up to people and say what I wanted. I began writing more often and didn't feel guilty or ashamed by it. Not only was it therapeutic, but also a hobby I grew to love. I wrote mostly poems, stories, and songs, which I still pursue. It's something I will never give up. It has become a part of my life, which I'm grateful for.

The Music Battle

Annie Reuter

I realized that music was the one thing I was
stubborn about. I refused to listen to those who
didn't think I could make a career out of writing.

Music journalism was the only thing I ever fought for. The poster child for non-confrontation, I was always the kid who listened to her parents.

"Can I go outside and play?"

"No, Annie it's supposed to rain today," my mom would say on a perfectly clear day.

"Okay," I'd reply with no argument.

When my parents said no, I didn't question it. So, when they didn't understand why I took a third unpaid internship at *Rolling Stone* after I graduated college, I realized I was alone with my decision to pursue music journalism as a career.

This wasn't just rebellion, it was war.

You see, from the very first concert I covered in college I was hooked. Writing about music was my future. I had no Plan B. Sure, I understood their concern about another unpaid gig, but it was a foot in the door to the mecca of music journalism and a white flag of surrender I would not give them.

> "...but it was a foot in the door to the mecca of music journalism..."

I was just one step closer to touring with bands and interviewing my favorite musicians. Of course, it would take months of unpaid work to get there and a lot of inner battles of what dinners or birthday celebrations I could attend because having no money was a constant enemy. The victory, though, was always in sight for me: getting paid to do what I love.

I'll never forget that feeling of being published on *RollingStone.com* as an intern or that first freelance check I received in the mail months after my internship ended. As I gear up to attend my very first awards show, the ACM Awards this weekend in Las Vegas, I'm glad I never gave in. Victory is very sweet.

Angel Pizarro

YEARS AS MENTEE: 1

GRADE: Sophomore

HIGH SCHOOL:
 NYC iSchool

BORN: NY, NY

LIVES: NY, NY

Annie and I both have a passion for music, which has influenced much of our conversations. Sharing new music with her is one of the aspects I love when it comes to our weekly meetings. We both learn from each other and grow as writers. I look forward to new adventures with Annie and couldn't be more grateful to experience this journey with her.

Annie Reuter

YEARS AS MENTOR: 2

OCCUPATION:
 Music Journalist, CBS
 Local/Radio.com

PUBLICATIONS AND RECOGNITIONS:
AOL, Billboard, CBS, MTV, Rolling Stone

Working with Angel this year has reaffirmed my passion for music. Every week, we spend time talking about the newest bands we're listening to and her love of music is contagious. We attended her first concert together, Amos Lee at the Beacon Theater, and seeing the show through her eyes and excitement instantly reminded me why I've spent so much time pursuing this crazy and unpredictable career in music journalism. It's in our weekly pair sessions that I am constantly reminded that this isn't just a job, it's so much fun.

Origins

Kirstie Plasencia

*My mentor and I selected a series of words that I
used as prompts. During our editing, I expanded the
poem, writing about the moon, the sun and the earth.*

I.

You are fascinated by my intensity and my emptiness. My voice is seductive, always
whispering, murmuring, inviting. You float in the shallows and I wrap your body in
my soft close embrace. You listen to my voice, hear how it speaks to your soul. You
love my brackish tears, the beautiful shells I churn out,
my waves. You skip in the beauty you see at my surface.
You think you are an explorer, but you are simply a tourist who fails to navigate my true depths, the horrors
within me. At night, I swallow the sky and still my power
is no match for the moon.

> "You love my
> brackish tears, the
> beautiful shells I churn
> out, my waves."

II.

You watch me, you gaze at me, you hold your breath and stare. You want to believe my
light comes from your love, but I am damaged with a cratered greyness. I will never
satisfy your private prayers and hidden wishes, and yet you would slice your soul into
a million pieces to form a constellation beside me. I would allow it for a night, but
when the sun came up I would do nothing to save you.

III.

You believe that I can shed light on your dark places, believe that you are brave when
you fly close to the flames. But I warn you, do not confuse my brilliance with a gentle
touch, for my power is molten and wrathful. That inner darkness you possess, only
you can light. I say, stay away, do not blister and burn, keep your distance. Appreciate
my radiance and warmth, and I will melt your fears, make the grass soft under your
feet, give you flowers to smell.

IV.

You close your eyes against your own handiwork, against the cracks, the holes, the
mounds, the barren places. If you stop to listen, this is what you will hear: an awesome pulse, an undying heartbeat. If you stop to look, this is what you will see: every
single color ever known in nature. You are alive for a single turn, but I am the one who
flourishes, who is full of life, a constancy of growth and bloom. Raw beauty that should
take your breath away. One day, when you have closed your circle, I will envelop you
whole, and you will see the entire tapestry, a woven blend of beauty and peril.

Leaving the Land

Cherise Wolas

*I challenged myself to create a tiny, stand-alone
excerpt from a 10,000-word story. I selected a small
chunk and refashioned it entirely, until I teased out
a new story that retained hallmarks of the original.*

Her apartment was newly shorn of every interior wall when Peck found the old photo album. Across the front was *Traynor*, her last name, in decayed silver leaf. When she was younger, during visits home, Peck sometimes stole for pleasure. Would she have hijacked her father's emulsified memories, or was it sent in the box from Devil's Creek along with her childhood things? She remembered lifting the lid, and finding her father's fragile hopes inside that she could recall from whence she came, her name at birth, the innocence she once possessed, the baby now loved by strangers.

Her father's family — in black and white — angular and steadfast on their land. Peck knew them only as gravestones, sepulchral limestone markings where they rest, sayings that summed them up. The last picture was oversized, her parents kissing, a silvered courtship kiss given before marriage, before she and Margo and T.J. were born, before bad times were anecdotes told by others. Peck touched the picture and felt something underneath. An unexpected envelope, small and sealed, with the name *Annabelle* written in her father's hand. When she lived on Traynor land, Peck would have acted, but flight had taught her the art of hesitation. She knew her father's words would be precise, but she wasn't ready for his sage, silly, hopeful or dumb advice written — who knew when.

> "An unexpected envelope, small and sealed, with the name *Annabelle* written in her father's hand."

Peck stripped naked and plunged her home into darkness. She tossed the old boxers into the bin, heard the swish of ancient love. The boxer-boyfriend hit her once, up on the Devil's Creek bluffs, an open-handed palm across her cheek that sent her tumbling to the ground. She had crawled away, he following behind, adoration in his eyes.

She stood at the window. Despite the unholy hour, the moon was still invested and lively, and she thought of the boyfriend who had said, "Naked, you are a bass clef, empty as intended, the spaces between your dots making clear that you're an F below middle C." Gorgeous talk that made her want to inhale him, but instead she had spoken the truth: "I don't have a clue what you're talking about."

Her apartment, once a warren of constricted rooms, was now open and vacant, nearly a womb. Down on the avenue, the traffic whooshed like the river back home when it crested its banks. Her father's letter fluttered to the floor. For now, she held close the belief that untethering herself from the land had been vital, a necessary freedom to give flight to her stories about lives blown apart on that land, about faith eliminated.

One day, she would read her father's words, as a fortune freed from a cookie or a message from beneath a grave, and Peck wondered, only briefly, if she would find she had slipped into her father's hopes or discover that his dreams no longer mattered, disappeared like the walls she had torn down. She breathed and waited to break the skin of a new day.

Kirstie Plasencia

YEARS AS MENTEE: 1

GRADE: Senior

HIGH SCHOOL:
Urban Assembly Media
High School

BORN: NY, NY

LIVES: NY, NY

COLLEGE: University at
Albany, State University
of New York

SCHOLARSHIPS:
Excellence Scholarship &
Opportunity Programme

My breakthrough moment this year with Cherise has been to discover how much I enjoy writing from prompts. Last year, I often found myself staring at a blank page, stuck and unable to manifest something from nothing. Or the idea in my mind was overly large, a novel perhaps, rather than a short story. Working with prompts has allowed me to focus intensely on only a few words, and I find myself amazed when a story naturally emerges.

Cherise Wolas

YEARS AS MENTOR: 2

OCCUPATION:
Writer, Editor, Lawyer,
Director and Executive
Producer of a UK-based
media company

PUBLICATIONS AND RECOGNITIONS:
Narrative Magazine

When I grapple with my own work, I eventually remember what Kirstie has focused on this year: the power of a single word. I return to the beginning of the sentence, the paragraph, the chapter and leave behind what came before. I search for that solitary word to commence the ripple. And when I find it, I search for the next word, and the word after that. In that patient way, a breakthrough of a kind occurs, effervescent and wondrous, as language and character furl together and I am able to move forward.

Untitled

Tema Regist

I'm recognizing the will power these successful
women exerted to break through the trials and
tribulations thrust upon them.

With pearls that glisten on their chocolate skin,
Clothed in African jewels,
Tribal patterns that hug their hips and their curves.
They uttered:

I am an African woman.

A woman that is a delicate flower with roots,
Roots as strong and as rich as the history of her people.
A woman that is the ying to every yang.
A woman that is a foundation.
A woman that is the backbone inside every man.
A woman that is a queen with a village that follows.
A woman that is the sweet sound of birds singing on a Sunday morning
A woman that is black and is proud.
A woman that is a treasure, a keepsake, a jewel.
She comes from a place of diamonds and gold.

She is a diamond.

Their chocolate legs strut fiercely with pride through trials and tribulations!
Determination led them to their successful pedestals.

Educated and opportunistic.
Dynamic and influential.
Strong and powerful.
Graceful and Elegant.

I am Michelle Obama
I am Oprah Winfrey
I am Angela Davis
I am Jennifer Hudson
I am Diana Ross
I am Madame C.J. Walker
I am Rosa Parks
I am Harriet Tubman

I am Lena Horne
I am Bessie Coleman
I am Ida B. Wells
I am Aretha Franklin
I am Billie Holiday
I am Mary McLeod Bethune
I am Maya Angelou
Not only are you African women,

You are African queens!

Pilot Script for Cougar Café

JoAnn DeLuna

*I wrote this screenplay during the Girls Write Now
Screenwriting workshop. Our group picked "café" as
a setting and we each wrote a different scene using
the same characters.*

*Connie, a 42-year old woman falls on hard times and is forced to go to work for her
daughter at her café as she figures out her life and tries to rebuild her relationship
with her daughter.*

Hillary: Um, Connie... these *organic gluten-free almond tofu-nut* croissants are
totally not gluten-free or tofu — these aren't even croissants! Where did they come
from?

Connie: Oh yeah, well they were out of those, so I swung by the Dunkin Donuts and
picked up a dozen assorted donuts.

Hillary: Connie, we are a gluten-free, nut-free coffee shop catering to the organic-
loving, gluten and nut intolerant demographic of the city. That's our USP.

Connie: Our US-what?

Hillary: Our USP — our *Unique Selling Point*. It's what we sold our investors on when we raised money on KickStarter and it's what we must deliver! We can't be an organic-loving coffee shop catering to the gluten and nut-intolerant population without organic, gluten-free, almond tofu nut croissants!

Connie: Well I can whip you up some of this [pats butt]. It's 100% gluten-free.

Hillary: Mom, you're fired.

Tema Regist

YEARS AS MENTEE: 3

GRADE: Senior

HIGH SCHOOL:
Midwood High School

BORN: Brooklyn, NY

LIVES: Brooklyn, NY

COLLEGE:
College of Staten Island

PUBLICATIONS AND RECOGNITIONS:
Scholastic Art & Writing Awards Silver Key for Poetry; Girls Write Now Poetry Ambassador; Poet-Linc Poetry Slam at Lincoln Center

My relationship with JoAnn has opened me up to taking my writing on journeys and exploring different topics and styles of writing. Our relationship taught me the lesson of not being afraid to put myself out there and this continuously motivates me to try new things. A breakthrough moment that I had with JoAnn was when we first met. Every question she answered of mine was the same answer I had. We both enjoy poetry. JoAnn works in journalism for a living and I have the hope of going into fashion journalism in the future.

JoAnn DeLuna

YEARS AS MENTOR: 2

OCCUPATION:
Associate Editor,
Business Travel News

PUBLICATIONS AND RECOGNITIONS:
Wergle Flomp Humor Poetry contest, *The Bodega Monthly Anthology* and *Boundless Anthology*

I'm always learning right alongside Tema. We try different genres, forms and styles of poetry together. Probably the biggest breakthrough we had this year was that we got to host one of the Girls Write Now CHAPTERS Readings Series. We were both incredibly nervous and were pushed way beyond our comfort zone — but we did it! And I'm so glad we did. The best part was that we got to perform a poem together that we had written in one of our weekly pair sessions. Yup, I think we're ready to host the Academy Awards — piece of cake!

Interrogation of Adelaide

Sara Reka

I see this piece relating to the theme of "Breaking Through" because it explores the mindset of a teenager whose eyes are opened to the corruption in the world.

My shackles glimmered in the dark as his badge spoke;
Officer, protector, man in blue.
The corners of my lips rose ever so slightly into a smirk;
The city's defender had found himself seventeen year old bait,
myself, chained for a quick buck, a speedy promotion.
Way to keep the city clean, officer.
Maybe it'd be better if I were a killer found with unholy weapons
and bloodstained hands.
Alas, my palms only reeked of marijuana and ink.

Heat waves rolled off his masculine body and engulfed my entity.
My face paled as his aroma taunted me,
challenged the rising hairs on my body.
Despite my goosebumps, I held his eyes in place.
The government's German Shepherd had his teeth bared.
Where is the safety in a maul, officer?
He was awaiting his kill, toying with his prey.

How did you end up in shackles?

I ran my tongue across my bottom lip, tasting the salt of blood and bruise.
Duly noting his sarcasm, I remembered the chase.
The figure of authority had bashed my face into the cement with ease.
My only regret was not leaving a print.

You chained me.
Confess.
To what?
*Being undeserving of my services, being the scum of the city,
the chewing gum beneath our feet!*

I do not regret my youth,

or the flow of passion continuously separating brain from body;
I sweat mischief from my pores and my fingers stay ink-stained.

The graffiti piece was worth a shiny penny,
you should have seen the sunrise break free from the attention-deprived wall.

I could have sworn the German Shepherd growled just then.
As he orbited around me I noted that his eyes were
empty vessels frozen solid in an interrogation room.
What a ferocious wolf man.

I saw the sharpness of his bones daring to break skin,
they shone dully, enough to betray the secret that
human skin was not good enough for the uniformed man.

What color are your veins?
Blue.
How many lies have you told?
One.
What was it?
That my veins are blue.
What color are your veins?
Red.

I am different from you, wolf man.
The world is separated into you and us,
and you know nothing of us.
You, the blue-veined, money-ruled,
the empowered figures of government.
Us, the red-veined, passion-ruled,
the disempowered citizens of your country.

Vrksasana*

Kathleen Kraft

*This poem was a breakthrough in the sense
that I have only started writing about my yoga
experiences in the last year or so.*

Hello, self, body rising —
Limbs I make, leaves I grow.
I inhale lifting, leaving much behind
for this temple of twisters, our mats of imagined
grass. Aligned natures — hips, backs, arms
flowing, divining.
Reach higher again and again —
Reach into this endless practice —
Lift your heart
My upper branches open —
Root to rise
We are knobs of root surfacing —
we are of the same glad soil,
parents to selves
I taste my thoughts, from nowhere they fall
like summer rain, now steaming, now dry.
Leaves grow from my limbs
lush with life before me.
Tree Pose in Sanskrit

Sara Reka

YEARS AS MENTEE: 2

GRADE: Senior

HIGH SCHOOL:
NYC iSchool

BORN: Durres, Albania

LIVES: NY, NY

PUBLICATIONS AND RECOGNITIONS:
Poet Linc Poetry Slam at Lincoln Center

Kathleen's hugs are always great. Whether they are given after a long editing session or upon arrival, I can say that I always look forward to them. This has been a significant year for both myself and my mentor. I believe that through my writing, I've allowed myself to meet the level of self that I was searching for. I now write about issues that matter to me: feminism, police brutality and the wonders of life. I would have never matured to this level of thinking or writing were it not for my patient mentor, who aided me with every piece of writing and with every kind suggestion. With Kathleen's editing suggestions, my visions came to life, and my breakthrough occurred.

Kathleen Kraft

YEARS AS MENTOR: 2

OCCUPATION:
Teacher of Writing,
Yoga, and Movement

PUBLICATIONS AND RECOGNITIONS:
Five Points and Five Points Blog

It has been so wonderful to be Sara's mentor. She is always engaged and passionate in our discussions about life and poetry, and she has grown so much as a young woman in the short time I've known her. Wow! She has also been a friend to me, supportive and encouraging of the recent changes I have made in my life.

Unconditional Love

Tiffani Ren

I fictionalized my relationship with my mom,
adding details and quirks. I hoped by writing about
Charlotte trying to break through, I would as well.

Charlotte slides into the seat, feeling the cold creeping through the fabric of her black denim jeans, and slams the car door.

She sighs, closing her eyes with the tired weighing them down.

"Why your face is like that?"

Her mother looks at her through the rearview mirror, her eyes hard, her eyes challenging.

because i still have to do five essays for health and watch an hour-long documentary about whether or not the bombing of hiroshima and nagasaki were war crimes and write a freakin' position paper for ap us history and study for physics or else i'll fail and my grades are going to drop and i feel like i'm falling all the time now lagging behind as everyone's accelerating and i feel like collapsing AND YOU'RE MAKING ME GO TO SAT PREP.

Charlotte crosses her arms tighter around her chest and over her feelings. She looks out the window, letting out an angry puff and making the glass frost over.

"If you don't want to, you don't have to go to tutoring," her mom says.

YEAH RIGHT i know you you won't let me stop you'll never let me take care of myself and make MY OWN mistakes you always try to control my life i KNOW IT FUCK just leave me alone.

Charlotte glares at all the cars going past, almost glad that she's quiet and usually doesn't talk to her mom and her mom has long stopped expecting a response, because they'd be arguing all the damn time and it'd just be too much, too much work, too much effort, too much screaming.

"I know that you aren't going to pay me back."

JUST LET ME MAKE MY MISTAKES.

...

"I know that you're going to leave home when you go to college and get a boyfriend."

... what

Charlotte looks back and stares at her mother.

Her mom keeps her eyes on the road. "And you're never going to come back and take care of me and your daddy when we're old, and pay us back for all we gave you."

"...but her mother doesn't look at her as she pulls away."

She stops the car at the tutor's driveway and Charlotte lets herself out. She tries to catch her mom's eyes so she can nod her usual *thanks* but her mother doesn't look at her as she pulls away.

Charlotte steps slowly toward the door of her tutor's house.

what? why is she doing all of this then? why does she spend her saturday nights driving me to prep school when she could go dancing with her friends why does she give up her lunch so that she can save it for me even though i don't NEED the freakin' extra food and

"Mrs. Tom?" Charlotte calls out into the stairwell. "I'm here."

i don't understand i don't understand if she doesn't expect repayment why does she do all of this for me I'M SO MEAN TO HER i don't even thank her properly half the time i never hug her or tell her that i lo — care .... about her?

The phrase unconditional love comes into Charlotte's mind.

except wtf does that really mean and it doesn't sufficiently explain how she still does all of these things for me even when i'm a freakin' ASSHOLE to her and i can't ever really talk to her or tell her my true feelings.

Charlotte sits down on a bright pink knitted seat cushion and she takes her glasses off because she's starting to tear up.

because, the only time i really talk to her is when i talk back, and become defensive and offensive and regressive and this whole mad, angsty teenager image would clash with a heartfelt talk about feelings my feelings how i understand her feelings i understood all this time her sacrifice except right now i can't understand why she's doing it for me.

Her tutor walks in with her cane clicking on the marble floor, holding a gigantic blue college board SAT book in her right hand. "How are you?"

Charlotte smiles, courteously taking the burden of the SAT book out of her tutor's hands. "I'm fine, thanks. And you?"

and that was the problem with being mute, not talking to her.

there's like this barrier built up over time and it's too hard to overcome it the moment we need it most and i'm too freakin' embarrassed to talk to her REALLY seriously to talk to her with an open heart and overcome that barrier

of misunderstanding and dislike i've helped build between us, and it's my fault it's my fault it's my fault i can't even ask my mom why she loves me still when i've given her no reason to.

Flying Up

Stacy China

It took years for me to feel comfortable with the
title of woman. I was female, not a child, but being
comfortable with being called "woman" took time.

Describe the moment when you knew you were a woman.

I remember when I stopped fighting it.

When I stopped picking up the armor to wear.

I remember the various sets of interlocking tin — tomboy, baggy pants, deep voice, cutting voice — all presented with no war paint. I remember putting them on. I remember using them to cut, to contain, to restrict, to push away.

And I remember being really, really angry. And not knowing why.

Years past before I noticed the weight of what I was carrying. I remember becoming distinctly aware of its constriction — on my shoulders, on the small of my back, on the backs of my legs. There was a sharp realization of how hard it was to take a deep breath. Then the eventual realization that breathing had almost stopped altogether.

> "...the eventual realization that breathing had almost stopped altogether."

In time, the desire to breathe became more important than the fear of what that living, breathing air might bring. I remember consciously forgetting to pick up one piece of armor, then another. Tin falling away. Body becoming lighter.

And when I stopped, I remember that the world didn't stop. The earth under my feet didn't give way and swallow me. But it did settle still. And the spirits — young and old, living and dead, subdued and fiery — rose up to meet me.

Rooted in the earth. Light enough to fly.

Tiffani Ren

YEARS AS MENTEE: 1

GRADE: Junior

HIGH SCHOOL:
 Stuyvesant High School

BORN: Queens, NY

LIVES: Queens, NY

PUBLICATIONS AND RECOGNITIONS:
Scholastic Art & Writing Awards Silver National Medal, Gold Regional Key

I used to be embarrassed and I hid things I thought would drive the people close to me away. Since I've started writing a memoir this year, I've found that opening up brings people closer. Stacy reads my pieces and not only critiques the writing, but talks to me about the experiences in my piece. When I get insecure and too hard on myself, Stacy is always there to reassure me, show great empathy, and give great advice when I talk about parents, boys and teachers.

Stacy China

YEARS AS MENTOR: 1

OCCUPATION:
 Freelance writer

Occasionally, I come across a writer who writes exactly the way she speaks. Tiffani does one better — she writes exactly the way she thinks. The entire stream of consciousness is on display. She's brave and forthright and incredibly generous to her reader. Through watching her write (think), I've considered how to better explain things in my own writing. And I'm skeptical of writers who insist on being taken seriously without displaying that kind of courage. No one will do it like she does, of course. But we should all engage in our own brand of bravery on the page.

Lost

Jade Rodriguez

In joining Girls Write Now, my writing has
become more descriptive. I'm taking risks and
breaking through.

Adam

I walked into Jason Richards's house and caught a whiff of the weed. Why did Chloe have to come to this party? I made my way up the stairs and walked through each room on the second floor, each room filled with drunken, horny kids. It was disgusting. I entered what seemed to be a bedroom and saw my friend Robbie from student government.

"Hey, bro, I didn't know you were going to be here."

"Yeah, just looking around for Chloe. Have you seen her?"

"Last time I saw her she was with Jason."

A pit formed in my stomach. I couldn't move. She was with Jason.

"Thanks, man. Talk to you later."

"See ya."

Robbie walked away and I continued to walk throughout the house. I walked down the stairs to see Lexi. Her flaming red hair stood out of the crowd. She was chugging down a beer and standing in a cloud of smoke. I walked over to her and tapped her shoulder.

"Adam, what are you doing here?"

"I'm here to see Chloe. She's not answering her phone."

"She's over there."

Lexi pointed behind me and there was Chloe; her long, usually straight, brown hair was perfectly curled and she was wearing a skin-tight dress. She was with Jason Richards. His broad arms were wrapped around her; they were kissing. I felt my heart break, I felt weak.

Lexi

"Adam why are you here looking for Chloe? She is obviously fine."

"Did you get her drunk?!"

"Listen, I didn't force her to drink and besides she's having a good time. Let her be."

"She's drunk, Lexi! You know how Chloe is."

"OMG! If you're going to act like this, then leave. You're killing my vibe."

"I'm just looking out for her."

"So am I."

"Well, you're obviously not doing a good job. Look at her."

I turned my head toward Chloe and smiled.

"She's having real fun for once in her life. Leave her alone."

"This is not real fun, she has no idea what she is doing."

"Just Leave, Adam!"

"Not without Chloe!"

"You're not taking her, so just leave her alone and go home!"

Chloe

Over the loud music I heard a familiar voice.

Adam.

I looked up to see him. I was confused. Why was he here? This wasn't his type of scene, this was barely my scene. He was arguing with Lexi. It looked pretty heated. Adam's face was turning red and Lexi's eyes were getting darker and darker. This was serious. Why were they arguing? They never argue like this. I was about to get up but Jason pulled me back down.

"Where do you think you're going?" he asked.

"Just going to talk to Lexi real quick."

"Talk to her later. Wouldn't you rather just be doing this?"

He pulled me into a deep kiss.

"I guess I could talk to her later."

I turned really quick to see Adam walking away from Lexi and toward the door. I needed to find out what they were arguing about. I turned back to Jason.

"Babe, I have to use the bathroom, be right back."

"Hurry up!" he said in an annoyed voice.

I got up and speed-walked to the door. Jason wasn't looking, so I quickly walked out. I stepped out and could see Adam's signature olive green jacket as he walked down the driveway.

"Adam!"

He turned and smiled once he saw me.

"Chloe, please leave with me. I don't have a good feeling about this party."

"Adam, I can't. I'm having fun. I love it here. Why were you and Lexi arguing?"

"You."

"Me! Why were you guys arguing about me?!"

"I was just saying that you're drunk and need to be taken home, but she said to just leave you alone and go home."

"Oh, Adam, I'm alright, I'm having fun."

Adam looked down and pulled his glasses up from the bridge of his nose.

"Are you and Jason together?"

"We haven't put a label on it, but I guess we are."

"What do you see in him Chloe? He is just like every other jock. Please just leave with me."

"I can't go Adam, I have to get back. "

"Please, just leave with me."

I was going to say something back but then I heard a deep voice behind me. It was Jason.

"She's not going anywhere, bro, just leave."

"Jason, I was just coming back inside."

"I thought you said you were in the bathroom."

"I just really needed to talk to Adam."

"Chloe! Don't apologize to him."

"Dude, just leave before something bad happens."

"No, not without Chloe."

"Adam, just go," I said with tears appearing in my eyes.

"Fine, Chloe, just please be careful. I don't trust this guy," Adam said as he turned to leave.

I turned to Jason once Adam was out of sight.

"Jason, I'm so sorry for lying to you."

Jason didn't say anything. He just stared at me with cold eyes. He lifted his hand and slapped me across the face. "Don't you ever lie to me again!"

Fitting Out

Linda Corman

This is a raw, unfinished response to one of the "I remember" prompts in Girls Write Now's Slam Poetry workshop. This is about a person who had a lot of breaking out to do.

I remember wishing my hair was as straight as Susie N's and Susan C's;

I remember feeling like I had to swim slower so people wouldn't think I was showing off;

I remember feeling like I was being a tiresome scourge when I wanted to walk or bicycle rather than drive;

I remember feeling like I wanted to shrink into myself because the boys were all shorter than men, my

teeth stuck out, and stray hairs stuck out from my braids;

I remember feeling like hiding my ankle socks at dancing school.

Jade Rodriguez

YEARS AS MENTEE: 1

GRADE: Freshman

HIGH SCHOOL:
Urban Assembly Bronx
Studio School for Writers
and Artists

BORN: NY, NY

LIVES: Bronx, NY

PUBLICATIONS AND RECOGNITIONS:
Writer for "The BSSWA Bulletin"

My relationship with Linda is great. Linda is always challenging me and lending her opinions. She has helped me learn to put my guard down with my writing. This has really opened me up and given me a chance to present my work. When I first read Linda my piece, I was terrified because it was very rough around the edges. When she said that she loved it, it made me realize that putting my work out there is okay. Linda helped me break out of my shyness and I appreciate her for that.

Linda Corman

YEARS AS MENTOR: 4

OCCUPATION:
Editor at Jennison
Associates

Jade is always surprising me with her liveliness, her playfulness, and her thoughtfulness. I usually think of her as a daughter; then she'll say something that makes me feel like she's more of a friend than a teenager. Often it's something very thoughtful and endearing. We were in Starbucks and I couldn't get online on my computer so we could send in our anthology submission. She asked someone for help and my computer still didn't work. Jade asked me, "When is your birthday?" I told her and asked why she wanted to know. "You should ask for a new computer," she said.

You are...

Najaya Royal

I began to think about the difference between
associates, friends and best friends; best friends are
the most valuable because they uplift you and help
you break through and better yourself. This poem is
dedicated to my best friends.

Have you ever been told how much you mean to someone?
Have I ever told you how much you mean to me?
But it may exceed my limit for this anthology piece
You are the one who keeps me high
You are my perfect melody
The soundtrack to my happiness
Would like to hate you sometimes
But my emotions say otherwise
You are my motivation
The perfect persuasion
I would define your importance
But allow me to speak a little more
You are a lullaby to a restless mind
Confidence for the unconfident
I love to like you
My "Corazon Sin Cara" *Prince Royce Voice*
My Superhero
My heartbeat
You are the extra loud laugh that blurts out unexpectedly
You are the blush that turns my brown skin red
How do you do that?
You are the past I pass constantly in my mind
And when the world decides to place its weight upon our shoulders
You are the love that adorns me
You are undefined beauty in a beastly world
You are my orange soda
I guess that makes me Kel
You are my 90's baby if you understand
Understand that you mean what others don't

You keep me sane in an insane world
And you may say the same
You are the one to say "We got this!"
You are the reason I'm not afraid
You are my best friend
I love that

A Place
Called Home

Anuja Madar

The first draft was my usual view on love in poetry —
pretty depressing — but I decided to push myself to
take a more positive outlook, and I'm glad that I did.

My smile and your laugh collide
We pull back from impact
Discover an unknown place called home

Winds of change bring seeds to my garden
Settling into soil they take root
Giving life to once barren land

Connect on common ground
Explore uncharted territory
Find there is a home where this heart is

Warmth yet no sun
Satisfaction with no appetite
Flight without wings

There are no gates
We let walls touch
Trade secrets under a rising sun

Disruptions but not destruction
Tend to wounds with tender touches
Safety in the number two

An impatient past
Savoring the present
Hoping for a future

Najaya Royal

YEARS AS MENTEE: 3

GRADE: Junior

HIGH SCHOOL:
Benjamin Banneker
Academy For Community
Development

BORN: Brooklyn, NY

LIVES: Brooklyn, NY

PUBLICATIONS AND RECOGNITIONS:
The Scholastic Art & Writing Awards Silver Key in Poetry

Anuja is like my big sister and a best friend to me. She always encourages me to do my best and if something is difficult, she tells me not to give up on it. I learn from her all the time, and she is always by my side, especially when I need to vent. I never feel down when I am around her, and this is one of the many reasons why I love her. I dedicate my poem to her.

Anuja Madar

YEARS AS MENTOR: 7

OCCUPATION:
Content Strategist,
Marriott

At the Girls Write Now CHAPTERS Reading Series, I saw something different in Najaya: a confidence and maturity that told me what I always knew — she's not a girl anymore, she's a woman. This realization came at a strange time. I've always cared for Najaya, but this year I found myself feeling internally protective of her, much like I imagine a parent would feel. Here she is getting older —and I guess I am, too.

Step

Angelica Rozza

I've been inspired to write the hardest truths.

"A line can be straight, or a street, but the human heart, oh, no, it's curved like a road through mountains." — Tennessee Williams

On my street, growing up, it took under 32 steps to walk straight to any store. After school, as I passed my friends walking together, or with their parents — knowing my mother was home in bed — I counted the steps it took to get to each store so I would know how fast it would take to get home. Back in my apartment, after putting away bags of whatever I purchased for my mother, I would read stories to her that I had written. Trying to get her to smile, I used theatrical gestures and my best storytelling voice. Growing up with a mother who has bi-polar disorder, no day was a straight or level line. But even on days I was needed at home and wasn't able to join my friends, no day went by without my writing stories.

I wrote at a desk by a window that faced the stores on the street. Picking up my mother's prescriptions at the pharmacy took 31 steps. The market took 24. When my mother was not able to work and things got rough with money, we had to barter with the landlord by buying him food as payment for rent. In the market, I weighed bananas and apples, and whatever fruit cost the least. I learned how to be observant and resourceful, to take charge, and to value caring for someone else. Though I didn't realize it at the time, all those steps I took on my street have shaped me into who I am today.

Learning to pay attention to details and cues that signaled my mother's needs allowed me to transfer this awareness to my writing. I tried to tap into the heart of each character I created. Every day, I wrote pages about different characters, creating adventures and stories about their lives. This gave me a sense of connection to a world outside my home life that I often didn't feel growing up.

But there were times growing up when I enjoyed my mother's company. During the summer of my first year of high school and the last summer with my mom's Honda, we drove into Queens. Although we didn't have much to say to one another, we walked in and out of small antique shops, both falling in love with antique picture frames and salt-and-pepper shakers.

As the day progressed and the sun boiled above us, her irritability began to surface. I knew that the best thing to do was leave before she had a full-blown episode. Instead she walked into a hole-in-the-wall bookshop. The place was crowded with thick books on uneven, wooden shelves. Greeting cards and bookmarks collected dust on the main desk in front of the brass cash register.

My mom told me to look around. The mustiness of old books gave me an instant headache. I decided to pick up the closest book with the most interesting cover. A hard cover, with a purple slip caught my attention. I ripped it out from a tightly packed shelf as quickly as I could without pulling the whole shelf down. My mother grabbed it from my hands and the cashier rang it up. Twelve dollars. Before I could escape the embarrassment and snatch it back from the cashier with a swift excuse, my mother began fishing through her pocket. First came the crumpled five-dollar bill. Then came the handful of change. And without as much as a blink of the eye, my mother counted. The cashier waited for every quarter, dime, nickel, and penny, and then dumped the handful of change into the brass register that clanked with every coin. The book was mine. As we left the store, with the book tucked under my arm, my mother turned to smile at me. Without much thought, I grabbed her hand and crossed the street with her to the car. Those were steps I walked with joy.

My mother is the woman who taught me to stand on my own two feet. And for every time the silence grows too loud between us, I'll remember that she spent her last handful of coins on me in that bookstore. I'll remember that she has always tried her best to make me smile. I've learned to cherish my time with her, because for every bad day, there was a good day that made it all worth it again. And despite all the rough patches her disorder created, her faith in me, and my passion for writing, will always motivate me to move forward.

Out of Nowhere

Joanna Laufer

I've been inspired to be more courageous, more prolific...

"A line can be straight, or a street, but the human heart, oh, no, it's curved like a road through mountains." — Tennessee Williams

On my street, growing up, it took under 32 steps to walk straight to any store. Maybe 32 is not an accurate count. As I tried to keep up with my mother's violent, quick pace, I might have fumbled the counting I sometimes did to try to keep from thinking.

The closest store on that street sold Chinese antiques. To me, each piece looked as fragile as my mother's tenuous rage. But because she had a happy childhood in Tientsin and Shanghai, in this store she was nostalgic and sedate. She had shown me photographs of her childhood pasted on cardboard pages in albums that were falling apart, pictures of her waving goodbye from ships and smiling on the steps of her school, a photo of her in a rowboat on a street in Shanghai during a flood that turned that street into a river.

When my mother was in good spirits she would talk about what she loved about China — her American father trading fur, playing in a park that was fenced-in under a roof, built to look like a pagoda. The elegant ship she traveled on called the Nitta Maru, the beauty of the water and land.

But when the rage came out of nowhere, she walked and talked fast. From any store on that street she took me home. If she wasn't venting about me, or about someone else, her stories about China changed. She would talk about beggars sleeping on boats, on crowded sampans shallow as rafts. People sleeping on streets. Cripples and the poor. She'd say when she passed beggars on the street in Tientsin holding out their hands, she'd always feel at least one of them touch her.

Once I left home, from college on, I left my fear of her behind, though I lived with a love/hate rage for her. I had every intention not to see her, but I visited a lot, somehow believing that walking with her, browsing in stores, or shopping together for holiday meals would erase the erratic outbursts from the past. At best, she showed disinterest. I held onto my rage, but I still longed for a straight-line connection, heart to heart.

> "...I left my fear of her behind, though I lived with a love/hate rage for her."

After I married and my daughter was born, the three of us often walked with my mother on that street. She bought my daughter ice cream from a store next to the Chinese antique shop. She held my daughter's hand and mine. My husband and I helped as she struggled to take far fewer than 32 steps. Gradually, she couldn't even take one. The past few years I have come to see that things that seem harmless often cause the most harm — air, the sun, time. Now in a wheelchair, with dementia, she remembers only the past. Not the beggars but the beauty of the land. No matter what time has done, it has made her level and kind. Time has made me love more freely.

Angelica Rozza

YEARS AS MENTEE: 3

GRADE: Senior

HIGH SCHOOL:
Long Island City
High School

BORN: Brooklyn, NY

LIVES: Brooklyn, NY

COLLEGE:
State University of New
York at New Paltz

SCHOLARSHIPS:
Merit Scholarship to
State University of New
York at Potsdam

PUBLICATIONS AND RECOGNITIONS:
Scholastic Art & Writing Awards Gold Key

This year, I realized how completely lost I would be without my mentor, Joanna. Without her support and motivation, senior year and the college application process would have been a nightmare. Although this is our last year together at Girls Write Now, I know we will always be a pair. With every meeting we had in coffee shops and over Skype, not only has our friendship grown closer, my confidence in writing memoirs has as well. For two years, she has inspired me to write the hardest truths and to have the strength to never give up.

Joanna Laufer

YEARS AS MENTOR: 2

OCCUPATION:
Writer and Editor

It has been a privilege to work with Angelica for two years. We got through writing college essays together with brownies and almond tarts. Her fiction and memoirs about high-stake subjects moved me to raise the stakes in my own work. In coffee shops, or during snowstorms by Skype, we exchanged vivid details about our families and lives, both verbally and on the page. What might seem different is often almost the same. At the heart of our stories and memoirs we found common themes. We took risks writing about subjects we had avoided. Angelica has inspired me to be more courageous, more prolific, and our strong connection keeps growing.

Untitled

Lawrencia Terris

*This piece relates to the theme of "Breaking Through"
because I have never written a journalism piece; I
branched out of fiction writing. I am usually a shy
person, so asking a stranger a ton of questions was a
new experience.*

He dug through a large bag woven from plastic. "I have this card somewhere," he kept
repeating without tearing his eyes away from the bag. His white hair was spread out
across his scalp, with some parts sticking up and others lying flat. His fingernails were
long and chipped. The scooter in which he sat was something you would see on the
streets of Italy, a cherry red color with two mirrors placed on either side. Carmine
Santa Maria is a large and intimidating man.

I sat in on a merengue and tango class taught by Carmine on a chilly Wednesday
night. "Surely there won't be much of a turnout," I thought, as we waited in the Bensonhurst middle school auditorium. To my surprise, half an hour after the class was
scheduled to begin, his students started to come down the ramp in pairs. The group
consisted of middle-aged and elderly Russians, Chinese and Italians. "They all get
along," Carmine said. "The pupils help each other."

Not only is this man a dance teacher, he's also an important figure in Brooklyn
news. Before he started writing columns for *Brooklyn Daily*, Carmine made a name
for himself as an activist. He's most proud of rallying against the MTA. It all started
when he moved to an apartment near the Bay Parkway subway station. He found the
screeching noise to be unbearable, a noise so loud, "It was possibly illegal!" After
going to the *New York Post* with complaints of the trains, Carmine realized he would
need more people on his side. "Do the work yourself and people will back you up,"
he told me. At the end of this battle, Carmine came out as the winner when the MTA
agreed to put rings onto the wheels of the train to lessen the noise. "I was always cam-
paigning for what I wanted."

But Carmine was more than a train activist; he also acted on behalf of children in
the New York City public school system. "The guy running the school board was a
political hack," he recalled. "I ran against him just to get him out." Carmine ended
up enjoying his job. During his term as school board president, he sold tickets for
events, fundraised, and visited all the schools in District 21. "Did you know I was the
best Santa there ever was?" he said, turning once again to rummage through his bag,
in search of a card with a photo of him wearing his homemade Santa costume. "This

was around the time schools were getting intermingled," Carmine explained. "I broke them into the American tradition of Christmas."

The students danced to the sound of ballroom classics, so loud I had to bend to hear what Carmine was saying to me. It had been an hour and a half and they were still twirling around like they'd just arrived. Most of them had never danced or had any Latin dance training before attending Carmine's free, weekly class. Because there was a different group every week, the newcomers had a harder time catching on. The veterans would position their hands and legs in the right way. An Asian woman showed an elderly Asian man who had arrived late how to do the steps properly. Carmine sat in his scooter, watching with observant eyes. He spotted errors quickly — any wrong turn, footstep or miscount was seen by him. "The first thing I say is, 'Can everyone count to eight? If not, get out!'" He looked content watching his students dance though he was unable to join them. "If you can't dance, you teach," he said. "Pass on the fruits of your labor to others."

Carmine spoke with fondness when asked about his family. He was born to a large Sicilian family and developed a love for dancing early on from going to what he calls "football weddings," weddings with so many people, sandwiches had to be thrown into the crowd like

> "Dance became a common language in a house with a language gap..."

footballs for dinner. Carmine had sisters with whom he danced and attending these events only deepened his passion for it. Dance became a common language in a house with a language gap; his father didn't speak any English and Carmine couldn't speak any Italian.

After three hours, the students were still dancing without any trace of fatigue. At the end of each song, they looked to the stereo and waited for the next one to begin. Music by Frank Sinatra came on and Carmine started to sing along into a microphone, his voice resonating through the auditorium. Toward the end of the song, he abruptly stopped singing and yelled, "Go home!" to signal the end of class. Though class was over, and the dancers were leaving, Carmine was still looking for the card with him dressed as Santa Claus to show me. "I never say no to anyone who needs my help," he said. Though he sees himself as someone who helps others, some kind of Santa Claus, Carmine needs help, too. When class was over, he needed help getting home.

5 Green Juice Recipes for the Juice Beginner

Juliet Werner

I've been amazed by the number of people drinking green juice. It seemed like one day people were drinking Coke, Gatorade and water, and then overnight, green juice was everywhere. Rather than dismiss my reaction to this trend as trivial, I decided to trust my instincts and write something. To my delight, a week after I wrote this, The New Yorker *cover featured a lion drinking a kale smoothie.*

Recipe #1
spinach, kale, cucumber, ginger, lemon, 4 apples
Note: Yum!

Recipe #2
spinach, kale, cucumber, ginger, lemon, 3 apples (If you can handle going down to three apples, go down to three apples. Otherwise, stick to the four.)
Note: As you reached for that fourth apple, did you tell yourself, "An apple a day keeps the doctor away?" Thought so. The predictable thought process of a person who lets his peers venture into new juice territory while he sits idly by drinking the juice he drank as a child.

Recipe #3
apples
Note: No, I'm not kidding. Apples only. You just don't seem ready.

Recipe #4
I actually left the piece of paper with this recipe on it at the beach. But due to having drunk it myself, I don't experience regret. My life is anxiety free. And my fear of failure has disappeared. I think it had kale.

Recipe #5
spinach, kale, cucumber, ginger, lemon
Note: Congratulations. You've made it to where you no longer need apples to make this drink palatable. Now you're on your own.

Lawrencia Terris

YEARS AS MENTEE: 2

GRADE: Senior

HIGH SCHOOL:
Arts and Media
Preparatory Academy

BORN: Castries, St. Lucia

LIVES: Brooklyn, NY

COLLEGE:
Syracuse University

My experience with my mentor has opened me up to new things in the two years that we have known each other. I tried new foods and learned things I never knew before. Ironically, the first breakthrough moment we had was an attempt to interview a coffee shop barista. Needless to say that didn't turn out too well. This time, writing these pieces, we had better luck with journalism.

Juliet Werner

YEARS AS MENTOR: 2

OCCUPATION:
Segment Producer,
"The Daily Show with
Jon Stewart"

Lawrencia had expressed interest in trying journalism so I brought her attention to The Brooklyn Paper events calendar. Together, we honed in on a ballroom dance class. On the night of the class, we traveled separately to Bensonhurst, and by the time I arrived Lawrencia was already interviewing her subject and taking copious field notes. One woman waved us over and told us she relies on a cane to walk, but can manage without it during these classes. We both listened politely, until she hit us with the money quote, and then Lawrencia, who was reporting for the first time ever, discreetly opened her notebook and jotted down the line.

Things I Wish Someone Had Told Me

Iris Torres

*This poem was a major breakthrough for me
because I had never written something personal
before. I detached myself from every piece I wrote to
ensure that it never coincided with my personal life.
With this piece, there was no detachment because I
couldn't hide the facts.*

I stare back into my younger cousins' eyes seeing
innocence that I wish I still had
14, 12, and 8
they could do no wrong
Their questions putting me in tough spots, the eldest one asking,
"What's it like being in love?"
But I can't answer because I'm afraid I'll look too stupid
or I won't give her the picture perfect answer she's looking for
The 12 year old complains about how difficult school is
The eight year old struts in heels bigger than the ones
I am supposed to wear
I look back at them and think about the things I wish someone had told me
Like how depression is an ugly
monster that takes the more you give to others
That your "best friend" won't be there
forever, and that you won't be her bridesmaid at her wedding
like she promised in the third-grade
that crying at 3 a.m. is normal
and so is having your tears lull you to sleep
That making decisions is so difficult
especially when it involves severing ties
with people you once considered family
That boys and girls are going to
come in and out of your life
but your mother will never leave your side

I wish someone had told me to set up a swear jar

because I'd have enough money to pay for a round trip to

Japan and back

I wish someone had told me that people will hurt you

and try to take advantage of you

because they know you're a good person

I wish someone had told me that there's no such thing as a

reliable definition of a

good person

I wish someone had told me what the fuck love even is

I wish someone had told me it's okay to fall in love with whoever you want

and that gender doesn't matter when someone makes

you feel elated and important

even if that person happens to be

your best friend

but that's okay

I wish someone had told me that religion should protect you

and not make you feel

afraid of what you don't quite

understand

I wish someone had told me that youth,

innocence, and freedom should never

be abused

My aunt had the answers for me

I once watched her straighten her luscious curls and paint her lips and face before

leaving the house

And I watched as motherhood robbed her from me

but rewarding me with another smiling, beautiful face that

relied on me for answers to questions she couldn't ask her mother

when the time comes sooner than she expects

But I will never have the answers for them

Not for Ivette

Not for Kiara

Not for Alexis

Not for Samara

and

Not for

Myself.

Sitcom Poem

Heather Kristin

*I was inspired by the Girl Write Now's Sitcom Writing
workshop and my mentee helped me break through by
connecting to the personal and turning it into poetry.*

1. An energetic and ambitious violinist from Ohio wins a scholarship to Juilliard where her conservative Republican beliefs clash with those of fellow artists.

2. A historical novelist attempts to write a TV series with her two best friends who are sketch comedy writers. Will their relationships survive or will comedy turn into tragedy?

3. A spunky and smart poet from New York discovers her family's dark past in the Ukraine. Does she reveal it to her Bosnian teacher openly or reveal the poem below to her class?

Brown was her name
Bright were her wings
Lights brought black dreams
To be seen and heard
On a screen
That the world thought was everyone.
Don't they know it just crushed men?
And left women slick with oil
On their bodies, barefoot and shining
The flame burns on and more generations ooze.
They dance and sing not knowing where to trod, their lipstick's smudge on each other.
They are mixed as one.
Don't trade yourself for the glow, let it go, get deep.
Words will be rewarded, toil and soil, can change the world.

Iris Torres

YEARS AS MENTEE: 3

GRADE: Senior

HIGH SCHOOL:
Young Women's
Leadership School

BORN: NY, NY

LIVED: NY, NY

COLLEGE:
Rider University

SCHOLARSHIPS:
$16,000 Dean's
Scholarship

PUBLICATIONS AND RECOGNITIONS:
Scholastic Art & Writing Awards Honorable Mention

Heather has always encouraged me to try new things and with-out her, my writing would have remained stagnant. She has taught me how to become more personal with my voice while still having fun with what I'm doing. Hearing her own personal stories under the bright lights of Caffe Bene in New York defi-nitely made me feel a lot more comfortable with myself as not only a writer, but as a woman.

Heather Kristin

YEARS AS MENTOR: 7

OCCUPATION:
Writer

PUBLICATIONS AND RECOGNITIONS:
As a little girl wandering the streets of New York City, at times homeless and home-schooled, I never dreamed 25 years later I'd be honored by the State of New Jersey General Assembly for my dedication to woman's issues, write for *Salon* and other publications, and be interviewed by Oprah

Iris and I had a major breakthrough this year when we learned to trust each other by revealing our true selves. She taught me to be a better listener and to think outside of the box. I can't wait to see what her future holds!

A Scream of Smoke

Moie Uesugi

This piece was a product of trying to carve out my own space and voice rather than pleasing an audience. By confronting this expectation, I feel that I was able to break through walls.

"The soft, trembling petals within me were bent around the edges." As she typed, she felt her pace slow as she neared the end of the line, finally coming to a halt as her pinky slid onto the period key. She stared at the blank, white canvas of the Word document that lay open before her.

"As I exhaled, I felt a wisp of whimpering smoke rise from their center," she typed, then slumped back in her chair. *That could work*. But then, with one look at the glaring white screen before her, she backspaced all of her words. Each of the pixels, only white as a combination of every possible shade of red, green or blue, seemed so much like her — but as she looked at them, she felt anything but solace and comfort. Instead, feeling like them meant she was pressured only to be so much whiter, so much more writerly, than she thought she was.

> "All she had was a confetti of words…"

All she had was a confetti of words, and all she could do was string them together like beads on a bracelet. But every time she looked into the glare of the screen, she felt she lacked a scream inside of her, the scream against injustice and men and hate. But at the same time, she had only ever heard snaps for fierce anger and fear and love — things she had declared, after countless battles like these, that she did not have.

But she told herself to be persistent, and let her mind turn inwardly instead. "The door slammed behind him as he left, all stubborn smiles and promises," she typed. She felt like a liar, only letting words slip off of the tips of her fingers instead of her tongue. And instead of excuses, these were reasons — reasons to be respected as a powerful girl who overcame difficulty and hardship or as someone who deserved a voice. She knew that these were the anguishes that received awards and the tears that led to applause. But she still couldn't choose between getting fake praise and giving real boredom.

She felt her eyes close in defeat, their lashes heavy and unpoetic. It was already two in the morning. And there she was once more, telling herself she didn't have anything to write. She closed the lid of her computer screen and went to sleep.

The Dressing Room

Amy Gall

*This excerpt was originally written during the Girls
Write Now Romance Fiction workshop. I specifically
chose a prompt in that workshop that involved
an interracial couple because I wanted to break
through my own discomfort with writing about
race. That brief exercise has since grown into a full
story and has helped me be more honest in the rest
of my writing.*

Harold picked at the skin on his thumb. It calmed him, seeing the red rawness underneath the dry layers. He avoided looking in the long row of mirrors. Some man with a
high voice and waxed eyebrows had covered Harold's face with something that made
him feel like his pores had been filled in with cement.

Delilah was across from Harold getting her hair done by a different high-voiced
man wearing some kind of cape dress who seemed perfectly content to tell strangers
his entire life story. "Swear to God, he set the bed on *fire*."

Delilah gave an easy, rolling laugh, "Oh my goodness," and pressed her hand to
her cheek.

The high-voiced man gasped. "As I live and breathe,
will you look at those cheekbones?" He turned his head
towards the hall. "Julian. Come here and look at Miss
Delilah's cheekbones."

> "The high-voiced
> man gasped. "As I live
> and breathe..."

A large, blue, bouffant appeared in the doorframe.

"Like a statue, am I right?"

The bouffant nodded vigorously and then disappeared.

High-voiced man grinned at Delilah and moved some of her hair behind her ear.
"Like a Greece statue."

Harold snorted. "Greece" statue. Perhaps, in order to qualify for the job of head
hair fluffer, one only had to learn his shapes and colors.

After the dressing room emptied out, Harold moved his chair next to Delilah's.
"It's Greek. Greek. And my wife is not a naked white man."

Delilah moved her chair farther away. "They're kids, Harold. And it's a compliment. Must you always sift around for the hidden insult in everything?"

Moie Uesugi

YEARS AS MENTEE: 2

GRADE: Junior

HIGH SCHOOL:
Bard High School Early
College Queens

BORN: NY, NY

LIVES: Brooklyn, NY

PUBLICATIONS AND RECOGNITIONS:
Scholastic Art & Writing Awards Honorary Mention

Amy and I spent this year changing in many ways. We became genre-travelers and perspective-hoppers. We broke through the stubborn veil that covers our surroundings. We ventured out of the fiction world and examined what exists around us, what could exist around us, and who we are as writers.

Amy Gall

YEARS AS MENTOR: 1

OCCUPATION:
Program Assistant,
National Book Foudation

One of the most exciting and humbling aspects of my relationship with Moie is how many of our huge breakthroughs have come as a result of small, shared moments: a joke, that turned into a writing exercise, an off-hand comment about a Spanish paper that evolved into a practice of listing our "proudest moments" for each other every week. I've experienced so much joy, satisfaction, and a shared sense of accomplishment from one hour a week of simply listening and being present. I will carry that breakthrough with me for the rest of my life.

A Mother's Love

Mya Watkins

*This poem is dedicated to someone who has carved
me into the woman I am. A mother's love can
sometimes go unappreciated, but I was inspired by
the theme of "Breaking Through" to truly appreciate
the care and affection she has given me. My mother
is more angel than human.*

Mama, I wish your confidence was contagious
Because you fill the room.
Boisterous and happy
People gravitate to you like a drug.
Possessing a bravery that cannot be questioned
You're the heroine of every story I could tell,
Slaying the insecurities.
You are a force to be reckoned with.
You keep me from being swallowed into a pit of my own creation.
With your fearlessness
Façades fall, ceasing to exist.
It feels good to feel safe.
The sweet solace of your words guide me
In directions I never dared to imagine,
Giving me a passage to new adventures,
Constructing a home in the experiences.
You immerse yourself in joy and bring me with you.
It's scary to be vulnerable,
But then I see the effortless way you open yourself up to life,
And it is beautiful.
How freeing it would be to express my opinions without being scared of judgment.
You are magical,
Rescuing me from enemies of the mind that block out the warmth.
You are the warmth,
Helping me to let go of every battle my mind has conjured.
I promise to never take you for granted,
For there would not have been a me without a you.
So I will make every tomorrow worthy of you.

And years from now disregard gray hairs
Because a soul as magnificent as yours must be forever.

My Father Is a Magician: And Other Stories I Tell Myself

Jeanine Poggi

As children, we believe our parents are superheroes.
When we grow up we may discover they are
profoundly more powerful than we ever imagined.
Then there's the breakthrough that comes when we
realize our parents are only human.

My father is a magician. He can make himself disappear with a flick of his hand and a silent wink. He took to performing this signature act on my seventh birthday. I expected my father to emerge on my birthday with a cape and wand and declare me his beautiful assistant as he attempted a daring act that none of my friends should try at home. But instead he simply vanished — no "abra cadabra" or "hocus pocus" — not even a puff of smoke to signal he had once been here. He nailed the disappearing act, but still hasn't been able to perfect his return.

My father is the homeless man on the corner I pass every day on the way to the library. His hair has grown wavy and his mustache unruly. He clutches a tin can with stained yellow fingernails. Dirt so permanent. As he whispers to himself he exposes a gap where his front teeth should be. I stop buying myself ice cream and instead put the money into his tin can. I like the way the nickels and dimes sound as they clink together. This is our song.

My father is a superhero on a mission to protect my family from monsters. I hear them at night, shuffling in the dirt, crawling up the trees, gently tapping at my window. But my father vanquishes them to faraway forests. They call him Mr. Invisible. His superpower is the ability to disappear, allowing him to sneak up on his prey. He doesn't need the suits and ties of his Wall Street persona — instead, my burly father wears a cape and spandex tights. I try to suppress my selfishness — it's unfair of me to wish to see him in the clearness of daylight when other families, other little girls, need him to rescue their puppy or lift a car that fell in a ditch.

My father is an astronaut, floating in space. His body, weightless, not burdened by the realities of earth. Surrounded by darkness, he can't see beyond the glittering supernovas that are his world now. Protected by his spacesuit, he bounces carefree, star-to-star, unconcerned about the earth below. How can he be blamed for being in awe of the beauty of something larger than himself, bigger than my mother, more powerful than me? Who am I to challenge the importance of outer space?

> "Who am I to challenge the importance of outer space?"

I wish any of these stories were real. But these were merely the lies I told myself, concocted on warm summer days in the hopes that if any were true, it meant my father's disappearance had nothing to do with me. The truth is, 20 years later I still have no idea where he is. I see him every day waiting for the bus, briefcase in hand, tie perfectly knotted. I pass him every Sunday morning mowing his lawn as his children run barefoot through the sprinkler. And I make up stories about the lives he leads and the one we never had.

Mya Watkins

YEARS AS MENTEE: 1

GRADE: Sophomore

HIGH SCHOOL:
Brooklyn Technical
High School

BORN: NY, NY

LIVES: Queens, NY

Jeanine has helped me better myself as a writer. Working together has opened me up to all the possibilities and opportunities the world of writing has to offer. The workshops and pair meetings have introduced me to new genres of writing beyond my comfort zone. It has been such an enjoyable journey and I can't wait to see what's next.

Jeanine Poggi

YEARS AS MENTOR: 2

OCCUPATION:
Reporter, *Advertising Age*

Does she think my jokes are funny? Am I talking too much? During our initial pair sessions these questions nagged me. I worried Mya's quietness would clash with my chattiness. Yet, sometimes there's beauty in silence and a bond that can form in writing instead of speaking. This happened when Mya shared a poem with me that made our difference in personalities and the 15-year age gap between us disappear. We didn't need to find commonality in chatter, her poetry did that for us.

P.R.O.M.

Carmin Wong

I wrote this trying to stay true to myself as a writer
while tackling something unfamiliar.

P.
P is for the pigment in our skin
The name calling in the words
That resonates into thin air
As we act like we do not hear
It's for the plenty of times
We've heard the
"You so black you blue,"
And
"Maybe if you loved yourself
They'd love you, too."
It's for prosperity
In the white man's land
As he digs ditches
Into our gold minds
And we act like we do not see
It's the tone in our voice
When we have nothing
Left to say
When we know
Not who we are
Nor where we have come from
And our only perception
Of tomorrow
Is that it hasn't come yet

R.
R is for "Remember that time
They called you foreign?"
And
To them
It was a complement
It was like saying

"You look
Like nothing
I've ever seen before"
But all you wanted to do
Was spit intelligence
Into the brains
Of the ignorant
And backhand them with
A word that offended them
Ten times worse
But see
Nowadays a nigga
Is a nigga
A nigga is a black man
And it won't be soon
Before Webster coins the
Masta's phrase
Like murders
Swept under the rug
Like the secrets
The government refuses to tell us
Because we very well might:
Travel out the country
Go to war for decades
Imperialize —
And take over
Millions of acres of land
That do not belong to us
But we do because of greed —
And convert believers
To believe what I say goes

O.
O is for opportunity
When opportunity knocks
You welcome it in with both hands
In the air
Like cops yell at you to do while
They're feeling up on you
Or wait
I think it's called searching —
No frisking —

You for some answers
That were never there to begin with
O is for "Oh, I'm sorry"
When he's done
And
The memory you have
Reliving that very moment
Ten years later
While lying in bed
Watching Law and Order
And realizing that what he did
Was a crime

M.
M is for my reason for writing
These words
Not for a poem
But awareness
To the unaware
About the accounts of our people
Nationally
Globally
We have held out tongues
We have victimized ourselves
M is for making a difference
Graduating high school
Going to prom
Protesting for those
Who never had the chance
M is for material items
People die for every day
The things we cannot afford
Yet
Still wish to have
M is for my ticket out of the hood
Out of patriarchal environments
And subway running rats
M is for the one midnight
I can be the Queen of my own castle
Shining light
On those I enlighten
M is my one night to

Represent myself
My school
My history
My culture
My one night to be alive
My journey
My Prom

Because I'm a Girl

Hadia Sheerazi

*Growing up in Pakistan, I spent most of my young
life breaking through social, cultural and economic
barriers. This piece salutes the indomitable girl
who persevered despite the odds, and a tribute to
all girls everywhere.*

"Pink is in aisle three," says the owner of the hardware store, the light shining off his bald head. "What about yellow ... or blue?" asks my pregnant mother, who is seven months. "You said you're having a girl didn't you?" he replies. "Yes," she smiles. "So, aisle three," he repeats as he struggles with five paint cans. "But," begins my mother as he starts walking away. He turns back to look at her and says, "Pink. Because it's a girl."

"Pink. Because it's a girl."

"Aww look at her tiny hands ... she's beautiful!" coos the supervisor with the dark red lipstick at the daycare as she leans over the baby basket. "But why aren't her ears pierced?" she asks with surprise. "Why would they be?" asks my mother. The woman responds matter-of-factly: "Because she's a girl."

"But I don't want a boy cut!" I protest loudly at the salon. "Your teacher said that you were playing with your hair in class," replies my mother patiently. "No I wasn't!" I argue with her, twisting around in my chair, my feet dangling high above the floor. "I was just trying to braid it," I try reasoning with her. "No distractions," says my mother firmly. "But she's a girl ..." the hairdresser tries interjecting weakly. "And she'll still be one," says my mother and resumes the reading of her book.

"Ha, ha! Hadia looks like a boy!" The taunts ring in my ears as the third-grade boys stand around me in the playground, smiling gleefully. "Shut up!" I retort angrily, my face flushing with embarrassment. "Or what?" jeers Ahmad, as he swings upside-down from the monkey bars. "We're not afraid of you," he continues, sticking his tongue out at me, "you're just a girl."

"Why do I have to wear these horrible things?" I ask my mother in dismay as I hold up the shapeless *shalwar*. "Because you're 12 now and can't go outside without covering up," my mother tries explaining. "But why?" I insist, looking down at my legs, wondering if they had suddenly become hideous. "Because you're a girl ..." she replies quietly, not quite meeting my eyes.

"Why can't we practice with the boys?" I demand of the pot-bellied coach as I stand on the sideline with a basketball under my arm. He glances briefly at my sunburnt face, pauses chewing tobacco long enough to say dismissively: "Because you're girls."

"You're letting her go to America for college all by herself?" asks my dentist incredulously. "Yes, why?" replies my father glancing up from his newspaper. The dentist's eyes widen over his facemask, and he waves his surgical pliers for emphasis: "Because she's a girl!"

It's graduation day. As the Dean introduces the Student Marshall and Valedictorian for the Class of 2010, one of the professors standing behind me whispers to her colleague, "How did she manage to do all that in just four years?" As I hear the applause from the sea of 20,000 people, I turn around, smile and say, "Because I'm a girl ... "

Carmin Wong

YEARS AS MENTEE: 2

GRADE: Senior

HIGH SCHOOL:
Boys and Girls
High School

BORN:
Georgetown, Guyana

LIVES: Queens, NY

COLLEGE:
Howard University

PUBLICATIONS AND RECOGNITIONS:
Honorable mention for Scholastics Arts & Writing Awards, Poet-Linc 2014 Anthology, Invictus Youth Essay Writing Competition Winner, Student journalist for *The Informer* newspaper (Macon, GA), Urban Word Teen Poetry Slam

Hadia encouraged me to keep it up and no better words than "break though" could express my journey as a writer this year. Looking back at it all, I'm not quite sure what led me to have a successful year as a writer and performer, but I began exploring spoken word poetry (something I had long idolized). I never thought I would be good enough to compete with my poems. I didn't always win, but Hadia's words of encouragement were always comforting. We both taught each other that we are women of action, and we can tackle anything we desire. And truthfully, we do.

Hadia Sheerazi

YEARS AS MENTOR: 2

OCCUPATION:
Development Assistant,
Grameen America Inc.

These last two years with Carmin have been incredible to say the least. There are so many moments, big and little, that will always be wonderful memories for us. Whether it was trying a new dessert or trying out a new style of writing, she has always been up for an adventure. I have seen her grow and develop a distinct and strong voice, and as a teacher and friend, it has been an honor and a pleasure to be a part of her journey. I cannot wait to see her take on the world. And she will!

Her

Luljeta Kulla Zenka

This poem came from listening to songs and reading
books about amazing women.

Sweet Nyx covers her
in the darkness.
Hides her for months,
away from the air of morality
For she is a blessing to others,
a treasure to keep.
A mother looks at a child,
the giggling and laughing creature,
with eyes bright and young.
She whispers promises,
and hopes the scribes of fate listen.
And she is a mother who cannot
do anything except hope.
Helios is waking and she is the sun.
Painfully, lovingly, she climbs through
the tortuous terrain and comes out,
bright.

It is an era where the mouth
is wide and full.
Words fall out.
Where roots are firm and limbs grow,
like branches.
Spindly.
Where eyes let out anger
suppressed by quieting shushes.
Eyes wet with tears, dimmed from the sparkling stars
of nonage.
And with the Twelve Labors,
she is forced through difficulty.
Named Felicia and Amy,
from the mouth of him.
With advice from old women,
with mock respect.

And she is the black sheep
of a herd of misguided peers.
Anger flows through for all of it.
Resentment.

Let her be the Penthesilea of all women.
Conquer in ripe age.
Rule with youthful eyes.
In a world where,
she is reminded of danger.
And no fruit, even Hades' crops
that sting the mouths of others,
can push her away from eternal
light.

I will accept her like Demeter
accepted spring,
when it came back to her,
with its loving smile.
She will laugh at the
Icarus of men, who does
not have the touch of double X.
And there is a smile on
a face that was prophesied to be danger.
Every flower wilts and
her time comes as winter
weaves into the ground and,
suffocated the life out of Persephone.
She tells tales of her time,
when they are at the end of her timeline,
it comes out like lies
yet there is truth,
and when she laughs,
the wise eyes twinkle.

She is not sad for
Charon's coming,
but instead welcomes his company
for she knows,
that a legacy is what she
gave to the world as a gift.
A wonderful gift.
A new sun, Penthesilea, Persephone.

Regretful Rhythm

Lizz Carroll

I used to play the drums, so this poem is about my
relationship with percussion and how I miss playing.

A dull Pearl drum set donated to a charity
Finally
Couldn't lie to myself any longer

One drumstick,
warped and useless
Found under a shelf when I moved out of my parents' house
Covered in dust bunnies
My name in purple marker

I haven't sat behind a drum set in decades, but
It stays with me
The rhythm, the heartbeat of music, the soulful guide
That sets the pace

It's a part of me

The haughty thud of the hefty bass drum, a foot rocks to the beat
Snares clap and crack
Rimshots cut the air
Their metallic footsteps echoing

A hi-hat exhales...haaaaaaah....tttsssssss
With every open and close
Ting ting-a ting ting-a ting
A drumstick bounces off the bell of a cymbal

Thump shhhhh
Thump shhhhh
A brush suggests a bassline
Treading lightly with finesse and subtlety

A fill on the toms punctuates the drum solo
Digga digga digga digga digga digga dun
Crash
Blam

Questlove, Tito Puente, Sheila E, Cindy Blackman,

Ray Barretto, Max Roach, Rick Allen
Creating beats that inspire hips to sway & jiggle
And cause heads to nod in raptured appreciation

Bebop, hip-hop, Afrobeat, Latin
Syncopated beats
Frenetic beauty of heavy metal basslines
An old friend knocks at my door, in time

It sinks into my skin
That rhythm created by others
Still flows through me
The musical pulse of memory

Luljeta Kulla Zenka

YEARS AS MENTEE: 2

GRADE: Junior

HIGH SCHOOL:
Susan E. Wagner
High School

BORN: Brooklyn, NY

LIVES: Staten Island, NY

PUBLICATIONS AND RECOGNITIONS:
Scholastic Art & Writing Awards Silver Key in Short Story

I've known Lizz for two years now. We're always cracking jokes and laughing together — both over the phone and when we meet up. We're so close and you can see that during the Girls Write Now workshops; we're sitting together, with our shoulders touching, whispering every now and then to each other and laughing. I know she cares for me and that she'll help me. I feel I can go to her for anything. She even puts up with me whenever I rant and cry about TV shows. She's just that amazing.

Lizz Carroll

YEARS AS MENTOR: 2

OCCUPATION:
Community Content
Manager, The
Foundation Center

Luljeta and I laugh a lot and we just get each other. I think the best part of our friendship is that we are always learning from each other. She awakens my creativity and I even think that I've become a better writer. When I'm with her, I fall in love with creative writing all over again. Every time we meet, we exchange three writing prompts and work on them for the opening of our meeting. We end up high-fiving each other.

Streetlights and People

Rachel Zhao

Writing a play is appreciating the subtleties in everyday language. New York is an extremely familiar place for me to write in.

(Midnight on a subway car. Train halts on a bridge. AUDEN presses her palm against the window as between sharp bursts of static, they announce that there is train traffic ahead.)

TRAIN CONDUCTOR: Dekalb Avenue, next stop. This is the Brooklyn-bound Q train.

AUDEN: *(frowning)* Dekalb? I've need heard of Dekalb before…

(She glances around, noticing for the first time the emptiness of the cabin. An old man wrapped in a coat lounges on one of the benches nearby. AUDEN quickly looks away before making eye contact. She eases herself off the seat and quickly makes her way to a map.)

AUDEN: Hmm…last time I checked we were at Lexington Avenue. How the hell did I get to Brooklyn?

(She looks down the length of the car. Just the old man again. AUDEN winces as her combat boots catch the plastic of the floor, squeaking loudly. The old man doesn't seem to notice. He appears to be in his fifties, with thinning silver hair. He's slumped over, dressed in an oversized, fraying winter coat and mumbling to himself.)

AUDEN: *(clearing her throat)* Excuse me?

(The man continues to mumble. AUDEN sighs.)

AUDEN: *(a little louder, edging closer)* Excuse me!

(Man is still oblivious to her presence.)

AUDEN: *(shouting)* EXCUSE ME!

(The man jumps, looking at and acknowledging AUDEN for the first time.)

MAN: Hello, can I help you miss?

AUDEN: *(stares at him incredulously for a moment)* Yes, I'm a bit lost. I was supposed to get off at Astoria Avenue in Queens but this seems to be going to Brooklyn…

MAN: *(raises an eyebrow)* You're pretty far from Queens now. This is a Brooklyn bound train. You're going the wrong way.

AUDEN: *(Her face falls and she glances anxiously at her watch)* Can you tell me how to get back?

MAN: *(shrugs)* It's pretty simple, just ride this train to Dekalb and transfer to the Queens-bound Q train. It should be right across the platform.

AUDEN: *(nodding)* All right, thank you, sir.

(AUDEN collapses onto the bench next to the MAN, who resumes mumbling to himself. She furrows her eyebrows as she looks out the window. There's silence for a moment before the quick jerk and shudder of the train car and then stillness.)

> "...the quick jerk and shudder of the train car and then stillness."

SPEAKER: Due to construction between Atlantic-Barclays and 7th Avenue, trains are running with delays. We thank you for your patience.

(AUDEN crosses her arms and sinks deeper into the seat. They wait for a while, the slow hum of the air conditioner filling the silence. Then there's a click of a door, and quick footsteps that follow. A TEENAGER with sagging jeans and large black sneakers swaggers in. He heaves boxes on his shoulder sealed with masking tape.)

TEENAGER: Candy! On express delivery! I've only got Snickers left now for a limited-time offer!

(AUDEN sits up quickly, fumbling for a dollar. She opens her mouth to ask for one when...)

MAN: I'll take you up on that offer, one Snickers bar-please.

TEENAGER: Smart choice, kind sir. That'll be $2.50

MAN: What? That's such a rip off. Give it to me for a dollar.

TEENAGER: Come on, man, it's the end of the day and it's the last one in the box. It's either you get this or you wait this out hungry.

MAN: And it's close to midnight so you're probably not going to find any other customers. I'll give you $1.50.

(TEENAGER grudgingly hands over the candy bar and pockets the cash before walking to the next car. AUDEN flinches at the sound of the wrapper crinkling as the MAN begins to feast. The smell of chocolate wafts through the air, making AUDEN press a palm to her stomach as her eyes fixate on the MAN chewing vigorously, with some of the chocolate making its way onto his beard. The MAN stays unaware of her plight as he works his way down to the last few bites, finally taking the time to glance at her, noticing her forlorn expression.)

MAN: Oh, would you like some?

(AUDEN quickly stares at the ground, feeling the building sting of tears. She violently wipes at her eyes as her breath begins coming in hiccups and her sinuses suddenly start clogging.)

MAN: *(looking stricken)* Uhm...are you all right, miss?

AUDEN: New York is supposed to have one of the most efficient transportation systems in the world. All I wanted to do was go to a lecture about Wordsworth and now I'm stuck on a train in the wrong direction.

MAN: *(muttering)* Of course it's Wordsworth, how can it not be Wordsworth?

AUDEN: *(tugs at her shoelaces)* What's wrong with Wordsworth?

MAN: Bit too convoluted for me, way too many metaphors.

AUDEN: *(sniffs)* Well, his poems were the ones that brought me here. *(glances out the window)* I've always wanted to see the city, "all bright and glittering in the smokeless air."

MAN: *(furrows his brow)* Wasn't that about London?

AUDEN: Well I could only afford a domestic flight, okay? I'm close enough.

(Silence for a few minutes.)

AUDEN: *(shakes her head)* I just wanted to write. I've never actually seen cities you know, it was always just open plains for me and ticks in the wheat.

MAN: You want to become a poet? Good luck. Hopefully you won't end up like the rest of them.

AUDEN: Like what?

MAN: You know, become a hermit or insane or something. Poetry brings the madness out in people. That's what poetry is, coherent madness.

AUDEN: *(snorts)* And you're some expert?

MAN: Actually, yes. I studied these people. I've taught them to pre-Meds and art majors. No one knows better what happened to those poets than me.

AUDEN: *(wipes her eyes indignantly)* But we need those people, we need people to write about beauty and space and nothingness for a few moments.

MAN: You're just like my students. But I guess, you'll write when you write and it's probably going to be a jumbled mess, but like I said, that's what poetry is.

(The train jerks forward and settles onto a steady rhythm of track. AUDEN smiles at the forward movement, relieved.)

END SCENE

Awake

Nina Agrawal

I had to stretch old muscles and tolerate discomfort
during the process of writing this, but the final
outcome was liberating.

Awake
We stretch our legs, wiggle our ankles
Muscles groan

Sleeping bags envelop warmth
Cool morning air laps at our skin

Not yet, not yet
I protest

Outside the rain stopped
It's quiet, calm
The mud breathes, expanding, contracting
Earth reborn

Fresh, moist
Verdure surrounds

Spider webs drip with dew,
Mist lingers on faces

Up, up we climb
Legs, arms, toes strain
Chests tight
Claiming the mountain
We sprint to the top

Empty
A quilt of fog
Where…?

Sitting in blindness
Senses alert
No sign of change

Rest, rest
before descending

Wait —
The fog clears
Mountains, lakes, sky, valley
Focus into place

Gladness
At starting
Climbing
Waiting

Alive

Rachel Zhao

YEARS AS MENTEE: 2

GRADE: Junior

HIGH SCHOOL:
  Millennium High School

BORN: NY, NY

LIVES: Brooklyn, NY

Nina and I never name our characters until the very end. Naming means taking responsibility for a character. "She should be wearing neon colored shoelaces," Nina suggested, and I hurried to scribble down a note to myself. Brainstorming sessions are a series of questions and half answers of a fragmented story. As we speak, we add in small, random details of clothing or facial expressions — bright pink tights or a large overcoat — and the story pulls together.

Nina Agrawal

YEARS AS MENTOR: 2

OCCUPATION:
  Policy and Communications Coordinator,
  Every Hour Counts

Pair sessions with Rachel insert a much-needed pause and a breath of levity into the relentless pace of life in New York City. I'm forced to focus, concentrating on the writing task at hand and allowing no distractions. At the same time, we get to chat; we laugh about Rachel's hipster English teacher, make plans for college, commiserate or co-revel in the weather. In the end, it's that mix of focus and friendship that allows us to break through in our writing.

Ready, Set, Write!

Prompts and writing exercises for individuals and groups.

2014: THE YEAR OF BREAKING THROUGH

Breaking through: It's something that the girls and their mentors from Girls Write Now do every day. We break through stereotypes at school and work; we empower each other to make our voices heard, redefining what it means to be women and writers in New York City.

This year, our "Breaking Through" theme encouraged us to turn expectation on its head. Why not take on a stereotyped genre like romance fiction? Why not cast ourselves as savvy women journalists in the male-dominated field of science? Why not break through our own inhibitions with a show-stopping poetry slam?

These writing prompts are designed not just to inspire individual creativity, but to harness the energy of a group of women writing together.

They can be used as they are, by a solitary writer or adapted by teachers, mentors, tutors — anyone interested in writing — to generate ideas and pieces of writing of all kinds and genres.

Below each exercise is a brief explanation of how Girls Write Now went about it in workshops and pair sessions. Recommended reading lists are also provided, allowing the interested reader to go further down the rabbit hole or helping teachers, librarians, or workshop leaders develop lesson and assignment plans.

—JESS PASTORE & CLAUDIA PARSONS
Girls Write Now Curriculum Co-Chairs

AND KIRSTEN REACH & KARA THORDARSON
Anthology Editorial Committee Members

Rites of Passage

Girls Write Now begins every workshop with an "Opening Lines" prompt, to get a conversation started. "Rites of Passage" was one of these prompts — and much more than another play on 'write.' These can easily be done alone or as a group — just share your work with your writing peers.

How we can break through as women and as individuals? What has shaped your sense of self? Of being a woman? You can think about certain rites of passage in your own life, those you've experienced or want to experience, or about women who inspire and move you in your family or community.

For example, read Kiara Kerina-Rendina's "Second Smallest," p. 100.

Answer as many of the prompts below as possible. Write whatever comes to mind: words or phrases, a memory, emotion, or observation — anything! Don't judge what you write, just set a time for five to 10 minutes and let it flow until the time is up.

A woman is... _____

_____

_____

_____

_____

_____

If I could write a letter to the person I was as a child, I would say... _____

_____

_____

_____

_____

_____

I knew I wasn't a little girl anymore when... _____

_____

_____

_____

_____

_____

I used to think that... _____

_____

_____

_____

_____

_____

I want to be... _____

_____

_____

_____

_____

I want to know why... _____

_____

_____

_____

_____

A phrase or piece of advice that has greatly influenced me is... _____

_____

_____

_____

_____

Think about a woman in your life who inspires you — maybe your mother, an aunt, a grandmother, a teacher, or a friend. What have you never told her that you would like to say?

_____

_____

_____

_____

_____

_____

_____

_____

Use the writing in that prompt (or take inspiration from any of the other prompts) to write one sentence that completes the line, "My story begins..."

_____

_____

_____

_____

_____

_____

_____

_____

Tell Your Story

Each week Girls Write Now mentees and mentors meet for a pair session. This is when we get to know each other, write, edit, and hopefully, break through. Here are some ideas that can easily be used alone or in a pair, group, or class — again, just share with your fellow authors.

Write a letter to yourself or someone else, telling you/them something that you haven't been able to say to them/yourself out loud.

For example, read Xiao Shan Liu's "A Letter to My Friends and Family," p. 121.

_____
_____
_____
_____
_____
_____
_____
_____
_____
_____
_____
_____
_____
_____
_____
_____
_____
_____
_____
_____
_____
_____
_____

Write down a few things that make you really angry and / or really happy.

_____
_____
_____
_____
_____
_____

Our own lives make for our best work. Write down three events that had a dramatic impact on your life.

_____

_____

_____

Pick one event and answer the following:

Why is this topic important for your audience to think about? _____

_____

_____

_____

What do you want your audience to know? _____

_____

_____

_____

How do you want your audience to feel? _____

_____

_____

_____

With your piece in mind, answer the following questions:

How quickly should your piece be read? _____

_____

_____

_____

Which words should be said louder or softer?_____

_____

_____

_____

What emotion should your face show?_____

_____

_____

_____

What tone should you use when performing? _____

_____

_____

_____

continued...

Choose a word or phrase you find yourself saying often (for example, like, totally, hate, really, kind of) and write a poem using it as much as possible, turning it over and over, repositioning it, extending it, playing with its uses and the parts of speech into which it can be shaped.

_____

_____

_____

_____

_____

_____

_____

_____

_____

_____

_____

_____

_____

_____

_____

_____

_____

_____

_____

_____

_____

_____

_____

_____

_____

_____

_____

_____

_____

_____

_____

_____

Continue to find your speaking voice and practice articulation, using the piece you wrote or even works of prose. Use pages 10-12 of this site http://www.toast-masters.org/199-YourSpeakingVoice to get started.

Slam That Poem!

Each month, Girls Write Now has a workshop where we learn about and practice a certain genre, or type, of writing. One of the genre workshops for 2014 was slam poetry. This exercise taught us about writing constraints and how to use the poetic device anaphora to get going.

Rhythm can be found in many ways — through repetition and the use of constraints. Starting a line of poetry with the same word or phrase is a called an anaphora. A constraint is any rule you set for yourself while writing. Only being able to start a new line with the same word or phrase — anaphora — is just one example of a constraint.

In this exercise, don't be afraid to shake things up. Slam poetry often tackles heated subjects. Sometimes it means getting up and saying things that others might be scared to, or may be surprised by. Use this to your advantage and turn off your filter.

Choose one of the following prompts to write on. You can write it as a poem now, but you don't have to. You'll have a chance during the second part of the freewrite to turn your writing into a poem.

PROMPT 1:
Pick a moment when you remember feeling (or not feeling) like a woman. Write down everything you can remember about that moment, beginning every sentence with the two words, "I remember." (Maybe it was a time someone treated you differently for being a woman or a time when you felt connected to your grandmother.) Whatever it is, write about it, starting every sentence with "I remember."

For example, read Nakissi Dosso's "You Damn Immigrant," p. 58.

Example:

> I remember the bra around my back in the dressing room.
> I remember my mom talking to the attendant, embarrassing me.

PROMPT 2:

Think about what it feels like to be a woman walking down the street, in your school, in your workplace or with your family. Begin every sentence with with one of the five senses. Every sentence should begin with either the two words "I feel," "I see," "I hear," "I smell," or "I taste."

Example:

I feel men's eyes on me, as I walk past McDonalds.

I smell the french fries.

I hear one guy say 'Hey, baby.'

_____

_____

_____

_____

_____

_____

_____

_____

_____

_____

_____

_____

_____

_____

_____

Now take 10 minutes to look at what you wrote and edit your favorite lines together to write your poem. You can revise whatever you'd like — every line doesn't have to begin with your constraint word, though it can.

_____

_____

_____

_____

_____

_____

_____

_____

_____

_____

_____

_____

_____

_____

TO ADAPT FOR A GROUP

Form that group! You have 15 minutes to create a collaborative poem with your lines. Your collaboration can be simple — each individual taking a turn to read her line — or you can experiment with repetition, overlapping words, group lines, or more.

Use the space below to write your collaborative poem, if needed. As you practice reading the poem together, think about rhythm, tone, where you might pause, what words you want to emphasize, and the emotion you want to convey.

_____

_____

_____

_____

_____

_____

_____

_____

_____

_____

_____

_____

_____

_____

_____

_____

_____

_____

_____

_____

_____

TO ADAPT FOR A PARTNER — AND PERFORMANCE!

Find a partner. Spend some time editing your poem with them, imagining that you are preparing it for a performance. Try reading it aloud to your partner. Think about the rhythm, your tone of voice for different parts of the poem, the emotion you would like to convey, and any gestures you might use.

You can use the following symbols in your draft to indicate how you want to read your poem:

_   Underline words you want to emphasize

/   Use a slash after a word to remind yourself to pause briefly

//   Use two slashes after a word to remind yourself to pause for a little longer

Use a pound sign to remind yourself to stop or pause for a long time

/   Use this arrow to indicate you should raise your pitch or inflection

\   Use this arrow to indicate you should lower your pitch or inflection

Girl, Put Your Record On

Another genre we focused on this year was music memoir. We used the following exercise to explore how music can capture, shape, or elicit a memory.

For each question below, write a song name in the blank space (it's okay if you don't remember the exact song name — describe it as best you can!). Then expand on the prompt. Think about how each song you choose takes you to a particular memory, time, or place. Is the memory a tangible story, or is it an emotion, feeling or sense? Answer as many of the prompts below as you like.

For an example of how music conjures strong memories, read Calayah Heron's "Every Little Thing," p. 86.

The song, _____, makes me happy whenever I hear it because it reminds me of...

_____
_____
_____

The first (or most recent) time I can remember wanting to dance or sing along, _____ was playing. I was...

_____
_____
_____

_____ always makes me sad, but I listen to it anyway because...

_____
_____
_____

The first piece of music I bought or downloaded was _____ .
When I hear it now, it brings me back to...

_____
_____
_____

I hate the song, _____, because it reminds me of...

_____
_____
_____

I always think of my _____ (family member/friend/other)
when I hear _____ because...

_____

_____

_____

The last time I fell asleep to music, _____ was playing and...

_____

_____

_____

I have listened to _____ a million times and will listen to
it a million times more because...

_____

_____

_____

TO ADAPT FOR A GROUP

As your fellow writers read aloud from these noted authors who were inspired by music, follow along.

Excerpt 1:
"Song of the Week: 'Don't Panic' by Coldplay," Annik Adey-Babinski
From: http://coldfrontmag.com/news/song-of-the-week-dont-panic-by-coldplay
Excerpt 2:
Excerpted from "How It Feels to Be Colored Me," Zora Neale Hurston
From: http://xroads.virginia.edu/~ma01/grand-jean/hurston/chapters/how.html

After reading these excerpts, discuss the following:

What role did music play in each of these excerpts? How did it allow the writer to enter the scene?

How did the authors use not just sound but the other four senses to describe the setting?

What exactly is a scene in memoir? How long or short does a scene have to be?

Did these pieces bring up any new memories about your own life and the role music has played in it?

Were there any lines or phrases you really connected to? Why?

Find the Moment

This exercise can be applied to virtually any story or piece you have written — it's all about adding detail. Again, it can be done on your own or with others who you share your work with.

Think of two characters about whom you have been writing or would like to add into a new or existing piece. Who are they? Using the five senses of taste, touch, smell, sight, and sound, describe the characters in the space below.

For example, read Arnell Calderon's "Pila," p. 24.

Character 1: _____

Character 2: _____

What is the relationship between these characters? What does their interaction sound and feel like? Where are they when they interact?

_____

_____

_____

_____

_____

_____

_____

Take us to a single moment of interaction between your two characters. How do your characters feel in this moment? What do they want/need? Do their wants/needs align? Now, write out this scene. Think about their expressions, their body language, and how the setting affects their ability to communicate.

_____

_____

_____

_____

_____

_____

_____

_____

_____

_____

_____

_____

_____

_____

Setting the Scene

Choose a prompt from the music writing exercise. Tell us what happened. Build out the narrative through the use of writing about character, action, dialogue, and music. Who was there with you? What was the main event, conflict, tension, or emotion in this scene? Think about the beginning and the end, and how to bring the story to life.

For example, read Tiffani Ren's "Unconditional Love," pg. 197.

_____

_____

_____

_____

_____

_____

_____

_____

_____

_____

_____

_____

_____

_____

_____

_____

_____

_____

_____

_____

_____

_____

_____

_____

_____

_____

_____

OPTION

Reflect on why that moment you just wrote about was important to you. How did you feel about it at the time? Have your feelings and recollections changed over time? Why do you still remember this moment? Why did a particular song draw you to it?

Recommended Reading

Here are some great reads and listens that relate to the exercises.

FOR SLAM POETRY

Aloud: Voices from the Nuyorican Poets Café, Miguel Algarin
I Remember, Joe Brainard
The Spoken Word Revolution: Slam, Hip-Hop & the Poetry of a New Generation (A Poetry Speaks Experience), Mark Eleveld
Words in Your Face: A Guided Tour Through Twenty Years of the New York City Poetry Slam, Cristin O'Keefe Aptowicz
Word Warriors: 35 Women Leaders in the Spoken Word Revolution, Alix Olson

FOR MUSIC MEMOIR

Bastard Out of Carolina, Dorothy Allison
High Fidelity, Nick Hornby
Love Is a Mix Tape, Rob Sheffield
Record Collecting for Girls: Unleashing Your Inner Music Nerd, One Album at a Time, Courtney Smith
Heavy Rotation: Twenty Writers on the Albums That Changed Their Lives, edited by Peter Terzian

ONLINE RESOURCES

Coldfront: Song of the Week
 http://coldfrontmag.com/?cat=1023
"Every Good Boy Does Fine: A Life in Piano Lessons," Jeremy Denk
 http://www.newyorker.com/reporting/2013/04/08/130408fa_fact_denk
"'Take on Me' by A-Ha," Sarah P. Grady
 http://www.mcsweeneys.net/articles/take-on-me-by-a-ha
"How It Feels to Be Colored Me," Zora Neale Hurston
 http://xroads.virginia.edu/~ma01/grand-jean/hurston/chapters/how.html

Girls Write Now Team
2014

BOARD OF DIRECTORS

Kamy Wicoff
Board Chair

Chelsea Rao
Vice Chair

Nancy K. Miller
Secretary

Justine Lelchuk
Treasurer

Unyi Agba

Marci Alboher

Sandra Bang

Gloria Jacobs

Sang Lee

Erica Mui

Maya Nussbaum

Ellen Sweet

STAFF

Maya Nussbaum
Founder & Executive Director

Tracy Steele
Director of Operations

Michelle Paul
Director of Development

Laura Stenson Wynne
Director of Programs

Laura Cheung
Communications Manager

Emily Coppel
Digital Program Manager

Rebecca Haverson
*Writing & Mentoring
Program Manager*

Aarti Monteiro
Program Coordinator

Lilia Epstein-Katz
Administrative Coordinator

Sarah Hubschman
Digital Program Coordinator

Molly MacDermot
Communications Advisor & Editor

Tara Bracco
Grant Writer

INTERNS

Sarah Andrew

Adina Applebaum

Olaya Barr

Sasha Bogoslowky

Amanda Feinman

Sarah Hubschman

Christine Kirby

Yasmina Martin

Brynnan Parish

Emily Turner

Natalia Vargas-Caba

Melanie Wang

Eryn Wecker

**PROGRAM ADVISORY
COMMITTEE**

Maria T. Romano
Program Advisory Chair

Claudia Parsons
Curriculum Co-Chair

Jessica Pastore
Curriculum Co-Chair

Demetria Irwin
Mentor Enrollment Chair

Rachel Cohen
Mentee Enrollment Chair

Kirsten Reach
Anthology Chair

Heather Graham
Pair Support Co-Chair

Katherine Jacobs
Pair Support Co-Chair

Heather Smith
Mentor Community Chair

Siobhan Burke
Readings Chair

THERAPY PANEL

Erin Baer

Betty Bederson

Simone Bloch

Stephanie Vanden Bos

Judi Evans

Sarah Gaffey

Cora Goldfarb

Peggy Horowitz

Judi Levy

Kristin Long

Julie May

Farrah Tassy

Eva Young

COLLEGE PREP PANEL
Lisa Commager
Yana Geyfman
Samantha Gross
Robert Gulya
Jamie-Lee Josselyn
Amanda Lorencz
Mark Maas
Sia Moua
Thomas Rabbit
Luvon Roberson
Ruth Sullivan
Josleen Wilson

YOUTH BOARD
Jeanette Anderson
Youth Board Chair
Swati Barua
Tuhfa Begum
Sophia Chan
Taysha Clark
Shannon Daniels
Teamare Gaston
Chandanie Hiralal
Karla Kim
Amanda Day McCullough
Ariana Nicolette
Idamaris Perez
Sade Swift
Natalia Vargas-Caba
Carmin Wong
Samantha Young Chan

MENTOR ENROLLMENT COMMITTEE
Jalylah Burrell
Nancy Hooper
Ashley Rose Howard
Joanna Laufer

MENTEE ENROLLMENT COMMITTEE
Sherry Amatenstein
Taysha Clark
JoAnn Deluna
Anne Feigus
Lynn Lurie
Elena Perez
Judith Roland

MENTEE TRAINING
Melissa Campbell
SPARK
Liz Cruz-Cortes
Urban Arts Partnership
Ramya Ramana
Youth Poet Laureate
Cheyanne Smith
Make the Road NY
KK Louviere
Rebel Diaz Arts Collective, Bronx
Emily Pilloton
If You Build It
Sarwat Siddiqui
Urban Arts Partnership

READINGS COMMITTEE
Alice Canick
Vivian Conan
Whitney Jacoby
Heidi Overbeck
Julie Salamon
Allison Yarrow

WORKSHOP TEAMS
POETRY (SLAM)
Simone Bridges
Ave Maria Cross
Margaret D'Poet
Morayo Faleyimu
Imani Ingram
Rachel Krantz
Anuja Madar
Marissa Quenqua
Peggy Robles-Alvarado
Mary Anne Rojas
Rory Satran

FICTION (ROMANCE)
Mala Bhattacharjee
Stacie Evans
Anne Heltzel
Colleen Katana
Katherine Nero
Perla Rodriguez
Alyssa Vine
Cherise Wolas

MEMOIR (MUSIC)
Jackie Clark
Rachel Cline
Linda Corman
Amy Gall
Heather Kristin
Raquel Penzo
Annie Reuter
Courtney Smith
Angela Szpak

JOURNALISM (SCIENCE WRITING)
Laura Barlament
Brooke Borel
Traci Carpenter
Rose Eveleth
Veronique Greenwood
Robin Marantz Henig
Gillian Reagan
Lilly O'Donnell

SCREENWRITING (TV SITCOM)
Stacy China
Darcy Fowler
Terri Minsky
Chana Porter
Juliet Werner
Avra Wing

WILDCARD (STORYTELLING)
Nina Agrawal
Alex Berg
Casey Donahue
Cyndi Freeman
Yvette Joy Harris
Mary Pat Kane
Amanda Krupman
Jeanine Poggi
Julie Polk

continued...

POETRY AMBASSADORS
Nakissi Dosso
Roberta Nin Feliz
Priscilla Guo
Bre'Ann Newsome
Sara Reka
Tema Regist
Najaya Royal

MARKETING/PUBLICITY COMMITTEE
Gloria Jacobs
Marketing/Publicity Co-Chair
Ellen Sweet
Marketing/Publicity Co-Chair
Marci Alboher
Morgan Baden
Mindy Liss
Susan Oehrig
Annette Orenstein
Tracy Perez
Cari Brooke Roberts
Karen Sughrue

FUNDRAISING COMMITTEE
Unyi Agba
Fundraising Chair
Samantha Carlin
Mentor Fundraising Chair
Sandra Bang
Nancy Gendimenico
Erica Mui
Ellen Sweet
Courtney Tuckman

FINANCE & AUDIT COMMITTEE
Chelsea Rao
Finance & Audit Chair
Liz Baker
Justine Lelchuk
Erica Mui
Julia Semrai

CRAFT TALK AUTHORS
Mala Bhattacharjee
Casey Donahue
Rose Eveleth
Cyndi Freeman
Darcy Fowler
Veronique Greenwood
Colleen Katana
Terri Minsky
Mary Anne Rojas
Courtney Smith

CHAPTERS READING SERIES KEYNOTE SPEAKERS
Ana Castillo
Farai Chideya
Amy Fusselman
Christina Baker Kline